SARAH KOCHAV

ISRAEL

SPLENDORS OF THE HOLY LAND

Thames and Hudson

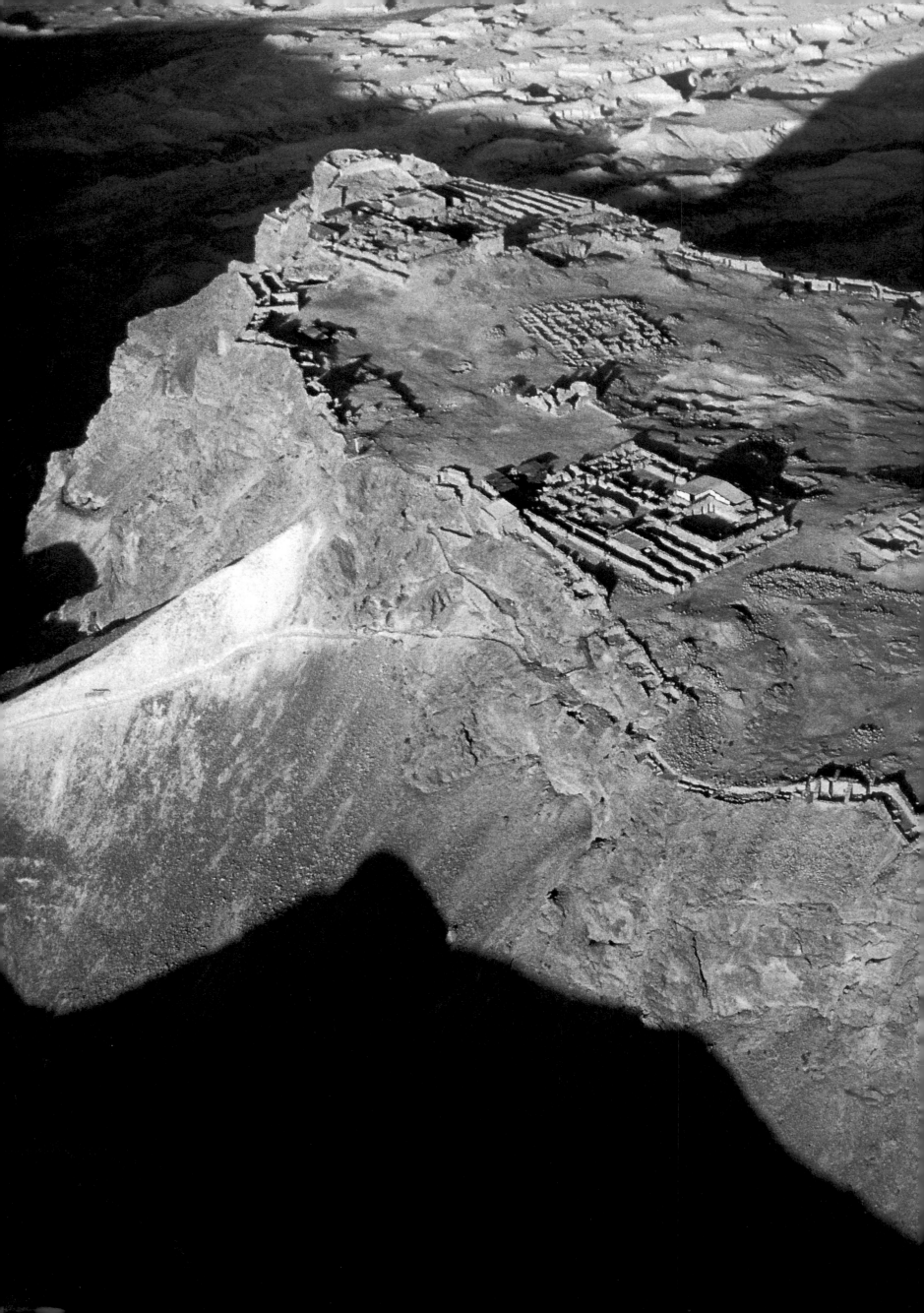

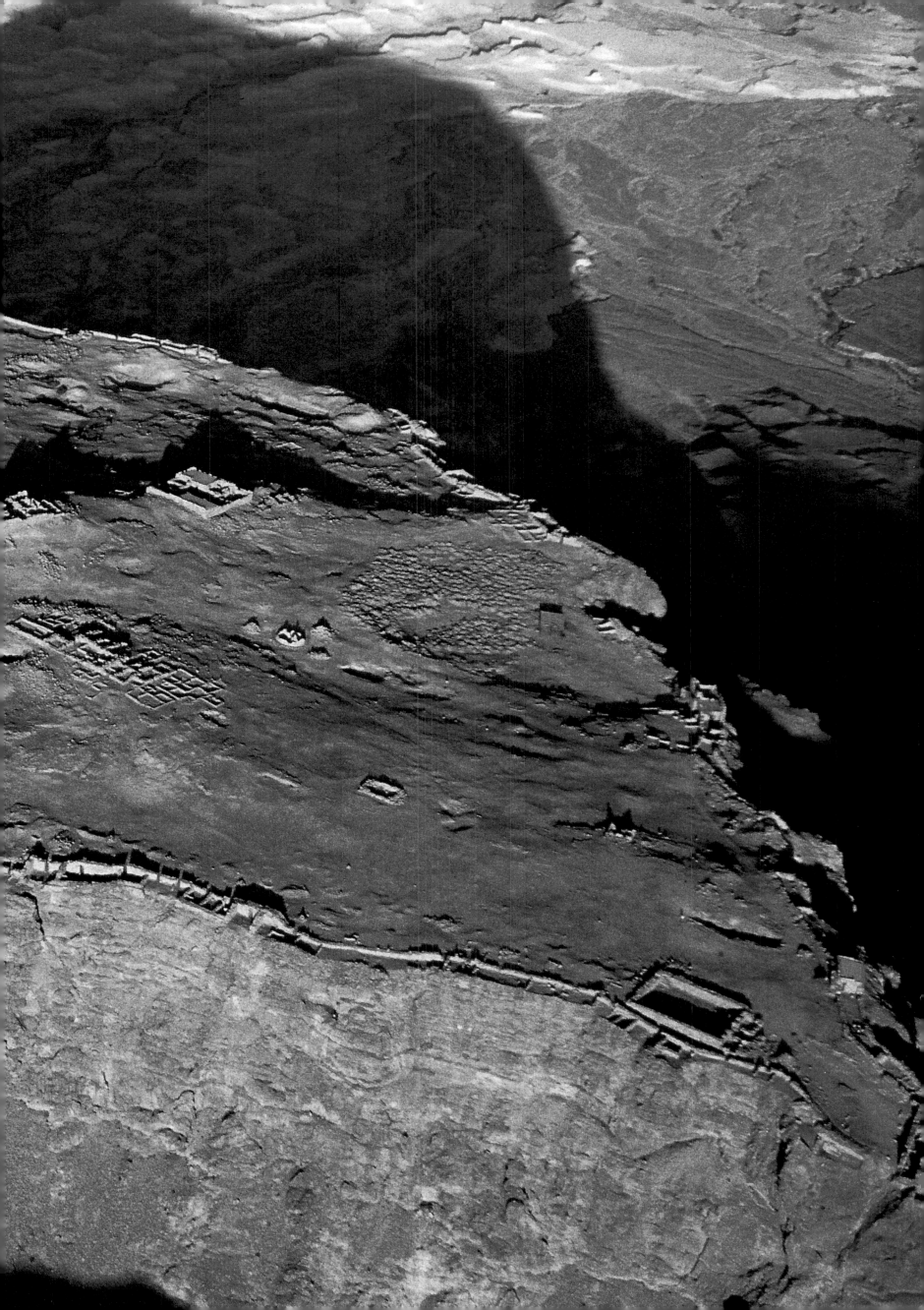

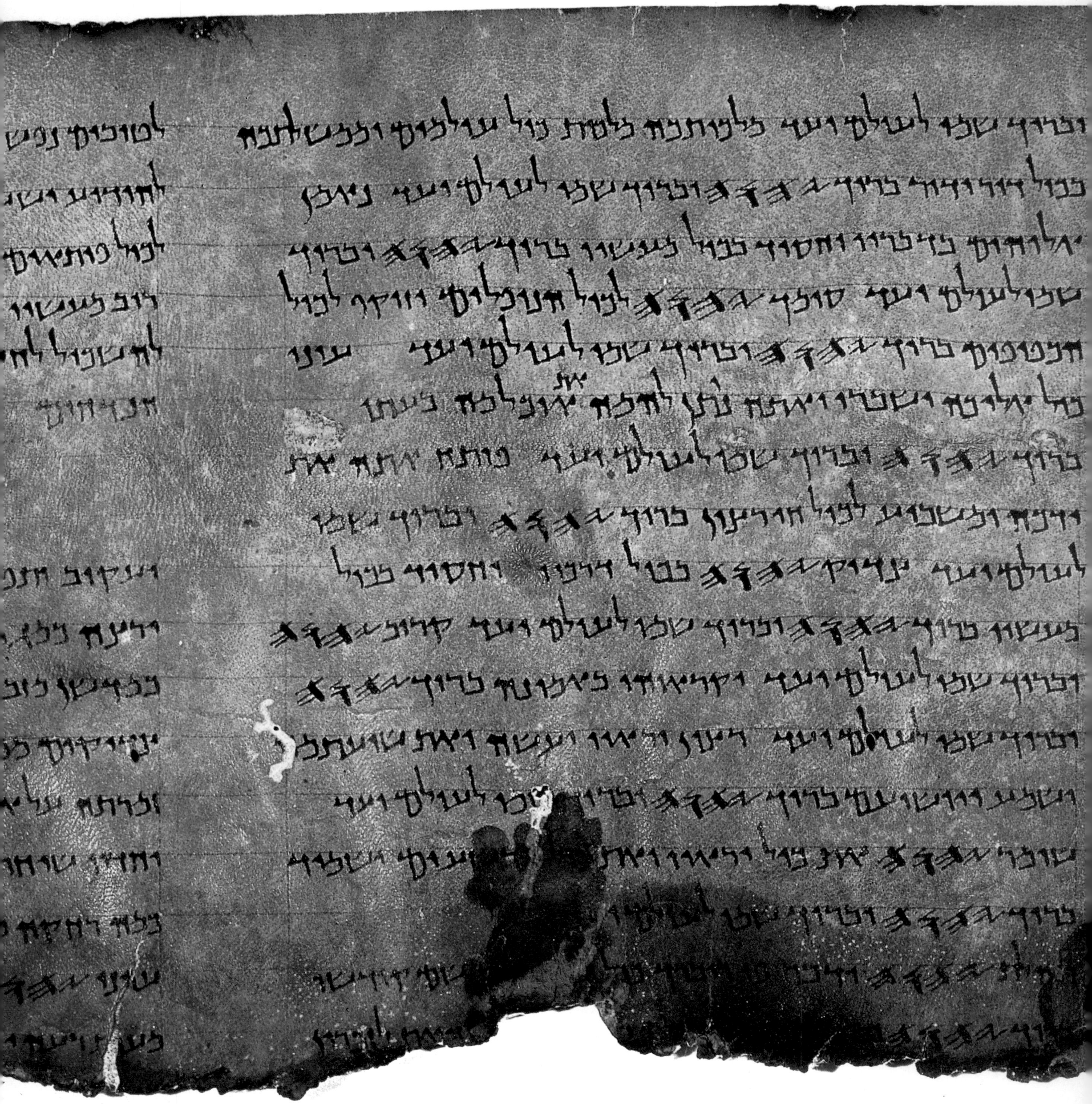

כי לעולם חסדו רעולש בי כי טוב בי ארדדדד הודו הסדו קרוי

רוח ורשועה ביאתלי עדיקיות ימן את רדדד עשה חיל יבון

את רודכח ימן את עשתת גבורת טוב לבמוה

בא דד א לבטוח באדק טוב לחסות בא דד בכטוב

בטירבוט טוב לבטוב בי א דד כבטוח באלף עם חודון

לעל דד כו טוב כו לעלילו חסדו חללוי

תמלח לרוגי ירומכבח . דד א אלהי הכלל

ויארבכח שבה לעולש וער ברוך דד א דד ובטוך שט

ברוך דד א דד א טי ברוך יום אברובה ואתלח שבח לעללו וער

טו דד א שם לעולש וילילו וברון

לעל דד א חזר ברו טוב דד א דד ובנוך שם לעללו וער

דדי לרוגי ישבחו בעשותו וגברתתוטו ו גברותו ברוך

וברוך שם לעולש וער דדד הדרבנו דדבק רדתרעדד א אלפ

ישוש ברוך שם א דד א וברוך שם לעולש וער

דדי יאברו דד א וילו לרוצה

Contents

Text
Sarah Kochav
Editor
Valeria Manferto De Fabianis
Editorial co-ordination
Fabio Bourbon
Laura Accomazzo
Designed by
Patrizia Balocco
Colour drawings
Luca Rossi
Black-and-white maps and drawings
Monica Falcone

The Publisher would like to thank: Giulio
Bourbon, Riccardo Cavaglion, Rupert Chapman,
Amos Goren, Yaron Niv, Jeff Rotman, Gino and
Valia Trionfo, Eva and Gimpel Wajntraub. Special
thanks to Rita Matichecchia and Piero Ruggeri for
their assistance with the colour drawings.

(Note: caption numbers refer to the pages where the illustrations appear.)

1 Jerusalem, depicted in a fifteenth-century copy of a manuscript by Burchard of Mount Zion.

2–3 Masada, on the Dead Sea, was one of King Herod's palace-strongholds. In AD 73 it was the last refuge of the Jewish rebels in the First Revolt, when 960 people took their own lives rather than surrender to Rome.

4–5 The first Dead Sea Scrolls were found in 1947 in caves in the Judaean Desert, west of the Dead Sea. They contain biblical texts and documents of the Qumran community.

6–7 A female figure representing the Hebrew month of Nisan in one corner of the zodiac mosaic in the fourth-century synagogue at Hammath-Tiberias.

8 This Phoenician ivory plaque, dating from the 9th century BC and found at Samaria, was probably used as inlay for wooden furniture. (Israel Museum)

9 A miniature bronze panther in the Hellenistic–Nabataean style of the first century AD. Found at Avdat in the Negev, it may have been a copy of an original in Alexandria, since other such miniatures were found in excavations. (Israel Museum)

10–11 The Old City of Jerusalem from the north. The tall tower of the Church of the Redeemer and the grey dome of the Church of the Holy Sepulchre are in the centre, while to the left is the golden Dome of the Rock on the Temple Mount.

12–13 The Western or Wailing Wall of the Temple Mount is the centre of Jewish religious life in Jerusalem. The wall, built of fine Herodian masonry, is part of the original platform on which the Second Temple was built.

14–15 The golden Dome of the Rock, one of the holiest shrines of Islam, was inaugurated in 691, approximately on the site of the Second Temple. Built according to a very exact geometrical design, it covers the Foundation Stone.

First published in Great Britain in 1995
by Thames and Hudson Ltd, London

First published in the United States in 1995
by Thames and Hudson Inc., 500 Fifth
Avenue, New York, New York 10110

© 1995 White Star S.r.l. – Vercelli, Italy.

British Library Cataloguing-in-Publication Data

A catalogue record for this book is available from
the British Library

ISBN 0-500-01668-2

Library of Congress Catalog Card Number
95-60282

Printed and bound in Italy

PREFACE

From the sands of the deserts, from the depths of the caves overlooking the Dead Sea, to the cities now lying in ruins and the magnificent buildings still standing, the history of the Holy Land can be traced in its stones and in the pages of the Bible. Israelite cities, Nabataean fortresses, Roman amphitheatres, Byzantine churches, Crusader castles and Muslim mosques are a testimony of the various peoples who have left their mark on a land sacred to Jews, Christians and Muslims alike.

Israel is situated at a crossroads between continents and nations and in a setting of great natural beauty. This volume takes the reader on a journey of discovery along the valley of the River Jordan and among the hills of the Galilee, from the shores of the Mediterranean to the sands of the Negev, in a quest to assemble the pieces of a mosaic that extend over the millennia.

Spectacular aerial views, art treasures, intriguing ruins and scenes of everyday life are all captured here by some of the world's finest photographers. A wide-ranging, thorough text complements the photographs, providing the reader with greater insight.

Maps and plans give further meaning to the mute stones of ancient ruins. Detailed architectural drawings show us what the camera cannot: how these great cities and buildings looked in the past. This book is a tribute to a land that has many and surprising faces to reveal, both to adventurous visitors and to armchair travellers.

16–17 A sixth-century bronze menorah *discovered at En Gedi. A seven-branched* menorah *was erected by the Israelites in the Tabernacle in the Wilderness and was one of the vessels of the Temple in Jerusalem.*

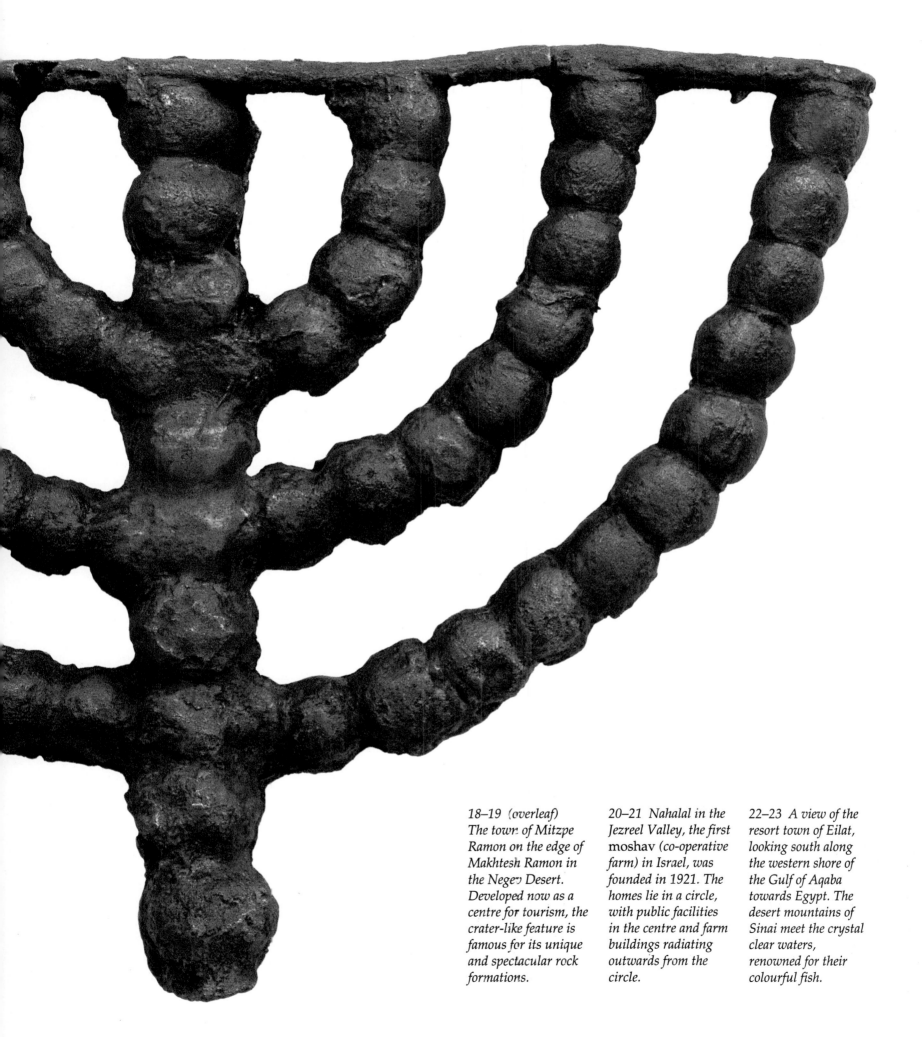

18–19 (overleaf)
The town of Mitzpe
Ramon on the edge of
Makhtesh Ramon in
the Negev Desert.
Developed now as a
centre for tourism, the
crater-like feature is
famous for its unique
and spectacular rock
formations.

20–21 Nahalal in the
Jezreel Valley, the first
moshav (co-operative
farm) in Israel, was
founded in 1921. The
homes lie in a circle,
with public facilities
in the centre and farm
buildings radiating
outwards from the
circle.

22–23 A view of the
resort town of Eilat,
looking south along
the western shore of
the Gulf of Aqaba
towards Egypt. The
desert mountains of
Sinai meet the crystal
clear waters,
renowned for their
colourful fish.

THE HISTORY
OF THE HOLY LAND

The history of the Holy Land has been largely determined by its location. The region consists of a long, thin stretch of land bounded by the Mediterranean Sea to the west, and mountains and deserts to the east. The shoreline is straight, with few natural harbours and the country therefore has been deeply influenced by its relations with the lands that lie north and south, and with the nomadic peoples who crossed over the deserts from the east. The land has retained an imprint of the many nations that have conquered it over the centuries, both in its ruins and also in the mosaic of the people who live there. It is called the Holy Land because it is the birthplace of the two great religions of western civilization – Judaism and Christianity. Islam, too, has strong claims on the Holy Land and its sacred places.

The names given to the Holy Land – or parts of it – have changed with each new conquering people; the boundaries, too, have changed. Geographically, the Holy Land is often described as Palestine, a name derived from the Hebrew word, *Peleshet*, or Philistia. Historically, the land has long been known as Palestine, but since 1948, when the Jewish people won an independent homeland for themselves, the Holy Land has been called Israel, a name that dates from the times of the Jewish Patriarchs.

As a bridge between two cultures – Mesopotamia to the east, with the rivers Tigris and Euphrates forming the Fertile Crescent, and Egypt to the south – this land was affected by trade along two major ancient highways. The *Via Maris*, or 'Way of the Sea', led north from Egypt, along the coastal plain and over a mountain pass to Megiddo, before splitting into two branches. One continued up the coast while the other led through Hazor, and on to Damascus. The second artery was the King's Highway, which ran along the east bank of the River Jordan.

Our knowledge of the history of the Holy Land comes from several sources. Archaeology provides much information through the investigation of the physical remains of the peoples who lived there. Most excavations in Israel are carried out on tells, mounds that represent the accumulated debris of successive settlements, sometimes representing thousands of years of occupation. It is the archaeologist's job to uncover layer after layer of these former habitations. The study of vast arrays of pottery, various types of tombs, and remains such as plant seeds or animal bones, all help to establish how the people of a certain time lived.

Another source of information is the Bible. The Old and New Testaments mention 475 geographical names, many of which can be matched to existing archaeological sites. Other sources include accounts by ancient historians. Perhaps the most useful is a Jew who became a Roman citizen, Flavius Josephus. Other valuable clues are found in the inscriptions from temples and tombs in Egypt, or in archives of clay tablets, such as the Amarna Letters. The Dead Sea Scrolls, discovered in 1947, have yielded an enormous trove of new information, at times prompting fiery debate among scholars.

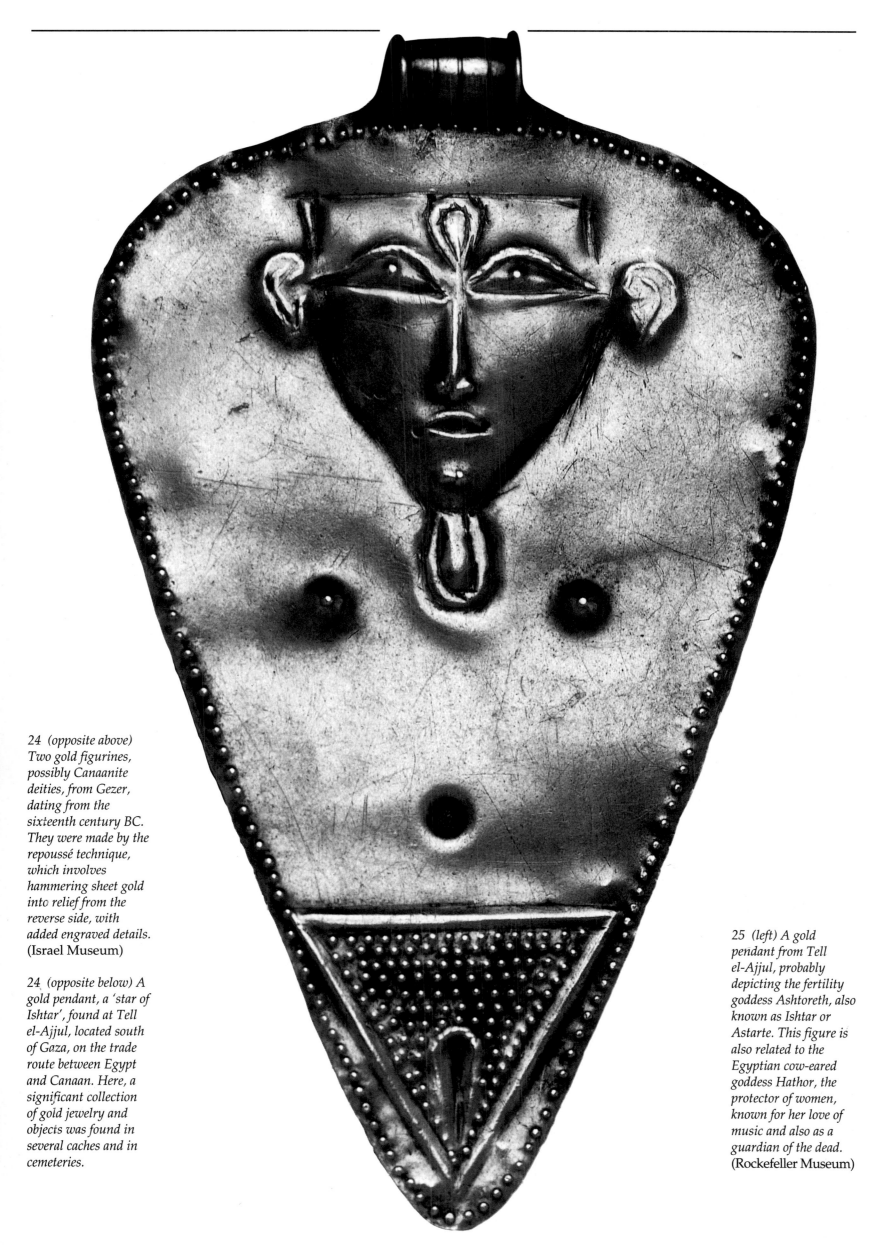

24 (opposite above)
Two gold figurines,
possibly Canaanite
deities, from Gezer,
dating from the
sixteenth century BC.
They were made by the
repoussé technique,
which involves
hammering sheet gold
into relief from the
reverse side, with
added engraved details.
(Israel Museum)

24 (opposite below) A
gold pendant, a 'star of
Ishtar', found at Tell
el-Ajjul, located south
of Gaza, on the trade
route between Egypt
and Canaan. Here, a
significant collection
of gold jewelry and
objects was found in
several caches and in
cemeteries.

25 (left) A gold
pendant from Tell
el-Ajjul, probably
depicting the fertility
goddess Ashtoreth, also
known as Ishtar or
Astarte. This figure is
also related to the
Egyptian cow-eared
goddess Hathor, the
protector of women,
known for her love of
music and also as a
guardian of the dead.
(Rockefeller Museum)

MAP OF THE HOLY LAND

RIVER JORDAN

BELVOIR

BETH SHEAN

SHECHEM

BETH ALPHA

SEBASTE

S A M A R I A

MEGIDDO

MOUNT GERIZIM

TAANACH

DOR

PLAIN OF SHARON

CAESAREA

HAMMATH GADER

CAPERNAUM

GAMLA

TIBERIAS

SEA OF GALILEE

CHURCH OF THE
BEATITUDES

TABGHA

HAMMATH-TIBERIAS

MOUNT TABOR

SAFED

MERON

NAZARETH

LOWER GALILEE

SEPPHORIS

BETH SHE'ARIM

CARMEL CAVES

ATLITH

ACRE

HAIFA

MEDITERRANEAN SEA

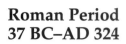

| Bronze Age c. 3150–1200 BC | Iron Age c. 1200–586 BC | Babylonian and Persian Period 586–332 BC | Hellenistic Period 332–37 BC | Roman Period 37 BC–AD 324 |

Bronze and copper come into general use for tools and weapons. The first fortified towns appear, although the end of the Early Bronze Age is marked by a return to a nomadic way of life. Urban life revives at the beginning of the second millennium BC. For much of the period, the coastal plain and other large sections of Palestine are held by Egypt. Canaanite culture begins to develop, strongly influenced by Egypt. Common artifacts include cylinder and stamp seals. New innovations are made in pottery with the introduction of the potter's wheel. Olive trees and vines appear.

Egyptian Execration Texts mention 'Jerusalem'
(c. 1850–1810 BC)

Tuthmosis III begins campaigns in Palestine; Battle of Megiddo (c. 1479 BC)

Amarna Letters (c. 1350 BC)

Merneptah's battle with Israel (c. 1238 BC)

Beginning of invasions by Sea Peoples (c. 1220 BC)

The Sea Peoples, including the Philistines, invade the coastal regions and displace the Egyptians. The Canaanites are still a powerful force. David conquers Jerusalem and extends his control over most of Palestine except for the Philistine stronghold on the southern coast. Solomon succeeds to the throne of the United Monarchy. After his death, his kingdom splits into Israel and Judah. The Egyptian pharaoh Shoshenq invades Palestine. King Ahab is defeated by Shalmaneser III of Assyria. The Assyrians conquer Israel in 722 BC and the Tribes of Israel are dispersed. Judah pays tribute to Assyria. The Assyrians are defeated by the Babylonians. Jerusalem surrenders to the Babylonians in 598 BC. The city and the temple are destroyed in 586 BC.

Kingdom of David (c. 1004–965 BC)

Solomon ascends the throne (c. 965 BC)

Divided Kingdom (c. 928 BC)

Shoshenq invades Palestine (923 BC)

Israel falls to Assyria (722 BC)

Sennacherib captures Lachish (701 BC)

Jerusalem falls to Nebuchadnezzar (598 BC)

Destruction of the Temple; beginning of the Exile (586 BC)

Jerusalem is taken by the Babylonians in 586 BC, the city and Temple are destroyed and the people of Judah are sent into exile to Babylonia. King Cyrus of Persia takes Babylon and the Jews are allowed to return in 538 BC. The city remains impoverished, although the Temple is slowly rebuilt. Nehemiah is appointed governor and orders the rebuilding of the walls of Jerusalem.

Proclamation of Cyrus; return of the Jews (538 BC)

Temple rebuilt (520–515 BC)

Ezra returns (458 BC)

Walls of Jerusalem rebuilt (445 BC)

Alexander the Great conquers the Holy Land in 332 BC. After his death his general Ptolemy controls Egypt and Palestine. The Ptolemies and Seleucids battle over Palestine and in 198 BC the Seleucids gain control. Beginning in 167 BC, a revolt led by Judah Maccabee succeeds in setting up the Hasmonaean kingdom. Internal conflicts threaten to destabilize the Hasmonaean kingdom and the Romans take control in 63 BC. With the aid of the Parthians, the Hasmonaean Antigonus briefly becomes King of Judaea.

Alexander the Great conquers Palestine (332 BC)

Ptolemy I gains Palestine (301 BC)

Antiochus III conquers most of Palestine (198 BC)

Antiochus IV plunders the Temple (169 BC)

Maccabean Revolt begins (167 BC)

Judah Maccabee takes Jerusalem and rededicates the Temple (164 BC)

Pompey takes Jerusalem (63 BC)

Parthian invasion (40 BC)

Herod, son of Antipater, conquers Jerusalem in 37 BC and places his permanent stamp on the country with numerous, grand building projects. After his death in 4 BC, his sons do not exhibit the same qualities and Palestine is ruled by a series of Roman procurators; this is a period of considerable unrest. Jesus of Nazareth is crucified around AD 30. The First Jewish Revolt begins in AD 66 and Jerusalem and the Temple are destroyed in AD 70. Hadrian's plans to rebuild Jerusalem as a pagan city provoke the Second Jewish Revolt. Hadrian quashes the rebellion, and rebuilds Jerusalem, naming it Aelia Capitolina. The Galilee becomes the centre of Jewish life.

Herod the Great (37–4 BC)

Rule by procurators in Judaea (AD 6–41)

Pontius Pilate is procurator (AD 26–36)

Death of Jesus (c. AD 30)

Herod Agrippa I (AD 41–44)

First Jewish Revolt (AD 66–70)

Destruction of Jerusalem and the Temple (AD 70)

Second Jewish Revolt (AD 132–135)

27 An anthropoid coffin from the cemetery at Beth Shean. Modelled in the style called 'grotesque', it is similar to Egyptian-influenced coffins discovered at Deir el-Balah, south of Gaza. (Israel Museum)

SYRIA

MOUNT HERMON

GOLAN

CAESAREA PHILIPPI

NIMROD

SOURCES OF THE JORDAN

HAZOR

KADESH

BAR'AM

BEAUFORT

MONTFORT

UPPER GALILEE

LEBANON

TYRE

SAREPTA

SIDON

Byzantine Period
324–640

The conversion of Emperor Constantine to Christianity in 313 changes the religious landscape of the Holy Land. In 324 Palestine is made part of the Christian Eastern Roman Empire. Churches are built at all the holy sites named in the Gospels. Jews and Samaritans revolt against Gallus in 351. Samaritans revolt again in 529. Justinian introduces new legislation. The Samaritans and the Jews aid the Persian invasion, Christians are massacred and churches destroyed. Jerusalem falls to the Persians in 614 and the Jews are given control of the city for three years. Emperor Heraclius negotiates a peace, but full Christian life does not resume; in 638 Jerusalem surrenders to the Arabs.

Church of the Holy Sepulchre dedicated (335)

Revolt against Gallus (351)

Emperor Justinian (527–565)

Samaritan revolt (529)

Persian invasion (614)

Heraclius restores the True Cross to Jerusalem (629)

Jerusalem conquered by the Arabs (638)

Early Arab Period
640–1099

Jerusalem surrenders to the second caliph, Omar in 638. With the surrender of Caesarea in 640, the entire country is in Arab hands. The capital of the country is at Ramlah. Christianity is tolerated with the exception of a period of persecution under Caliph al-Hakim. Fatimids conquer Palestine in 969 and they have control at least of the cities. Much of the countryside is controlled by the Bedouin. By 1071, the Seljuk Turks capture Jerusalem in addition to other parts of the country. The Fatimids retake Jerusalem in 1098.

Prophet Muhammad dies (632)

Surrender of Jerusalem (638)

Dome of the Rock completed (691)

el-Aqsa Mosque completed (c. 710)

Fatimid dynasty in partial control (969–1099)

Seljuks capture Jerusalem (1071)

Fatimids retake Jerusalem (1098)

Crusader Period
1099–1291

Responding to an appeal by Pope Urban II in 1095, the Crusaders take Jerusalem on 15 July, 1099 and massacre all Jews and Muslims. With the help of the city-states of Genoa, Pisa and Venice, the coast is conquered by 1153. At the Battle of Hattin these victories are reversed by Saladin and the Crusaders are forced to retreat to Tyre. Richard the Lionheart succeeds in breaking the siege of Acre in July 1191 and regains the coast between Tyre and Jaffa. Frederick II negotiates the return of Jerusalem, except the Temple Mount, Nazareth and Bethlehem to the Crusaders. Jerusalem is conquered a second time in 1244. Baybars begins the campaign that finally drives the Crusaders from the Holy Land in 1291

Crusaders take Jerusalem (1099)

Baldwin I (1100–1118)

Saladin victorious at the Horns of Hattin (1187)

Jerusalem regained through diplomacy (1228–1244)

Baybars begins campaign (1265)

Fall of Acre; Crusaders leave the Holy Land (1291)

Mameluke Period
1291–1517

Palestine becomes a backwater in the Mameluke period. Many Crusader buildings in Jerusalem become Muslim religious institutions. Jaffa, Acre and other coastal cities are destroyed to prevent another Crusader invasion. Christians and Jews are granted limited rights. Special concessions are granted to the Georgian and Ethiopian Christians. The Franciscans return and buy a small house on Mount Zion in 1335. Jerusalem remains an unwalled city. Many Islamic religious institutions are founded and much Mameluke architecture in the city dates from this period.

Bahri Mameluke dynasty (1250–1390)

al-Nasir Muhammad (c. 1294-1340)

Fall of Constantinople to the Ottoman Turks (1453)

Burji Mamelukes (1382–1517)

Ottoman Turks occupy Cairo (1517)

Ottoman Period
1517–1917

The Mamelukes are defeated by Ottoman Turks in northern Syria in 1516. Suleiman the Magnificent rebuilds the walls of Jerusalem during the Golden Period of Turkish rule. Afterwards, the area enters a period of decline. Much of the countryside remains in the hands of the Bedouin or local rulers and heavy taxes are inflicted on the population. Napoleon marches uncontested from Egypt in 1799 until being routed outside Acre by Jazzar Pasha and the British fleet. The reign of Muhammad Ali of Egypt opens up the Holy Land to foreign consulates, missionaries, explorers and surveyors. Jews become the majority of the population. The Zionist movement lays the foundations of the modern State of Israel.

Ottomans conquer Palestine (1517)

Napoleon's campaign (1799)

Muhammad Ali of Egypt (1832–1840)

English-Prussian Bishopric (1840–1881)

Palestine Exploration Fund founded (1865)

First Zionist Congress (Basel, 1897)

Balfour Declaration (1917)

DEAD SEA

HERODIUM

EN GEDI

MASADA

ARAD

I D U M A E A

BETH GUVRIN

LACHISH

BEERSHEBA

TELL EL-AJJUL

JORDAN

MAMSHIT

NEGEV

AVDAT

SHIVTA

N

AL '95

34 *A marble head of the Greek god Hermes discovered in the seaport of Dor. Dating from the Hellenistic period, it shows the extent of the influence of pagan Greek culture in the city.*

TRANSJORDAN

MADABA

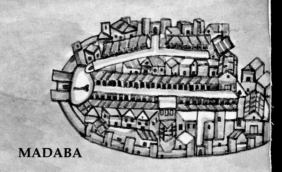

JERICHO

QUMRAN

MAR SABA

SHILOH

JERUSALEM

BETHLEHEM

EMMAUS

J U D A E A

LYDDA

GEZER

RAMLAH

JAFFA

ASHKELON

MEDITERRANEAN SEA

The Stone Age and the Chalcolithic Period

At some point between 11,000 and 6000 BC, society in what is now called the Near East was transformed from small bands of subsistence hunter-gatherers into settled communities raising food crops. In the Neolithic period people lived in small villages, cultivated grains and legumes, raised livestock and engaged in a limited network of exchange. The term Neolithic is Greek for 'new stone' and refers to the technology of making flaked and ground stone tools from flint and obsidian. The people of the early Neolithic, however, did not have pottery. The climate was then slightly warmer and more humid than it is today. The coastline lay to the west of the present shore; in some places the ancient coast is now submerged about 2.75 m (9 ft) below sea level.

One of the best known Neolithic sites is Jericho, in the Jordan Valley, 14 km (9 miles) north of the Dead Sea. The oasis of Jericho was first settled by the Natufian people, a culture found throughout Palestine and Syria between around 11,000 and 8500 BC. These people still lived mostly by hunting – the gazelle was their favourite prey – and gathering a variety of plants. At Jericho traces of structures built of mudbrick have been found. In the Early Neolithic the settlement at Jericho was surrounded by large protective walls, which have no parallels elsewhere at this date. Just inside one wall was a massive tower, around 8 m (26 ft) high, whose function is not certain. These remains have earned Jericho the title 'the oldest town in the world'.

36 (above) Remains of prehistoric man have been found in the Skhul, el-Wad, Jamal and Tabun Caves of the Mount Carmel range.

36 (right) In the el-Wad caves a rich collection of bone tools was found, belonging to the Natufian culture. This tool handle was fashioned into the shape of a young gazelle. (Israel Museum)

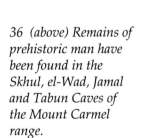

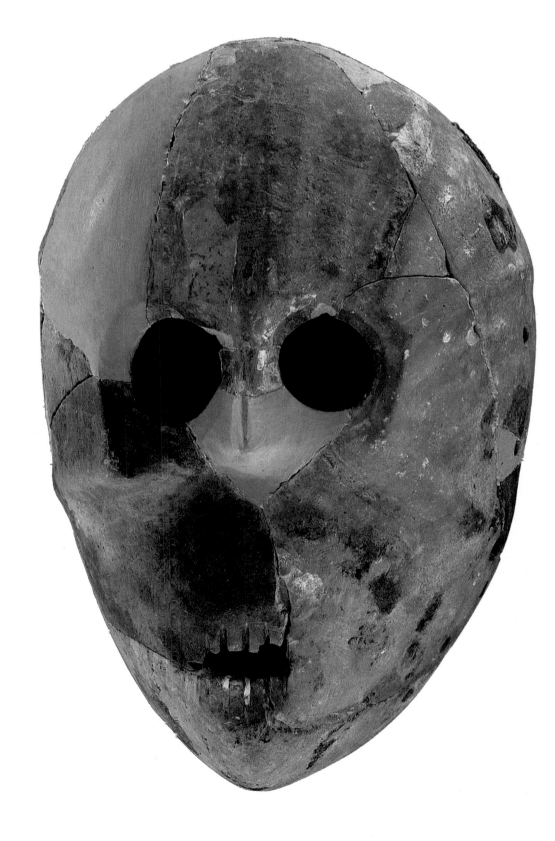

37 (above left) Pottery figurine of a seated woman holding a churn on her head and another vessel under her arm, from the northern Negev site of Gilat. It was part of a large collection of cult objects dating from the Chalcolithic period. (Israel Museum)

37 (above right) A hunting scene from Mount Karkom in the southern Negev, a Palaeolithic sanctuary containing over 40,000 petroglyphs. Here, two hunters can be discerned, with their prey, two antelopes.

37 (right) Stone mask from the cave of Nahal Hemar in the Judaean Desert. Probably used in an ancestor cult, the mask was decorated with green and red stripes and had a beard attached using asphalt. (Israel Museum)

The following, Chalcolithic, period, witnessed the first metalworking technology with the development of copper metallurgy. The name Chalcolithic comes from two Greek words, *khalkos* (copper) and *lithos* (stone). Though stone tools were still widely used, copper tools were introduced, indicating a new ability to smelt copper-bearing ores.

One of the main sites of the Chalcolithic period is Teleilat Ghassul in the Jordan Valley, 5 km (3 miles) northeast of the Dead Sea. This site gave its name to the 'Ghassulian culture', dating from the fifth millennium to about 3300 BC; by this point the use of pottery was widespread. There are also indications of exchange networks: basalt was brought from the north; shells from the Red Sea and the Nile; turquoise from the mines of southern Sinai; elephant tusks from Africa or northern Syria; and hippopotamus ivory may also have come from Egypt. Copper ores took one of two forms: regular copper from Timna, near the Gulf of Aqaba; or arsenical copper from Anatolia, Iran and the Caucasus Mountains. The latter, a copper ore with deposits of arsenic, is a naturally stronger material.

The sophistication of Chalcolithic metalworking is demonstrated by the hoard from the Cave of the Treasure, found by archaeologists in cliffs rising above the west shore of the Dead Sea, near Nahal Mishmar. At the back of this nearly inaccessible cave, hidden in a niche and covered with a thin mud wall, was a rich collection of over 400 objects, nearly all made of copper. Many appear to have had religious significance, such as crowns and maces or sceptres. Even remnants of basketwork survived in the dry conditions of the cave.

The people of the Chalcolithic period disappear from the archaeological record about 3300 BC and scholars do not agree on the reasons for this.

38 Ivory figurines from the Negev dating from the Chalcolithic period. The provenance of the female figure (left) is unknown, while the male figure is from Bir Safadi near Beersheba. The holes around its head probably held tufts of hair. These figures may be carved from hippopotamus ivory. At Bir Safadi remains of an ivory workshop, complete with tools, were found by archaeologists. (Israel Museum)

39 (below) An ossuary from Azor, south of Jaffa. Dating from the middle of the fourth millennium BC, these ossuaries were used to contain the bones of one individual in a secondary burial. They usually measure around 60 cm (24 in) in height, and often take the form of houses or stylized animals and frequently have a curious beaked nose on the front. Others were painted with red or brown, floral and geometric motifs. (Israel Museum)

39 (right) A Natufian necklace made of dentalium shells interspersed with bone, found in el-Wad Cave on Mount Carmel. Such necklaces were often found accompanying burials, the bodies usually laid in a tightly flexed position. (Israel Museum)

40 (right) This copper sceptre decorated with ibex heads is part of a hoard of over 400 copper objects found wrapped in a straw mat and buried in the 'Cave of the Treasure' at Nahal Mishmar, in the Judaean Desert.

Dating from the Chalcolithic period, these objects probably belonged to a cult centre nearby, possibly the shrine building found at En Gedi, and may have had a connection with fertility rituals.

40 (left) A crown-like object adorned with birds and animal horns mounted over what may symbolize a temple entrance. Ten such 'crowns' were discovered in the hoard.

40 (below) A sceptre-head cast in the shape of a bird. These ceremonial objects were made by the 'lost-wax' process, which involves modelling the desired form in wax and building a clay mould around it. The wax is then melted and molten copper is poured in its place. The finished objects sometimes had details engraved on them and all were highly polished.

41 *A copper sceptre-head with two ibexes. The arid conditions of the Judaean Desert also preserved a large number of household objects in the cave. Fragments of linen and woollen cloth and a weaving loom were discovered, as well as remains of a sandal and part of a leather garment. Basketry items used in the collection and preparation of food survived, as did grains of wheat and barley.* (Israel Museum)

THE BRONZE AGE: THE TIME OF THE CANAANITES

42 A silver goblet from a tomb in a Bronze Age cemetery at Ain Samiya. It is decorated in repoussé, with a mythological scene, possibly depicting an epic Mesopotamian creation myth, though the goblet may have been made in Syria. Two figures hold a band underneath a sun disk, while a snake writhes between them. In another scene, a Janus-headed figure with the legs of an ox holds a plant and wards off another snake or dragon.

The Bronze Age takes its name from the increasing use of bronze, an alloy of copper and tin. The Early Bronze Age began around 3150 BC and was marked by growing urbanization, as the population gathered into city-states consisting of a city or town surrounded by villages and farms. Some settlements were fortified and there is evidence of warfare between them. The economy was largely based on agriculture and the Early Bronze Age is marked by the appearance of the olive tree and the vine. There is evidence of trade with Egypt and since no port is known to have existed in Palestine prior to the second millennium BC, all this trade must have gone overland. During this period a recognizable Canaanite culture began to develop.

The end of the Early Bronze Age was marked by a cessation of trade with Egypt and a decline of urban culture. The reasons for the collapse of town life and the corresponding rise in nomadic and semi-nomadic ways of life are unclear. We do not know whether city dwellers were displaced by a new people, or whether a change in climate prompted a return to a nomadic existence. Urban life did not resume until the beginning of the second millennium BC, during the Middle Bronze Age. Canaanite culture revived and flourished; trade with Egypt grew.

The use of the potter's wheel, which had nearly vanished at the end of the Early Bronze Age, reappeared. New religious practices are evidenced by the construction of open-air *bamah* (raised platforms), or

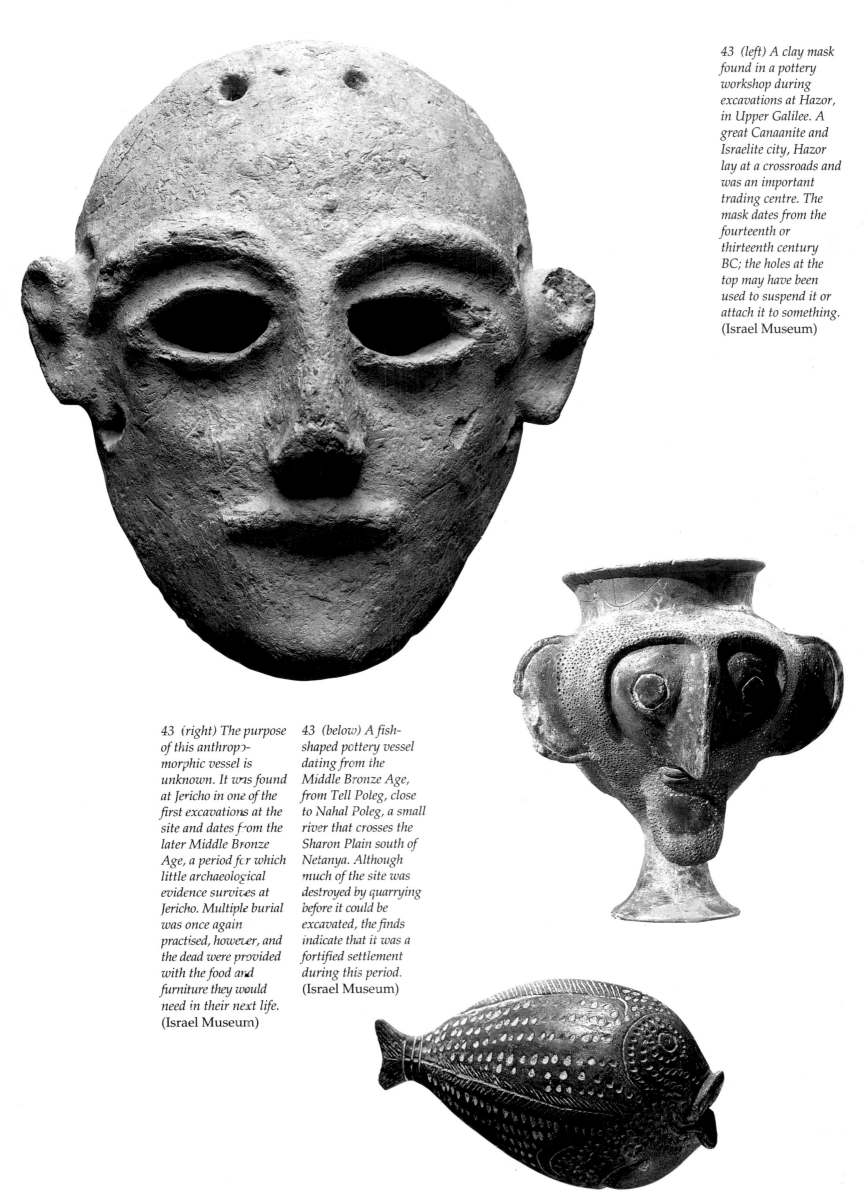

43 (right) The purpose
of this anthropo-
morphic vessel is
unknown. It was found
at Jericho in one of the
first excavations at the
site and dates from the
later Middle Bronze
Age, a period for which
little archaeological
evidence survives at
Jericho. Multiple burial
was once again
practised, however, and
the dead were provided
with the food and
furniture they would
need in their next life.
(Israel Museum)

43 (below) A fish-
shaped pottery vessel
dating from the
Middle Bronze Age,
from Tell Poleg, close
to Nahal Poleg, a small
river that crosses the
Sharon Plain south of
Netanya. Although
much of the site was
destroyed by quarrying
before it could be
excavated, the finds
indicate that it was a
fortified settlement
during this period.
(Israel Museum)

other open places of worship, featuring stelae – upright carved stone pillars.

Important information for this period comes from the Egyptian Execration Texts, of the Twelfth Dynasty. Written on pottery bowls and figurines, they listed city-states that had been cursed as they were considered hostile to Egypt. Among those listed in the land of Retenu – Syria-Palestine – is Jerusalem.

Settlements were well fortified; the most important city in northern Canaan was now Hazor. A new feature of the fortifications was the two-chambered gate; palaces also first appear during this period.

Canaanite culture was greatly influenced by Egypt and large numbers of Egyptian-style objects have been found, such as scarabs set in rings or gold jewelry. The Hyksos, of Canaanite origin, established a short-lived dynasty in Egypt, ruling from Avaris in the Nile Delta.

The Middle Bronze Age is seen by some scholars as the likely setting for the stories of Abraham and the Patriarchs; though this is a question that is much debated.

45 (below) An ivory cosmetics bottle found in a temple at Lachish, dating from around 1350–1250 BC. The lower part is made from a section of an elephant tusk, and the upper part, also made of ivory, was carved separately On top of the head is a spoon. (Israel Museum)

45 (above left) A limestone stela dating from 1500–1200 BC and depicting a deity worshipping the Tree of Life. It shows the marked influence that Egypt had on Canaanite culture.

45 (below left) An anthropoid coffin made of clay in the Egyptian style, from Deir el-Balah – an Egyptian garrison on the Gaza Coast, dating from the fourteenth to thirteenth century BC. These sarcophagi were made using the coil technique, with the lid cut from the base before firing. (Israel Museum)

44 (opposite) A basalt orthostat from Beth Shean dating from the Late Bronze Age, when the city was an Egyptian stronghold. A lion and a dog (or possibly a lioness) are locked in combat in the upper panel and a dog is attacking a lion in the lower.

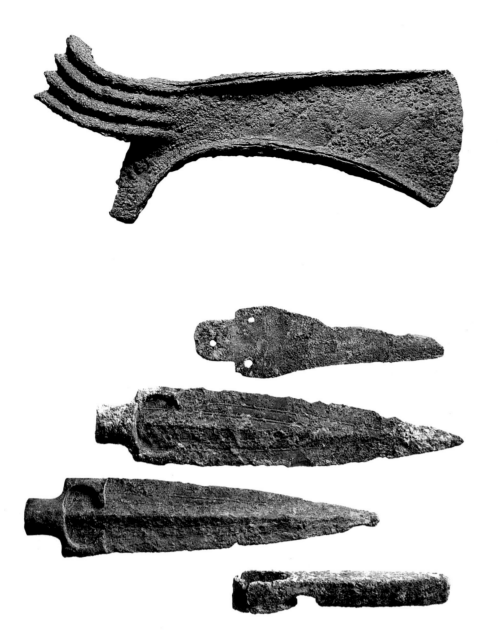

The Late Bronze Age in Palestine corresponds to the New Kingdom in Egypt. It was a time of renewal of Egyptian power and large parts of Canaan came under direct Egyptian control. Tuthmosis III (1504–1450 BC) waged several campaigns to extend Egyptian sway over Canaan; the most decisive of these culminated in his victory at the battle of Megiddo, when he defeated the united rebel forces of Canaan and Syria. One significant Canaanite achievement of this period was the development of an alphabetic script.

The Amarna Letters, an archive of over 350 clay tablets found at the site of that name in Egypt, are evidence of the turmoil at the end of the Bronze Age. Some of the tablets are appeals from Canaanite princes to the Egyptian pharaoh to come to their defence. Egyptian power, however, was in decline, resulting in the withdrawal of its forces and the loss of its empire in Canaan. This period was also marked by the advent of the so-called Sea Peoples in the area, and by the appearance of the Israelites in the hill regions.

46 (top) A bronze axe in the curious 'hand-shape' style, found at Shiloh. Made in a mould, this axe dates from between 1750 and 1550 BC and shows the great improvements made in casting techniques by the middle of the Bronze Age.

46 (centre) In addition to weapons like these spearheads and the notched axe (at the bottom), the Canaanite soldier was protected by a suit of mail made of metal scales sewn on to a leather jacket.

46 (right) A fragment of an Egyptian mask from a sanctuary dedicated to Hathor, dating from the reign of the Pharaoh Sethos I (1318–1304 BC). The temple was near Timna, north of the Gulf of Eilat–Aqaba, where copper was mined.

47 (below) A bronze figure of the Canaanite god Baal. The Bible contains many references to the worshippers of Baal, warning against the cult of this god of storm and weather. The worship of Baal was, however, very popular and was thus a constant threat to the religion of the Israelites. Archaeological evidence shows that the cult continued into the ninth and eighth centuries BC.

47 (left) An Egyptian bronze mirror from the Persian Garden graves near Acre. It was discovered in a tomb containing the skeletons of three people – two men and a woman – along with cylinder seals, gold beads, a gold ring, stone weights and other small objects. The large number of luxury goods may indicate that this was the grave of a group of wealthy travellers or merchants who had died and were buried by the side of the road. (Israel Museum)

48 and 49 A naked goddess holding lotus flowers and standing on the back of a horse is depicted on this plaque of beaten gold. Dating from the Late Bronze Age, the plaque was discovered in a temple on the tell at Lachish. Both the design of the temple and the style of the plaque show a strong Egyptian influence. At this time Lachish was an important Canaanite city. A destruction layer shows that in about 1130 BC the city came to a violent end when Egypt lost control of southern Canaan.

THE IRON AGE: THE DAYS OF THE JUDGES OF THE BIBLE

The term Iron Age is used for the period dating from 1200 BC until the destruction of the First Temple in 586 BC. It begins with the invasion of the Sea Peoples, among them the Philistines, along the coastline of Palestine, and sees the establishment of the Israelites in the hill country of Canaan. This corresponds to the time of the biblical Judges.

The reign of Saul, Israel's first king, has been dated from about 1020 to 1004 BC. According to the Bible, Saul defeated the Ammonites, the Moabites, the Amalekites, the Aramaeans and the Edomites, but finally lost his life to the Philistines in battle near Mount Gilboa.

Saul was succeeded by David, who as a boy had slain the Philistine giant, Goliath. David defeated the Philistines and united the tribes of Israel. He reigned for 40 years; his son and successor, Solomon, further consolidated the kingdom. He built the Temple in Jerusalem, which became the major religious centre, and fortified a number of towns, notably Hazor, Megiddo and Gezer.

50 A four-tiered pottery cult stand from Taanach dating from the tenth century BC, probably used for offerings or libations. On the top tier is a horse or calf with a sun disk above its back. Below, two ibexes are feeding from a plant, flanked by two growling lions. Two cherubim or sphinxes guard an opening on the next tier. The theme of growling lions is repeated on the bottom tier, where they stand on either side of a naked goddess. (Israel Museum)

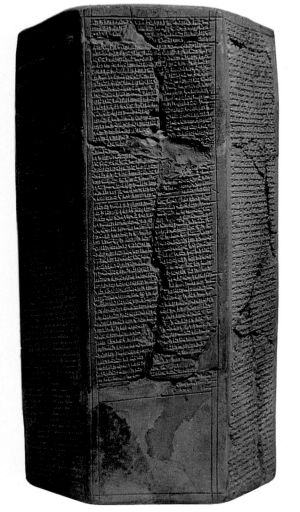

After Solomon's death, his son Rehoboam was unable to maintain the united kingdom and it split: he ruled over Judah in the south, while Jeroboam ruled over Israel in the north. This divided kingdom was further weakened by the invasion of Shoshenq (Shishak), pharaoh of Egypt, in 923 BC. According to an inscription at the Temple of Amun in Karnak, Shoshenq conquered various cities, including Gibeon and Megiddo and only spared Jerusalem when he received tribute.

While the kingdom of Judah remained under the rule of a single dynasty, the House of David, the kingdom of Israel saw nine different dynasties rise and fall. One of the northern kingdom's strongest rulers was Omri, who founded the city of Samaria and made it the capital of his kingdom. Israel survived until the year 722 BC, when it was conquered by the Assyrians. The story of the exile of the Ten Tribes of Israel and their replacement by foreign colonists finds confirmation in the annals of the Assyrian king, Sargon II. Although the Assyrians, now ruled by Sennacherib, laid siege to the city of Jerusalem the city did not fall, perhaps because of tribute paid by Hezekiah.

The Babylonians, however, under their king, Nebuchadnezzar, were more successful, and Jerusalem fell to them in the year 597 BC. King Jehoiakim was slain; his son and 10,000 of Judah's leading citizens were led off to exile in Babylonia.

Nebuchadnezzar installed a king of his choice on the throne, Zedekiah. Under great pressure from his countrymen, however, and with a promise of help from Egypt, Zedekiah decided to stage a revolt against his Babylonian masters. Following a siege of two years, the Babylonians took Jerusalem in 586 BC. Zedekiah's two sons were killed in front of his eyes before he was blinded and led away into captivity in Babylon. The walls of Jerusalem were levelled.

This biblical account can largely be confirmed by the archaeological record. The Iron Age, a name coined because of the appearance of the use of iron, is also called the Israelite period because of their dominance. However, there were other peoples of importance at this time: in particular the Sea Peoples on the southern coast and the Phoenicians on the northern coast.

The transition between the Bronze Age and the Iron Age was a period of crisis throughout the eastern Mediterranean. Egyptian power declined significantly, due in part to the incursions of the Sea Peoples. Egyptian-influenced Canaanite culture similarly went into a decline; many towns in Canaan were destroyed, among them Hazor and Lachish. Causes for these widespread changes have been sought in environmental factors – in particular, several years of drought.

The Philistines and other Sea Peoples invaded the southern coastal plains. The Israelites established a position in the central hill country. The Canaanites and their cultural descendants, the sea-faring Phoenicians, held sway over much of northern Palestine and the northern coastal plain. In the Transjordan – lands to the east of the River Jordan – the Edomites, Moabites and Ammonites increased their power.

The Israelites, because of their central biblical role, have attracted most attention from archaeologists. However, no consensus has been reached as to their origin. The Merneptah stela, of around 1220 BC, mentions a victory by that pharaoh over a people called Israel, but no

52 A Philistine cult stand found at Ashdod. Standing at windows cut in the base of the stand are musicians, including a flute player and a figure with cymbals. During the Iron Age, when this cult stand was made, Ashdod was a walled city; a gate has been excavated at the site similar in plan to ones found at Megiddo, Gezer and Hazor. These gates have been linked with the building projects of King Solomon. (Israel Museum)

sources outside the Bible tell us anything concerning the Israelites' origins. The whole question of the settlement of Canaan by the Israelites is much debated. Furthermore, it is hard to distinguish early Israelite sites from those of other peoples, such as the Gibeonites, Amalekites or Jebusites. A few general conclusions, however, can be drawn. The Israelites formed a sedentary society, largely made up of farmers and herders, living in small villages. Many of their customs were identical with, or very similar to, those of their Canaanite neighbours.

The archaeological record becomes clearer under the Monarchy and as well as the Bible, there are other sources, such as Egyptian, Assyrian and Babylonian documents, and inscriptions written on ostraca (sherds of pottery). Many fortified urban settlements have been excavated, which reveal a rise in the standard of living and the presence of luxury goods for the elite.

Only a very few fragments of the walls that Solomon built around the city of Jerusalem have been identified and the finest surviving examples of his work are found at Hazor, Megiddo and Gezer. Similar six-chambered gates have been excavated at these cities, as well as at Lachish and Ashdod. Another feature of these sites are so-called Solomon's Stables, with the best example at Megiddo and others at Hazor, Beersheba and Tell Masos in the Negev. While Solomon's magnificent palace in Jerusalem, so glowingly described in 1 Kings 1–7, has not survived, there are remains of palaces of this period at Megiddo.

Judah and Israel became markedly urban societies and the capital of each, Jerusalem and Samaria respectively, grew considerably. Other major cities, such as Lachish, were a fraction of the size of Jerusalem. In response to the threat of Assyrian invasion in the late eighth century BC the walls of major cities were reinforced. The chief siege weapon in the Iron Age was the battering ram and preparations were made to withstand it. Elaborate water systems, such as those at Jerusalem, Gezer, Megiddo, Gibeon, Hazor and Lachish were another feature of city construction.

In the early Iron Age, evidence for writing is quite scarce, but by the eighth century BC literacy was widespread – not restricted to a few scribes and aristocrats. This level of literacy was unusual in the rest of the ancient world. Evidence takes many forms: ceramic vessels were stamped or inscribed with their owner's name; the name of the deceased was inscribed on tombs, along with curses to frighten off aspiring grave

53 (above) A cult stand adorned with snakes and birds found in a tenth-century temple at Beth Shean. (Israel Museum)

53 (below) These two ivory lions from Samaria date from the tenth to ninth centuries BC. In the Bible Amos rebuked 'those in the mountain of Samaria… That lie upon beds of ivory.' (Israel Museum)

53 (below right) An Iron Age bull figure. Bull worship was common in Near Eastern religions and calves and bulls played an important part in the religion of the Israelites.

robbers; and seal stones were used to stamp clay seals fastening the strings tied around rolled-up documents.

In the last third of the eighth century, Assyria began systematically subjugating the kingdom of Israel. By 701 BC the Assyrians had conquered Israel and the plain of Philistia, and were exacting huge tribute from Judah.

These conquests are graphically depicted in many Assyrian reliefs, the best known showing the conquest of Lachish, originally carved on the walls of Sennacherib's palace at Nineveh. The ruins of Assyrian administrative buildings have been excavated at Megiddo, Gezer and Dor. Archaeological evidence of the Babylonian conquest is most graphic and plentiful in excavations in Jerusalem.

To the north of the city wall archaeologists discovered a large tower; among the burnt debris all around were many arrowheads, indicating fierce combat. In the City of David, excavations have uncovered artifacts of everyday life mixed with the arrowheads of both Israelites and their Babylonian attackers; everything is cloaked in a thick, charred layer of destruction.

54 (opposite left) A terracotta woman with a drum found at Shiqmona, on the Carmel coast, dating from the ninth or the eighth century BC. (Israel Museum)

54 (opposite right) A pillar figurine of the Israelite period. Of Canaanite-Phoenician origin and associated with fertility, these figurines are often found in excavations of private dwellings and may have been worshipped by women. (Israel Museum)

55 (above) An ivory plaque depicting a woman at a window, dating from the eighth century BC. The balustrade is made up of proto-Ionic capitals, typical of Israelite palace architecture and similar to ones excavated at Ramat Rahel near Jerusalem. (Israel Museum)

55 (right) A figurine of a pregnant woman in the Syrian-Phoenician style and dating from the sixth century BC. It was found in a cemetery at the port of Achziv. (Israel Museum)

THE BABYLONIAN AND PERSIAN PERIODS: THE EXILE AND THE RETURN

56 (below) Clay figures of warriors on horseback, from tombs at Achziv, north of Acre. Since the tombs also contained arrow-heads, it has been surmised that a small local garrison was stationed at the port. (Israel Museum)

King Cyrus of Persia added Babylon to his expanding empire in 539 BC. As part of his tolerant policy towards conquered peoples, he issued a proclamation in 538 BC which permitted the Jews to return to Jerusalem and rebuild the Temple. Leading the return were Sheshbazzar and Zerubbabel. It has been estimated that some 50,000 Jews returned, especially the poor; these returning Jews did not always get on with those who had remained behind. There was also conflict with the Samaritans as the returning Jews did not consider them truly Jewish.

Despite demoralization and tensions within the Jewish community, as well as a lack of resources, reconstruction of the Temple began in 516 BC, under the leadership of two prophets, Haggai and Zechariah. Later, in 458 BC, the prophet Ezra returned with a group of exiles. They began the work of codifying the Bible. Ezra also introduced new laws, some of which – such as the expulsion of foreign women from Jerusalem – were clearly aimed at halting the integration of Jews with other peoples. Nehemiah, an important figure in the court of Cyrus, was appointed governor in 445 BC.

Nehemiah rebuilt the walls of Jerusalem and imposed a covenant

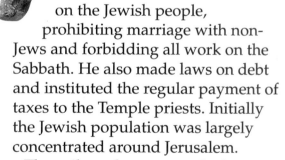

56 A silver 'Yehud' coin, with an eagle on one side and a lily on the other. These coins were used in the Jerusalem area during the Persian period. Yehud was the Aramaic name for the administrative district containing the city.

on the Jewish people, prohibiting marriage with non-Jews and forbidding all work on the Sabbath. He also made laws on debt and instituted the regular payment of taxes to the Temple priests. Initially the Jewish population was largely concentrated around Jerusalem.

The exile and return marked a new stage in the development of Jewish religion and culture, if only because many Jews did not return. Sizeable Jewish communities grew up in Babylonia, with smaller ones in Egypt. These Jews laboured and lived in their host country, but saw their spiritual homeland as Jerusalem. This was the beginning of the Jewish Diaspora.

57 This gold earring in the shape of a ram's head was found at Ashdod but was probably made in Persia and is an example of the Achaemenid style. Various goldworking techniques were used in its manufacture: the head was cast; granulation work was used for the neck decoration; and the horns are simple but effective twisted gold wire.
(Israel Museum)

THE HELLENISTIC PERIOD: THE RISE AND FALL OF THE HASMONAEAN DYNASTY

58 A menorah bronze coin of Mattathias Antigonus, the last of the Hasmonaean kings (40–37 BC). This seven-branched candelabrum, today the emblem of the State of Israel, also represents the menorah *that stood in the Second Temple.*

In 332 BC, Alexander the Great conquered the Holy Land. After his death in 323 BC, his empire was split between his generals. Palestine, part of a larger province of Syria and Phoenicia, came under the Ptolemies, who ruled Egypt. Judaea, the land of the Jews, was a hyparchy, an administrative unit, and the high priest of the Temple in Jerusalem was the political as well as religious leader. The area, however, was soon a battlefield in wars between the Ptolemies and the Seleucids, who ruled over Asia Minor. In 198 BC, the Seleucid ruler Antiochus III gained control of Judaea. His successor, Antiochus IV, was less tolerant of the traditional Jewish leadership: he doubled the taxes paid by the people of Judaea, appointed Hellenistic priests instead of orthodox Jews to serve at the Temple and plundered the Temple's treasure. A fortress called the Acra was built overlooking the Temple Mount, manned by a garrison to keep order. The last straw came when Antiochus decreed that Jews could no longer practice their religion, thus sparking off the Revolt of the Maccabees.

The incessant round of domestic revolt and foreign conquest was played out in the larger context of the growing influence of Greek culture – Hellenism – on the Jewish people and religion. Hellenistic culture dominated the eastern Mediterranean and influenced Jews and non-Jews alike in Palestine. Greek became the language of trade; many, especially the wealthy, adopted Greek dress and customs.

The Revolt of the Maccabees was led by a priest named Mattathias, of the Hashmon family, and his five sons, including Judah Maccabee. The Maccabees were aided by the Hassidim, or 'Pious Ones', and they even forged alliances with Rome in their battle for independence from the Seleucids. By 164 BC the Temple had been retaken for Jewish worship, though the Seleucids maintained control of the citadel of the Acra until 141 BC. In 140 BC, a great assembly was held in Jerusalem. Simon, the last of the brothers, was proclaimed high priest.

With this, an independent Jewish state was once more in existence, ruled by the Hasmonaeans. They, too, were now greatly influenced by Hellenistic culture, arousing the opposition of the orthodox Pharisees. The Hasmonaeans embarked on an expansion of their territory. Simon conquered lands that included both Gezer and Jaffa, thus creating access to the sea for Jerusalem. During the reign of John Hyrcanus (134–104 BC), the Hasmonaeans gained control of most of the Negev region and he forcibly converted many people, including the Idumaeans, to Judaism. The Hasmonaean empire reached its greatest extent under Alexander Jannaeus (103–76 BC): as far north as Banias; much of the Transjordan and the Moab desert to the east; and the coastal plain south of Ashkelon. Alexander Jannaeus was a cruel ruler who came into more conflict with the Pharisees, but his widow, Salome Alexandra was more favourably received by them.

59 (opposite) A Hellenistic pottery head depicting the Greek goddess Aphrodite, found at Dor. At this time Dor was a well-planned port city and its Phoenician origins had largely disappeared under Greek cultural influences.

60 (opposite) An oil lamp moulded in the shape of a satyr's head, from Dor, and dating from the Hellenistic–Early Roman period. A spirit of nature, mountains and forests, the satyr is characterized by a low forehead, a snub nose, protruding ears, and small horns. This example is wearing the pelt of a lion and its upper teeth, nose and ears can be seen resting on the satyr's head.
(Israel Museum)

61 (above) These two fine pottery heads, dating from the Hellenistic period, show the influence of Phoenician culture mixed with Greek features. Moulded terracotta items like these are common throughout the period and are found all around the Mediterranean.

After Salome Alexandra's death in 67 BC, the throne was fought over by her two sons: Hyrcanus, the older brother, who was supported by an Idumaean called Antipater; and Aristobulus. Civil war ensued, which lasted until 63 BC when the Romans intervened in the form of Pompey. He created a Roman province in Syria and marched into Jerusalem. He divided up the Hasmonaean empire and only those areas with a significant Jewish majority were retained by the Jews. Judaea was made an autonomous Jewish state, ruled by Hyrcanus II, who was given the status of ethnarch, or leader of the people,

in addition to high priest, but, significantly, not king. Judaea was no longer independent and the Romans kept a firm grip on their acquisition. The Idumaean Antipater became procurator and made his son Phasael governor of Jerusalem, and his son Herod governor of the Galilee. This aristocratic Idumaean family, which had been converted to Judaism, exhibited more loyalty to Rome than to the Jews. In 40 BC, the Parthians invaded Judaea and Hyrcanus was deposed as high priest. Antigonus, a son of Aristobulus, was put on the throne and named Mattathias. This state of affairs lasted only three years.

The Roman Period:
King Herod,
the Procurators,
and the Jewish Revolts

During the Parthian invasion, Antipater's son, Herod, fled to Rome. There he was made King of Judaea and returned to rout the Parthians in 37 BC. Herod took Idumaea, Samaria and Galilee with the help of the Roman armies. He then proceeded to Jerusalem and, after a five-month siege, captured the city. The Hasmonaean Dynasty ended with the execution of Mattathias Antigonus.

Herod could technically be considered a Jew, but, even though he went out of his way to observe Jewish customs and dietary laws, he was never accepted by the Jewish majority of Judaea who considered him to be first and foremost a vassal of Rome. Apart from his cruelty to his family and subjects, his reign is best remembered for his splendid architectural accomplishments, often on a very large scale. His projects included the fortress at Masada on the Dead Sea; a palace-stronghold at Herodium, south of Jerusalem; a winter palace at Jericho; a colony for his loyal soldiers at Sebaste near the ancient capital of Samaria; and the city of Caesarea, with its harbour Sebastos, named in honour of his patron, Caesar Augustus. The city of Jerusalem was transformed: Herod built himself a palace, three gigantic monumental towers and, most significantly, in 19 BC he began the construction of an entirely new and spectacular temple for the Jews.

After Herod's death, his three surviving sons partitioned his legacy: Archelaus received Judaea; Herod Antipas the Galilee; and Philip acquired all the territory to the northeast of the kingdom.

Herod's son Archelaus ruled over Judaea for a brief ten years. In AD 6 he was exiled and the state came under direct Roman rule. Named Judaea, the country was run by a series of governors sent directly from Rome. A first they had the title of *praefectus* but later the position was elevated to that of procurator. The best known procurator was Pontius Pilate, who, in the Bible, condemned Jesus to death.

The Jews enjoyed a greater degree of autonomy than they had under Herod; their supreme governing body and court was the Sanhedrin, which met in Jerusalem. However, there were divisions over the key issues of how to accommodate the overwhelming influence of Hellenistic culture and, on a political level, how to deal with Roman rule with its high taxes and oppressive regime. The presence of Roman troops in the holy city of Jerusalem was especially resented. The Jewish people were divided even among themselves and many were working in various ways against Rome. The ministry of Jesus must be seen

63 *A bronze statue of Emperor Hadrian, discovered at Scythopolis (Beth Shean). Hadrian travelled through Judaea in the summer of AD 129–130 and initiated many new building programmes. His plans to rebuild Jerusalem and the Temple on a Roman plan may have been the cause of the Second Jewish Revolt against Rome.* (Israel Museum)

62 *(opposite) A Latin inscription, honouring Emperor Tiberius, originally placed on a temple in Caesarea dedicated by the Roman procurator of Judaea, Pontius Pilate, c. AD 26–36. This is proof that he was in the province at the time of Jesus' death. It was found reused in the town's theatre.* (Israel Museum)

against this background of turmoil. Although Christianity later became a religion with appeal beyond national boundaries, it initially shared some characteristics with other sects that had their origins in Judaism. For instance the Essenes, a communal sect, were reported to have a following of at least 4000 people.

In AD 37 the Roman emperor Caligula appointed Agrippa I, grandson of Herod the Great, king of the territories held by his uncles, Philip and Herod Antipas. His rule, from AD 41 to 44, was a period of brief respite for Judaea as he accommodated better than any other ruler of the period the different peoples, religions and factions under his control. For instance, when Caligula ordered that his statue be placed in the Temple in Jerusalem, Agrippa intervened and delayed the execution of this edict. However, after Agrippa's death a series of corrupt Roman governors aroused great resentment, which came to a head with the First Jewish revolt of AD 66 to 70. According to the Jewish Roman historian, Josephus, the First Revolt was sparked off by a bitter dispute between Jewish and Greek residents in Caesarea, the Roman capital of the province. The Romans responded with force and the Tenth Legion was sent from Syria. Control over large parts of the countryside

64 Roman soldiers left behind many reminders of their occupation of Palestine, among them this bronze helmet. They lived in almost every town in Palestine, as shown for instance by the New Testament story of the Roman centurion living in Capernaum. They also settled in the new towns of Caesarea and Sebaste, founded by Herod the Great.

65 (top left) A **Judaea Capta** coin, depicting Rome standing triumphant over a vanquished Judaea.

65 (centre) A coin issued by the Roman procurator Pontius Pilate with the symbol of a curved staff, the mark of office of the Roman augur, a soothsayer who predicted the future. This blatant pagan symbolism was deeply offensive to the Jewish people and contributed to the outbreak of the First Revolt against Rome. The reverse of this coin shows a wreath surrounding the date of issue.

65 (left) A silver shekel coin of the First Jewish Revolt. One side is decorated with three pomegranates, with an inscription in Hebrew 'Jerusalem the Holy'. On the other side is a chalice with the words, 'Shekel of Israel, Year Two' (AD 67–68).

and much of the city of Jerusalem was lost to the rebels, and the province was in a state of unrest. On the Roman side were three legions which, along with the auxiliary forces, amounted to 60,000 men. The Jews were not only ill-equipped and badly trained as soldiers, they were also not united among themselves.

In the spring of AD 70, the Roman general Titus and his armies lay siege to Jerusalem. Josephus' account outlines the disunity among the Jewish defenders and the terrible suffering of the civilian population. When the Temple was finally taken it was levelled to the ground, as was the rest of the city. The Jews that were not massacred were sent away into slavery. Entry to the city was forbidden to the Jews, although this edict was not always strictly enforced. The destruction of the Temple in Jerusalem in 70 signalled the end of both a religious and cultural tradition that had been based in Jerusalem. It was an event that left a deep scar and is still commemorated by the Jewish holy day of Ninth Av.

However, Jewish cultural and religious life did not end. Rabbinical academies grew up around great rabbis, both in the Holy Land and in the Diaspora. Instead of the Temple, religious life was focused on the synagogue. Although the Jews could no longer live freely in Jerusalem, several other centres of Jewry grew up in other places in the Holy Land.

In 117 Hadrian became emperor and many of the changes he introduced further enraged the Jewish people. In 129 he visited Jerusalem and three years later he began to implement his plan for rebuilding it as a pagan city named *Aelia Capitolina*. Hadrian also changed the name of the country from Judaea to *Palaestina* or Palestine. The Second Jewish Revolt broke out in 132 and was led by a messianic leader, Simon Bar Kokhba, who promised the redemption of the Jewish people.

66 (above) The central panel of the mosaic floor in the synagogue at En Gedi on the Dead Sea, dating from the fifth century AD. Four birds are depicted in the central medallion, while in each corner is a pair of peacocks with a bunch of grapes.

66 (centre) The Oval Hall at the hot springs of Hammath Gader in the Jordan Valley. The springs were first mentioned by Strabo, the Roman geographer, in the first century, and became well known both for their medicinal qualities and as a place of leisure.

66 (right) A sarcophagus discovered in the excavations at Ashkelon, decorated with three bulls' heads, separated by a garland, a flower and a pair of lizards. Ashkelon was a centre of maritime trade and banking.

67 (opposite) The face of a youth from a mosaic floor discovered in the excavations of Neapolis (Shechem). This new city was founded by the Flavian emperors in AD 72–73, after the destruction of Jerusalem.

68 The eastern
Mediterranean, in
particular Sidon,
became the centre of
a new glass industry
based on techniques
invented in the first
half of the first
century AD. This
luxury glass became
a coveted item
throughout the
Roman Empire. In
the excavations of the
Jewish Quarter in
Jerusalem, a store of
broken glass was
found for reuse in a
glass factory.

69 (opposite) New
glass-blowing
techniques were used
in the production of
free-blown and mould-
blown glass. The
process of casting
entailed pouring
molten glass into
moulds made by the
lost-wax process,
similar to that used
in the casting of
metal. Glass pieces in
new colours also
began to appear in
mosaic work.

Coins were minted by the rebels bearing the façade of the Temple as it had looked over sixty years previously. The revolt lasted only three and a half years, and in the Roman suppression of the insurrection many thousands of Jews were massacred. Once the majority of the population, the remaining Jews largely retreated to the Galilee or fled throughout the Diaspora. The character of Jerusalem was substantially changed when Hadrian completed his rebuilding of the city on an entirely Roman plan, a plan which still underlies the layout of the city today.

70/75 The Old City of Jerusalem from the northwest. The Judaean Mountains and the Dead Sea can be seen in the background. The boundaries of the city have not always been the same. The area in the lower centre, now called the Christian Quarter, between the New Gate and the tall tower of the Church of the Redeemer, was unoccupied during Second Temple times.

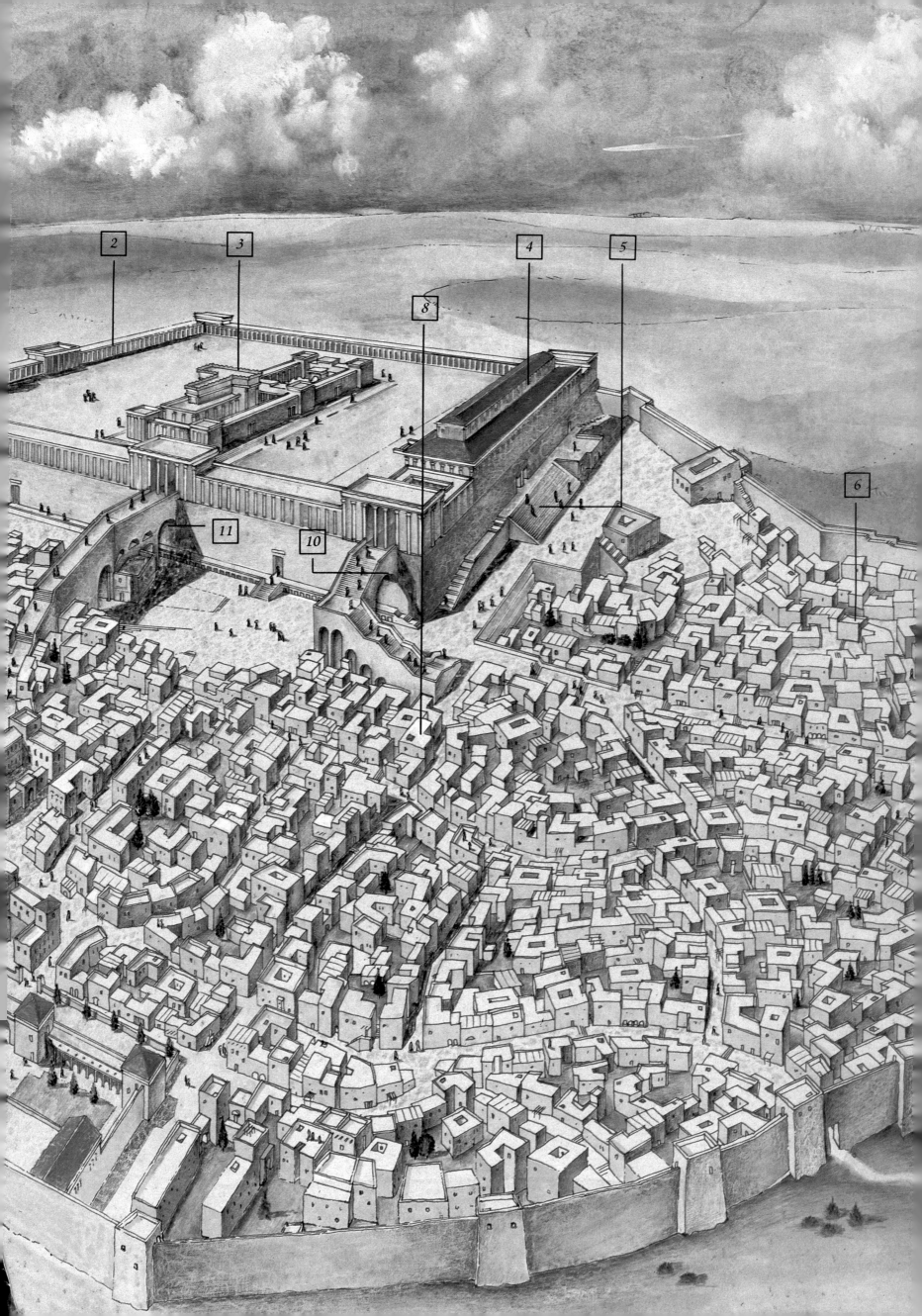

JERUSALEM IN SECOND TEMPLE TIMES

The reconstruction of the city of Jerusalem after the return from the Babylonian exile was a long, slow process. Only with the reign of King Herod did the city once more reach magnificent proportions. As this artist's impression shows, Herod built himself a fortified palace, with three monumental towers, named Phasael, Hippicus and Mariamne, after friends and family. On the northwestern corner of the Temple Mount, Herod rebuilt a fortress and named it Antonia, in honour of one of his patrons, Mark Antony. The Temple Mount was greatly enlarged, and on the southern side the Royal Stoa was built. Most significantly, Herod rebuilt the Temple, nearly doubling its size and adding lavish new embellishments.

76 (left) A terracotta
sculpture of Aphrodite
found on Mount
Carmel and dating
from the first century
AD. This statue of the
Greek goddess of love
is just one example
of the pervasive
influence of

Hellenistic–Roman
culture in Palestine.
The fashions of Rome
were most influential
on the upper classes,
including Jews, whose
religion prohibited the
worship of such pagan
images as this statue.
(Israel Museum)

76 (above) The art of
jewelry-making was
developed to a very
high level in Roman
society. These cameos
show in relief the
head of an unknown
Roman nobleman
and a mythical horse-
man figure.

77 (above) This cameo brooch, framed in gold and set with garnets, carnelians and emeralds, has been further decorated with another small cameo.

77 (right) A pendant gold earring with a pearl within a setting of cutwork. Three more pearls are suspended from triangles set with garnets and attached to two mythical beasts.

77 (below) This ring, set with an intaglio gem engraved with an elephant, could be used as a seal. The Hellenization of society meant not only the import of luxury items such as this jewelry, but also a new standard of living for the very wealthy. For example, the Herodian Mansions excavated in Jerusalem revealed a standard of living the rival of any other part of the Empire. The rooms were brightly decorated with plaster reliefs, frescoes and elaborate mosaic floors.

THE BYZANTINE PERIOD: CHRISTIANITY COMES TO THE HOLY LAND

78 This bronze menorah lamp (below) dates from the fourth century, as does the Christian one (centre), from Beth Shean. Lamps of such quality were used in religious ceremonies. (Israel Museum)

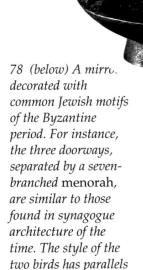

78 (below) A mirror decorated with common Jewish motifs of the Byzantine period. For instance, the three doorways, separated by a seven-branched menorah, are similar to those found in synagogue architecture of the time. The style of the two birds has parallels in several mosaic floors.

The Byzantine period was a time of relative peace, marked by the consolidation of the Christian population and Christian institutions in the Holy Land. The one man responsible for this change of fortune was Emperor Constantine. He made Christianity the official religion of the Roman Empire, and he and his mother, Helena, took a personal interest in the building of churches to commemorate the holy sites of Christianity.

In 326, Helena made a pilgrimage to the Holy Land. In Jerusalem she discovered the remains of the True Cross and in Bethlehem located the grotto where Jesus was born. The Church of the Holy Sepulchre in Jerusalem was dedicated in 335. The Holy Land became a place of pilgrimage for Christians and they helped to build large numbers of churches.

Although the short reign of Julian the Apostate (361–363) saw an attempt to restore the pagan pantheon of gods to its former glory, Christianity became the religion of the majority of the people of the Holy Land. More than a hundred monasteries were founded during this period, many of them in very remote desert areas. The best known was that of St Theodosius, who founded a monastery with a hospital, hospices and workshops for hundreds of monks in the desert near Bethlehem. The remains of many Byzantine churches can be seen in Israel today; their mosaic floors are especially beautiful.

There were at least 43 different Jewish communities in Israel during the Byzantine period. Within the Roman Empire, Judaism had the status of *religio licita*, a permitted religion, but this position was slowly eroded. It became a crime to convert to Judaism. However, in spite of restrictions, the remains of many large and impressively built synagogues indicate that the practice of Judaism was possible on a local level. There were few instances of open revolt by the Jews, the exception being the revolt against the Roman ruler Gallus in 351 which was quickly suppressed.

In 358, the area was divided into three administrative districts, a system which lasted until 429. *Palaestina Prima* included Judaea, Samaria, the Coastal Plain, Idumaea, and Perea, with the capital at Caesarea. *Palaestina Secunda* had its capital at Scythopolis (Beth Shean) and included the territory of the Galilee, the Golan and the Decapolis.

79 (opposite) Mosaic floors from the church at Kissufim, in the northern Negev. In the upper panel a lioness is grooming her cub and in the lower scene a hunter on horseback spears a leopard. Hunting scenes were common on Byzantine church floors, though some of the clergy opposed this as a form of idolatry.

ΡΓΟΝΑΛΕ3ΑΝΔΡΟΥ

The Decapolis included Beth Shean and nine other cities in Transjordan. *Palaestina Tertia* consisted largely of territory in the Negev, with its capital at Petra.

Another significant minority group, the Samaritans, attempted to assert their independence, and with the promise of help from the Persians staged two revolts, one in 485 and the second in 529. They briefly achieved an independent state, but this was ruthlessly crushed. The reign of Justinian I (527–565) was characterized by the building of walls and water supply systems, and also the construction of new churches. New legislation was introduced further depriving the Jews of many of their rights.

The end of the Byzantine period in Palestine was marked by the Persian invasion of 614. The Persians were aided by the Jewish population of Palestine, many of whom saw them as a kind of messianic deliverance from their oppressed state under Byzantine rule. The Persians first took Damascus, in 613, and in the following year captured the Galilee. From there they marched on to Caesarea and Jerusalem.

80 A seven-branched menorah, *carved in relief in stone, from Beth Shean. It is accompanied by a* lulav *(palm-branch), a* shofar *(ram's horn trumpet), an* etrog *(citrus fruit) and an incense shovel. These religious objects are also common motifs in the mosaic floors of synagogues.*

Many of the churches of Jerusalem were razed to the ground and the True Cross was sent to Persia as war booty. The Jews were given control of the city of Jerusalem, but after three years the Persians apparently reversed this policy in favour of the Christian population.

In the year 627, under threat from the Byzantine emperor, Heraclius, the Persians were forced to retreat, and in addition to suffering many persecutions, the Jews were expelled from the city. In March 630, Heraclius entered Jerusalem and restored the Cross to its place in the rebuilt Church of the Holy Sepulchre.

81 (above) A cross carved in relief in stone, from a Byzantine church. Around its base are vine leaves, a common Christian motif.

81 (centre) These gold earrings were discovered in a cemetery at Mamshit, in the central Negev. During the Byzantine period Mamshit had two churches. Its chief importance was as a trading town on the route from Petra and the Transjordan to the Negev.

81 (below) In early Christian art the fish was a symbol of Christ, here in the form of a pendant. While Christ was the fisher of souls and the first apostles were fishermen, the image is of an earlier origin. From the letters of the Greek word for 'fish', Ιχθυς, can be obtained the acrostic 'Jesus Christ, Son of God, the Saviour'.

THE EARLY ARAB PERIOD: THE INTRODUCTION OF ISLAM

82 (below) A female statue from the palace of Khirbet el-Mafjar in the Jordan Valley, north of Jericho. Commonly known as Hisham's Palace and dating to the Umayyad period, the complex consists of an elaborate reception hall, mosque and bathhouse. Left unfinished, it was destroyed by an earthquake in AD 749. (Rockefeller Museum)

82 (right) A carved stone and stucco window from Khirbet el-Mafjar. There is evidence that much of the stucco was painted in bright primary colours. These matched the lively mosaic pavements, laid in elaborate geometric designs, that decorated the interior of the palace and the bathhouse. (Rockefeller Museum)

The campaign by the Arabs to capture the land of Palestine was long and fragmented, beginning only after the death of Muhammad in 632. They began their attack from the south and from the east, and by 633–634 the Byzantine forces had lost control over much of the countryside and retreated to the walled cities and towns. Beth Shean was the first city to be abandoned by the Byzantine forces and by 637 or 638, Jerusalem surrendered after a siege of two years. Caesarea fell in 640 and Ashkelon in 641. The Arabs settled as agriculturalists in the countryside and colonies were set up in coastal towns to prevent them being reconquered by Byzantine forces.

While Arabic became the dominant language, the population of the towns remained largely Christian. The only predominantly Arab town was Ramlah, founded by the caliph Suleiman in about 715.

The Fatimid dynasty of Shi'ite Muslims from Egypt conquered Palestine in 969. Their success was short-lived, however, and almost the entire country was taken by the Qarmatians in 971. Although three years later they were routed by the Fatimids, they managed to return after a few months. This unrest gave the Byzantine forces an opportunity to invade. In what has been called the 'Byzantine Crusade' they captured Beth Shean in 975. The Qarmatians attacked again, and only in 977 were they finally defeated by the Fatimids.

However, the Fatimids were never in complete control of the countryside and large parts were dominated by Bedouins. The economic base of the country was primarily agricultural, although the years of unrest had weakened it, and trade in the entire eastern Mediterranean had declined.

In general, the minority Christian, Samaritan and Jewish populations were tolerated. One notable exception was the rule of the fanatic Fatimid caliph al-Hakim in the years 1009-1013. He enforced restrictions regarding the distinctive dress required for non-Muslims, as well as ordering the destruction of churches and synagogues. The Church of the

82 (opposite below) A reconstructed window from the courtyard at Khirbet el-Mafjar. The courtyard led to a large ornamental pool that greeted visitors on entry to the palace. From the design of the palace, it seems that its chief purpose was for the lavish entertainment of guests.

83 (above) A mosaic of a fruit-bearing tree with feeding deer, one of them being attacked by a lion. The style of this mosaic imitates an oriental carpet, with a border and tasselled fringe. From the diwan or reception hall, the other mosaics are all in geometric designs, also intended to resemble oriental carpets.

Holy Sepulchre in Jerusalem was one of those destroyed.

In the middle of the eleventh century, the weak position of the Fatimid dynasty was exploited by the Seljuks from Turkey. By 1071 they had captured Jerusalem as well as other parts of the country. The Fatimids, however, retained their hold on coastal towns and by 1098 had retaken Jerusalem. This victory was short-lived: the Crusaders took the city the following year.

THE CRUSADER PERIOD: THE HOLY LAND IS RETURNED TO CHRISTIANITY

84 One of five Crusader capitals in the Church of the Annunciation in Nazareth. They depict scenes from the lives of the Apostles and other religious themes. Made by artists from the south of France, they were never installed.

84 (below centre) The eastern lintel that stood over the entrance to the Church of the Holy Sepulchre in Jerusalem. Carved from marble in the Romanesque style, it depicts the snares that entangle the sinner. (Rockefeller Museum)

84 (below right) A cross incised on the walls of the Church of the Holy Sepulchre, probably as a sign of devotion by a pilgrim during the Crusades. The Crusader church has survived, although with many alterations, to the present day.

85 (opposite) A fragment of sculpture representing the Trinity, found in excavations on the site of the Church of the Annunciation in Nazareth, in 1867. Sculpted in the same style as the five capitals, it was concealed when the Crusaders surrendered Nazareth after the battle of the Horns of Hattin.

The Crusades began in response to an appeal made in 1095 by Pope Urban II to rescue the Holy Land from Islam. The knights of the first successful Crusade to the Holy Land arrived on the coast of Palestine in May 1099: by 7 June, Jerusalem was under siege. After little more than a month, the Crusaders succeeded in breaching the walls of the city. The Muslim and Jewish population, numbering between 20,000 and 30,000, were nearly all massacred and the few survivors were sold into slavery. Bethlehem was relinquished to the Crusaders by its Christian

population; Nablus, Jericho, Tiberias and Beth Shean surrendered with little bloodshed. Jaffa was the chief port of entry for the Crusaders, and, by 1153, the other coastal cities had fallen. This was achieved with the help of the Italian merchant cities of Genoa, Pisa and Venice. Large concessions were made in reward: grants of land, judicial autonomy

and certain commercial monopolies.

Baldwin I, first King of Jerusalem, gained control over the King's Highway route from Syria to Egypt in addition to the *haj* route from Damascus and Cairo to Mecca and Medina. At its height, the borders of the Kingdom of Jerusalem, as the Crusaders called their state in the Holy Land, extended from Beirut in

the north, to Ashkelon in the south, to Eilat, and Moab on the east side of the Jordan. To maintain these borders a series of fortresses was built.

The kingdom was short-lived, however. Saladin, Sultan of Egypt and Syria, reversed the Crusader victories and at the battle of the Horns of Hattin, in July 1187, soundly defeated the combined Crusader forces. Jerusalem fell in October 1187 and, by the end of that year, nearly all Crusader-held towns and fortresses in the interior had surrendered, and a withdrawal of the Crusaders to the port of Tyre was negotiated.

The fall of Jerusalem spurred on another Crusade. Richard I, the Lionheart, regained Acre in July 1191. In the peace treaty agreed in September 1192, the Crusaders were ceded territory along the coast between Tyre and Jaffa, and granted rights of pilgrimage to Jerusalem.

86 (top left) The remains of the Crusader castle of Atlith on the Carmel coast. The Knights Templar established a fort on this small promontory during the Fifth Crusade in 1218 and it was manned until after the conquest of Acre in 1291.

86 (centre left) The Nimrod fortress on the Golan Heights was of great strategic value, guarding the road to Damascus and overlooking Banias and the Huleh Valley. Very little is known of this fortress; its construction dates from before the Crusader conquest.

86 (above) The head of an angel on a fragment of a fresco executed in tempera, from the Crusader basilica of Gethsemane at the foot of the Mount of Olives. (Museum of the Studium Biblicum Franciscanum)

86 (right) The Crusaders arrived at Caesarea in 1099. Their imprint has survived to this day in the ruins of the fortifications, in the arches of a covered street along the city walls and in the Gothic vaults of the gatehouse.

After Saladin's death in 1193, his empire was dismantled, and although subsequent Crusades were able to reclaim limited territories, especially along the coast, Jerusalem remained Muslim until 1228 when Frederick II, Emperor of Germany, negotiated with the Sultan of Egypt. Many cities, including Nazareth, Bethlehem and Jerusalem, were returned to the Crusaders, but the Temple Mount was retained by the Muslims.

When Frederick returned to Germany, the Crusaders began to war among themselves. In the next two decades Egypt regained much of its lost territory and Jerusalem was lost again in 1244. The final campaign, by the Egyptian Mameluke ruler Baybars, began in 1265. In May 1291, Acre was defeated and Atlith fell in August; after two centuries in the Holy Land, the last Europeans were forced to return home.

87 (right) A twelfth-century gilded bronze crucifix found in Jerusalem. Originally fixed to a wooden cross, only the figure has survived. This crucifix is quite rare, since most ceremonial objects of the Crusader period were taken back to Europe after the Crusaders' retreat from the Holy Land. (Museum of the Studium Biblicum Franciscanum)

87 (right) This enamelled bishop's crozier comes from the Church of the Nativity, Bethlehem. Discovered in 1863, it is among the oldest examples of Limoges enamel work known, dating from the time of King Baldwin II. It is made in the form of a snake with the figure of Christ in the centre. (Museum of the Studium Biblicum Franciscanum)

THE MAMELUKE PERIOD: THE HOLY LAND IS RECLAIMED

The first years of Mameluke rule saw some building projects in Jerusalem but, in general, Palestine was not important to these Egyptian rulers. The economy remained much as it had been for centuries; among the major exports were fruit, olive oil and soap. Many of the coastal cities, including Acre and Jaffa, were destroyed to prevent the Crusaders regaining a foothold in the Holy Land. Large parts of Jerusalem lay in ruins and it is estimated there were only 4000 households. Instead, the centres of population had shifted to Ramlah, Nablus and Gaza.

The Islamic character of Palestine was established during this period and at least 50 *madrasas* (religious schools) were founded. The Christian and Jewish populations were allowed to coexist as long as the observance of their religions was very discreet. Laws prevented the expansion of any of the surviving Christian churches or Jewish synagogues; however, special concessions were granted to the Georgian and Ethiopian Christians. Other Christian groups had to resort to large payments to extend their rights over the holy places.

The most obvious reminder of the Mameluke period is the magnificent Islamic architecture of Jerusalem, and in buildings in Ramlah.

88 (left) One of the architectural gems on the Temple Mount, the Fountain of Qa'itbay was built in 1482, influenced by the great funerary monuments of Cairo. It was repaired in 1883 and new elements were added.

88 (centre left) The small Dome of the Ascension of the Prophet, built in 1200, commemorates the place where the Prophet prayed before ascending to Paradise. There is a theory that it may have been rebuilt from a baptistery dating from the Crusader period.

88 (centre right) The Mameluke Fakhriyya Minaret is one of the four square minarets that stand around the Haram al-Sharif. It is topped with a balcony for the muezzin, a copper dome and an alam, the decorative metal finial in the form of the Muslim crescent. The typical 'stalactites' which support the porch are called muqarnas.

88 (left) The 'Gindas' Bridge near Lydda was built in 1273 by the Mameluke Sultan Baybars. The lion, carved in relief on either side of the arch, was the symbol of Baybars. Here they flank a splendid inscription that commemorates the construction of the bridge.

*89 (above) An oil
lamp of the early Arab
period, decorated with
animal motifs. The top
was made by being
pressed into a mould
and it shows a dog
chasing a small
animal.*

*89 (above) A very
fine example of a
Mameluke war axe,
with the personal
blazon of a Mameluke
sultan incorporated in
the cut-out design
with exquisite
workmanship. The
lower edge of the
crescent-shaped blade
is attached to the shaft
to prevent it breaking
or twisting on impact.*

*89 (right) A
Mameluke-period
bronze candlestick,
probably used at one
time in the el-Aqsa
Mosque. The arches
in the circular body
recall the shape of the
arches of the Dome of
the Rock.*

THE EARLY OTTOMAN PERIOD: UNDER TURKISH RULE

Palestine passed into the hands of the Ottoman Turks after the defeat of the Mamelukes in northern Syria in 1516. The first half century of Turkish rule is referred to as the Golden Period and during that time Palestine was in part divided into four administrative districts called *sanjaks*: Jerusalem; Gaza; Nablus; and Safed; while mostly it belonged to the province of Damascus. Safed became a major centre for the Jews.

The major problem for the population of Palestine was the decline in security as the Ottoman government gradually lost direct control over the countryside. Also, the Ottomans imposed very high taxes and had a merciless system for collecting them. The minority populations of Christians and Jews were especially vulnerable. Disputes over the Christian holy places in Jerusalem and Bethlehem became part of the agenda of international relations as various European countries tried to gain concessions in treaties with the Ottoman government.

By the middle of the eighteenth century, Zahir al-Omar had gained control over much of the country before being killed by his own forces in 1775. The northern part of the country came under the control of Ahmad Pasha al-Jazzar. Jazzar was given the name 'The Butcher', because of his habit of cutting off the nose or ears of those who displeased him. Jazzar stopped the northward march of Napoleon in 1799 when, with the help of the British fleet, he repelled the siege of Acre and Napoleon was forced to retreat with his army to Egypt.

90 (top) The present walls of the city of Jerusalem were largely built on the orders of Suleiman the Magnificent in 1537. The Damascus Gate, on the north side of the city, is one of his impressive gates.

90 (centre) One of many medallions with geometric motifs decorating the walls of the Old City. Others take the form of rosettes, sometimes set inside geometric shapes.

90 (below) One of the pairs of lions that flank each side of what is now called St Stephen's Gate. The lions were the symbol of the Mameluke sultan Baybars and were reused by Suleiman when he rebuilt the walls of the city.

91 (opposite) The exquisite marble interior of the Great Mosque of Acre, built by Jazzar Pasha in 1781, decorated with very fine multi-coloured stonework in geometric designs.

THE BIRTH OF MODERN ISRAEL

The Holy Land had long been a dangerous country for the foreign traveller; however, during the reign of Muhammad Ali of Egypt (1832–1840), Jerusalem became more receptive to foreigners and several western countries opened consulates there. Missionaries – Protestants, Roman Catholics and Orthodox Christians – began their work in the city and Jerusalem became a great centre of pilgrimage. Numerous travel accounts brought the Holy Land to the attention of armchair travellers in Europe and America. The excavations of the Palestine Exploration Fund (founded in 1865) mark the beginnings of modern archaeology in the Holy Land, and their discoveries excited much interest. They also made very accurate maps, using the most modern techniques of the time.

92 (top) The foundation ceremony of the new city of Tel Aviv, on the sands north of Jaffa in 1909. Tel Aviv was the first all-Jewish city built in modern times and today it is the centre of a large metropolis.

92 (far left) Settled in 1878, Petah Tikvah was the 'mother' of Jewish settlements. It nearly failed because of hostility from the Turkish authorities, raids by Arab neighbours and the malaria-ridden swamps nearby.

92 (below left) General Allenby entered Jerusalem through the Jaffa Gate on 11 December, 1917, thus ending over 400 years of Ottoman rule. He chose to walk into the Holy City rather than ride on a horse.

The roots of modern Israel are to be found both in the nationalistic movements of Europe and within the community of Jews in Jerusalem. The first Zionist Congress was held in Basel in 1897, led by Theodor Herzl, when a consensus began to emerge, representing the many threads of the Jewish people. In 1901, the Jewish National Fund was set up to purchase land in Palestine.

92 (centre) The Haganah (Jewish underground army) ship, the Exodus, one of the immigrant ships that tried to smuggle Jews fleeing Europe to Palestine. After its arrival in Haifa in 1947, it was returned by the British to Europe, causing great international outcry.

While the people who made up the first *Aliya* (immigration) were inexperienced in working the land, those of the second *Aliya*, in the first decade of the twentieth century, possessed an ideology of labour: that by the toil of their own hands they could build a new society. This new society was based on socialist ideals and some of its institutions, like the communal societies of the *kibbutzim*, were unique to Israel.

Led by men like David Ben-Gurion, who would later become the first Prime Minister of the new state, its foundations were built not on labour alone but also on the creation of a new Hebrew culture. Eleazer Ben Yehuda promoted Hebrew as the language of the new land, as the only way for immigrants from many different countries to integrate into one united society.

The Balfour Declaration of 2 November, 1917 expressed the support of the British government for 'the establishment in Palestine of a national home for the Jewish people'. When the British General Allenby walked into Jerusalem a month later at the head of the conquering British forces, he found that the basis of this society was already in place. The new city of Tel Aviv had been founded on the sands north of Jaffa, the modern port of Haifa was under construction and many new agricultural settlements had been started. During the British Mandate, the institutions of a

modern Jewish state were established: the Histadrut Labour Union; the banking system; a modern secular education system; the Hebrew University of Jerusalem; and co-operative agricultural unions. On 14 May, 1948, when the British Mandate expired, the Jewish government proclaimed the foundation of the State of Israel, an event that triggered a violent reaction from the Arab world. The War of Independence was only the first of many conflicts.

93 (above) The Declaration of the State of Israel on 14 May, 1948. David Ben-Gurion, who would become the first Prime Minister of the new state, is in the centre.

93 (left) Young fighters in Jerusalem during the War of Independence. At the time of the declaration of the State, 51,500 people were serving in its armed forces.

Israel today

Israel today is still a young country with the legacy of a long past. Great importance is placed on the in-gathering of Jews from all over the world. The latest immigrations of Jews from Ethiopia and the former Soviet Union show how diverse peoples look to Israel as their national home. The absorption of new immigrants and the teaching of Hebrew are seen as essential.

The population of the country is nearing five million, and of that number more than 83 per cent are Jewish. Of non-Jewish Israeli citizens, Muslims make up about 78 per cent, Christians 14 per cent and Druze and other groups about 8 per cent. Most people live in urban settlements. While Jerusalem is technically the largest city in the country in terms of number, the majority of people live on the coastal plain in the metropolis centred on Tel Aviv–Jaffa. Other large centres of population are in the Haifa Bay region and in Beersheba in the Negev.

In its social and educational services, Israel is the equal of the countries of western Europe. Most children begin their education at the age of three or four in nursery school and many go on to one of the eight universities. Israel's medical services are among the best in the world.

The country has a parliamentary democracy – the 120-member Knesset is Israel's legislature. Moreover, the size of the country gives the people a sense of a common cause, no matter what their background or political or religious beliefs. Much of this unity can be attributed to the compulsory national service required of young men and women after they have finished school.

Israel's economy is based not only on new technologies like irrigation systems and computer-related products, but also on age-old Jewish professions. The diamond exchange in Ramat Gan is the largest in the world. Tourism, either to the holy city of Jerusalem or to the exotic fish and sun of Eilat, is growing in importance. Israel is an outward-looking country and one that is in the midst of a new kind of struggle – for lasting peace and reconciliation with all its neighbours.

94 (below) The resort of Eilat is popular with tourists who come to enjoy the beaches and the tropical fish of the Gulf of Aqaba. It has its own airport with direct flights from Europe.

94 (left) The city of Haifa, overlooking Haifa Bay to the north. It overtook Acre as the most important port of Palestine by the beginning of the twentieth century, and is now also a centre for industry.

94–95 (above) Tel Aviv, looking south towards the promontory of Jaffa. The beach front is lined with the commercial and residential centre and large hotels.

95 (left) The new city of Jerusalem looking towards Mount Scopus and the campus of the Hebrew University, which was established in 1925 and rebuilt after the 1967 war.

THE HOLY LAND IN MAPS AND PRINTS

THE BIBLE AND THE MAPPING OF THE HOLY LAND

The cartography of the land of Israel was not just the mapping of a certain part of the earth, it was also the matching of the land to the Bible.

The stories of both the Old and New Testaments are planted in the soil of the Holy Land in an area from 'Dan to Beer-sheva', measuring only 80 km (50 miles) wide and 240 km (150 miles) long. The Bible itself is a kind of verbal map, as for instance in Joshua 13–19, where the borders of the 12 tribes of Israel are laid out.

The mapping of the Holy Land was important for several reasons. There was great interest in the land which was central to three of the world's great religions: Judaism, Christianity and Islam. Jerusalem – believed by many to be the centre of the world, the navel of the universe, the gateway to Paradise – was at the middle of many ancient maps. Later, the printing of the Bible created a need for illustrated Bibles as well as works like dictionaries, encyclopaedias and biblical atlases.

96 This parchment manuscript of the mid-twelfth century is the oldest extant copy of the map of the Holy Land drawn by St Jerome in c. 385. In the centre, the two concentric circles represent Jerusalem, while in the lower right and left appear Alexandria in Egypt and Constantinople.

CLASSICAL MAPS AND THEIR INFLUENCE

Classical maps have not survived in their original form but have come down to the present day only as copies. For example, the Ptolemaeus maps were initially part of the geography of second-century geographer Ptolemy of Alexandria. Although no originals of his map are preserved, we do have copies made in the sixteenth and seventeenth centuries, when map-makers looked to the classical period. The maps of Ptolemy were orientated to the north and were drawn according to a scale on a grid using longitude and latitude.

The third-century maps of St Jerome, illustrating his Bible commentary, are more conceptual. As in later *mappaemundi* Jerusalem is the centre of the world and is much larger than the countries around it. Jerome was influenced by his contemporary, Eusebius of Caesarea, author of the *Onomastikon*, the first biblical geography. The Roman military road map, called the *Peutinger Table*, was compiled in the fifth century AD, although the earliest copy dates to the thirteenth century, now in the Royal Library in Vienna. It is essentially a long table of roads divided by mileposts showing the major routes between the cities of the Roman world, from Britain to Ceylon.

96–97 The work of Claudius Ptolemy influenced European cartographers up to the seventeenth century. The Tabula Asiae IV *was drawn on parchment in 1474 by Donnus Nicholaus Germanus for the first printed Ptolemaic Atlas, published in Ülm in 1482.*

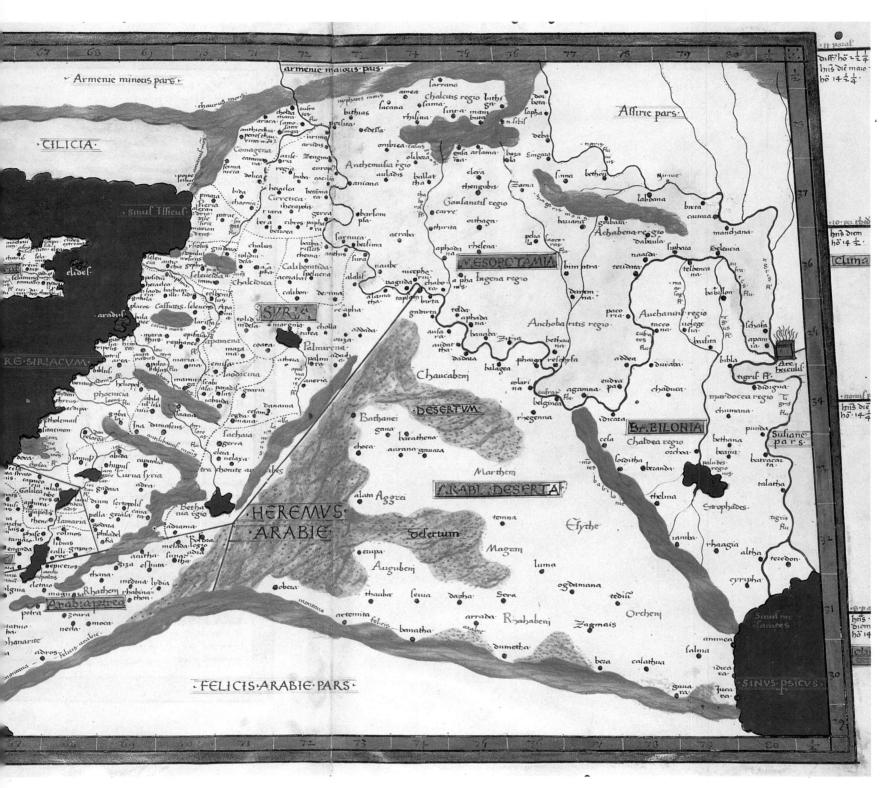

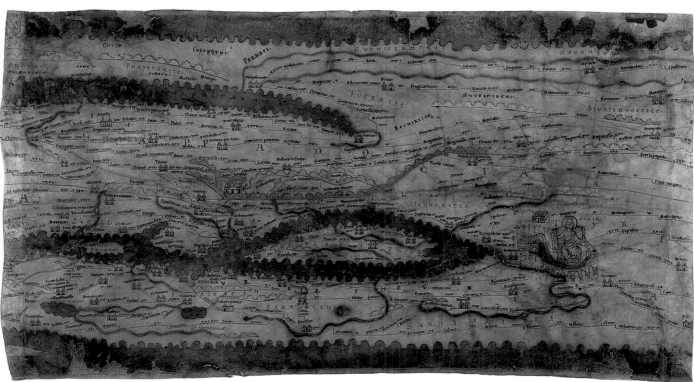

97 (left) The Tabula Itineraria, *better known as the* Peutinger Table, *from the name of one of its discoverers, the German Humanist Konrad Peutinger, is a medieval copy of a road map of the Roman empire drawn up in the middle of the fifth century AD. In the section reproduced here Palestine appears in the bottom left, below Rhodes.*

THE MADABA MAP

The Madaba Map is a mosaic floor discovered in 1896 in a Byzantine church in the ancient city of Madaba, 30 km (19 miles) south of Amman in Jordan. Although parts of the mosaic had been destroyed during the building of a new church after the mosaic was laid, the surviving sections (5 by 10 m or 16 by 35 ft), show the Holy Land from the Mediterranean to the far shore of the Dead Sea, and from the town of Salem close to Beth Shean to the mouth of the Nile River.

1 *Three fish swimming in the River Jordan; one has turned back after encountering the salty water of the Dead Sea.*
2 *A small gazelle being chased by a lion (only his legs survive).*
3 *Two ferries crossing the River Jordan.*
4 *A watchtower, mounted by a ladder, guarding the southern ferry over the River Jordan.*

5 *The Dead Sea. The Lishon Peninsula now projecting into its centre is not shown.*
6 *Two ships on the Dead Sea, manned by figures whose features have been destroyed by iconoclasts, people who objected to the pictorial use of the human figure. The northern boat has its sails rolled up and is carrying a cargo of what is probably salt from the Dead Sea.*

7 *The second boat is carrying a cargo of wheat or another yellow grain.*
8 *Bethabara is the place where John the Baptist sought refuge.*
9 Charachmoba, *or modern-day Karak, is shown here as a large Byzantine city.*
10 *Aravah, the desert south of the Dead Sea.*

11 *Jericho is shown as a walled town with four towers and two gates, enclosing three churches, and surrounded by palm trees, indicating that it is an oasis.*
12 Neapolis, *or modern-day Nablus, is represented as a large walled town. This part of the mosaic is badly damaged but the east–west cardo maximus can still be seen, as well as the main church of the town.*
13 *The Samaritan holy mountains of Gerizim and Ebal are labelled twice on the Madaba Map. After the Samaritans laid claim to these mountains, the Jews insisted on a different location. The artist has clearly tried to accommodate both.*

14 *Sychar, where Jesus conversed with the Samaritan woman (John 4, 5).*
15 *Gethsemane is the garden outside Jerusalem where Jesus was betrayed by Judas Iscariot.*
16 *Modi'in, the home village of the Maccabees.*
17 *Lydda, or Lod, is shown as an unwalled city; the east–west cardo and the large basilica are visible.*

18 Nikopolis, *or biblical Emmaus of Luke 24, 13.*
19 Bethlehem *is shown as a very small town with the Basilica of the Nativity.*
20 Eleutheropolis, *or Beth Guvrin, is represented as a walled city.*
21 Ashdod, *the ancient harbour with colonnaded street and church.*

22 *Ashkelon, shown as a very large coastal town, is only partially preserved on the Map.*

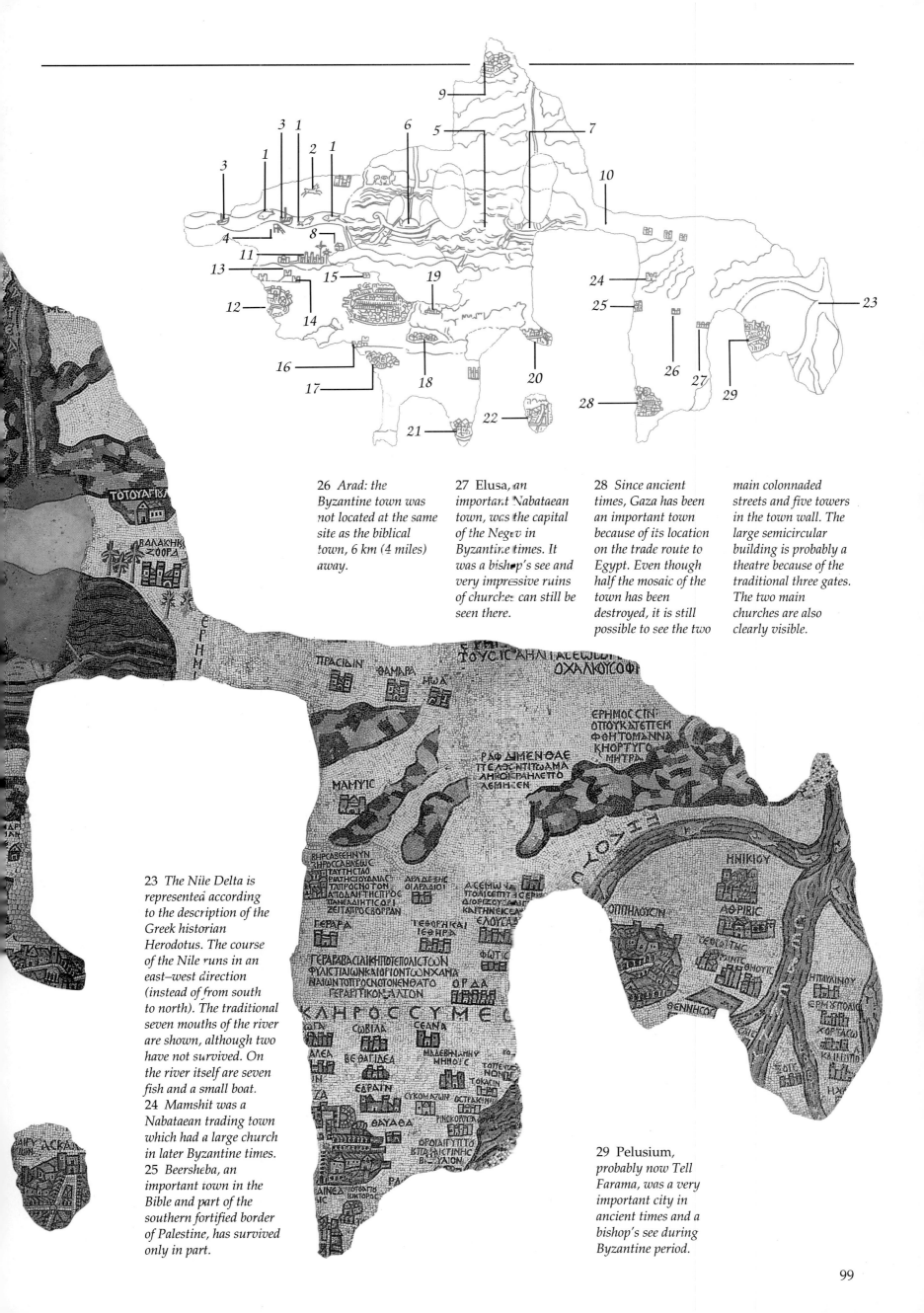

26 *Arad: the Byzantine town was not located at the same site as the biblical town, 6 km (4 miles) away.*

27 *Elusa, an important Nabataean town, was the capital of the Negev in Byzantine times. It was a bishop's see and very impressive ruins of churches can still be seen there.*

28 *Since ancient times, Gaza has been an important town because of its location on the trade route to Egypt. Even though half the mosaic of the town has been destroyed, it is still possible to see the two main colonnaded streets and five towers in the town wall. The large semicircular building is probably a theatre because of the traditional three gates. The two main churches are also clearly visible.*

23 *The Nile Delta is represented according to the description of the Greek historian Herodotus. The course of the Nile runs in an east–west direction (instead of from south to north). The traditional seven mouths of the river are shown, although two have not survived. On the river itself are seven fish and a small boat.*

24 *Mamshit was a Nabataean trading town which had a large church in later Byzantine times.*

25 *Beersheba, an important town in the Bible and part of the southern fortified border of Palestine, has survived only in part.*

29 *Pelusium, probably now Tell Farama, was a very important city in ancient times and a bishop's see during Byzantine period.*

The original map, probably measuring almost 7 by 22 m (23 by 72 ft), was made up of more than two million coloured cubes. Next to the sites, there are detailed explanations in Greek and also some biblical texts. A pictorial map, it is orientated with the Mediterranean at the bottom and the Nile at the right. The major features of Byzantine Palestine are readily identifiable; for instance, the ferry crossings at two points on the River Jordan are depicted. On the Dead Sea are two boats, with their occupants damaged by iconoclasts who objected to the depiction of the human form in a church. There are even fish swimming in the River Jordan – one of them has turned back with a sour look on its face after tasting the bitter water of the Dead Sea.

The map also includes significant biblical landmarks, as well as the borders of the areas of the 12 Tribes of Israel. The largest city, Jerusalem, is easily recognizable, as are nearly 150 other biblical sites. The major landmarks are laid out on a network of roads, probably derived from the *Peutinger Table*, while some of the smaller features could have been copied from the *Onomastikon* of Eusebius. The large amount of detail enables historians to date the making of the map to between AD 560 and 565.

One of the largest preserved sections is devoted to the city of Jerusalem, which is shown as an oval, even though the city was roughly square in shape.

The southeast corner of Jerusalem has been destroyed and so there is no information on the area south of the Temple Mount. The two main streets of the Byzantine city, clearly shown with columned porticoes, begin just inside the Damascus Gate in a large plaza marked by a tall column. In Roman times the column no doubt held a statue of the Roman emperor and during the Byzantine period it was reported to have been graced with a cross. Churches stand out clearly because they have been given red roofs, while other buildings have yellow ones. The three largest churches are especially evident. The Church of the Holy Sepulchre is shown 'upside down' in the centre and its main architectural features are visible: the rotunda over the tomb of Christ; the basilica; and the steps leading down to the *Cardo Maximus*. The Nea, or 'New Church', of Justinian is prominent in the right-hand part of the mosaic, and the Church of Mount Zion is depicted in virtually the same way.

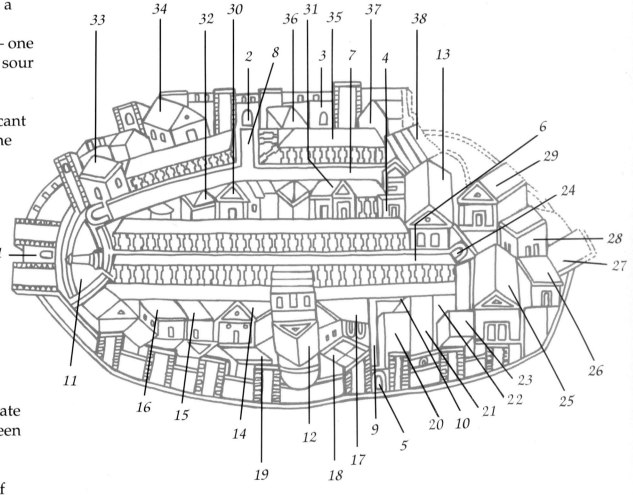

1 *Damascus Gate.*
2 *Lions' or St Stephen's Gate.*
3 *Golden Gate.*
4 *Nea Gate, perhaps the Dung Gate.*
5 *Jaffa Gate.*
6 Cardo Maximus.
7 *Roads of the Tyropoeon Valley.*
8 *Street leading to St Stephen's Gate.*
9 *Decumanus, leading from the Jaffa Gate. Today this is probably David Street.*
10 *Street leading to Mount Zion.*
11 *Plaza in front of the Damascus Gate with a column topped by a statue or a cross.*
12 *Church of the Holy Sepulchre.*
13 *Nea Church.*
14 *Palace of the Patriarch.*
15 *Clergy House of the Patriarch.*
16 *Hospital.*
17 *Forum.*
18 *Baptistery of the Church of the Holy Sepulchre.*
19 *Monastery of the Spudaei.*
20 *David's Tower.*
21, 22, 23 *Monasteries.*
24 *Gate leading to Mount Zion.*
25 *Church on Mount Zion.*
26 *Diaconicon of Mount Zion.*
27 *Clergy House of Mount Zion.*
28 *Baths above the Siloam Pool.*

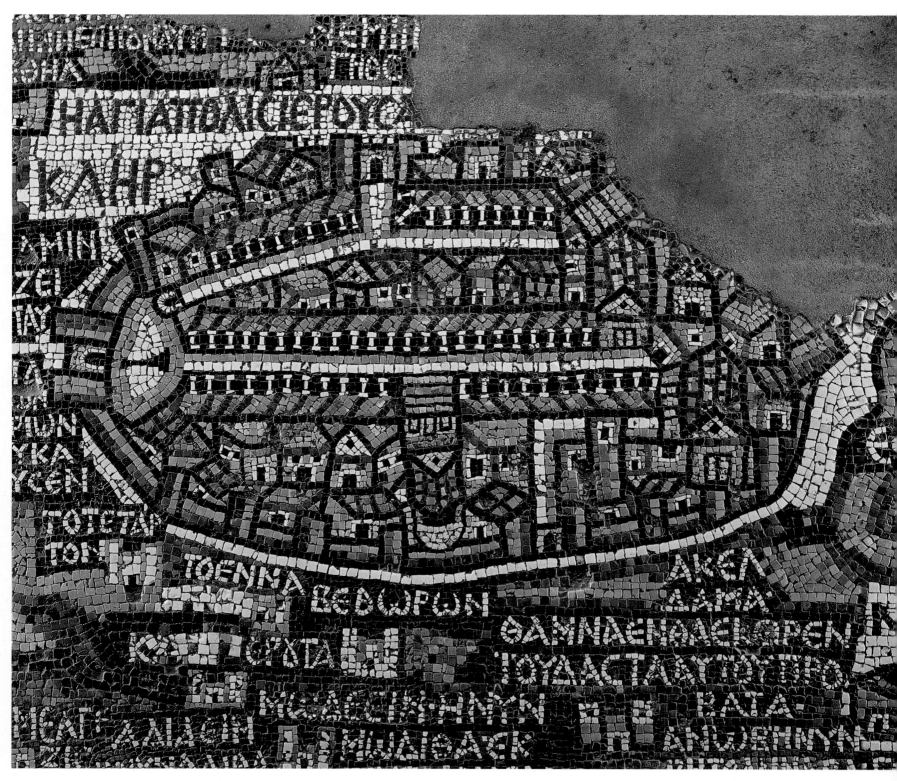

29 Church near the
Siloam Pool.
30 Probably the
Church of St Sophia.
31 Monastery of
St Cosmas and St
Damianus.
32 Public baths.
33 Palace of the
Empress Eudocia.

34 Church of the
Sheep Pool.
35 Temple area
(indicated only by a
single line of black
cubes).
36 Ruins of the
Antonia Fortress.
37 Church of
St James.

38 Some scholars
believe that this
represents the
Western, or Wailing,
Wall. Others think it
is more likely to be
the ruins of the wide
staircase in front of
the southern wall
of the Temple.

MAPS PRODUCED BY ISLAMIC GEOGRAPHERS

102 The Islamic cartographer Ibn Abd Allah Ibn Idrisi had a considerable influence on the work of his successors. This map is a sixteenth-century Persian copy of his map of Palestine drawn in 1154 and compiled in Arabic.

In accordance with Islamic custom, the map is orientated towards the south; while fairly detailed, it is nevertheless drawn in a somewhat picturesque style, making its interpretation anything but easy.

The maps drawn by Islamic geographers during the Golden Age of Arab culture in the tenth century were intended as aids for Muslim pilgrims as well as for merchants. The best example is that of the Persian geographer Istakhri. His atlas, compiled in 952, contains 21 maps. The map of Palestine is orientated to the south. Even though the map is based on the principles of Ptolemy, it is basically conceptual in nature. In the twelfth century, the Moorish scholar, Idrisi, was employed by Roger II, the Norman King of Sicily, to make an atlas of 70 maps. Also orientated to the south, the map of the Holy Land is largely impressionistic.

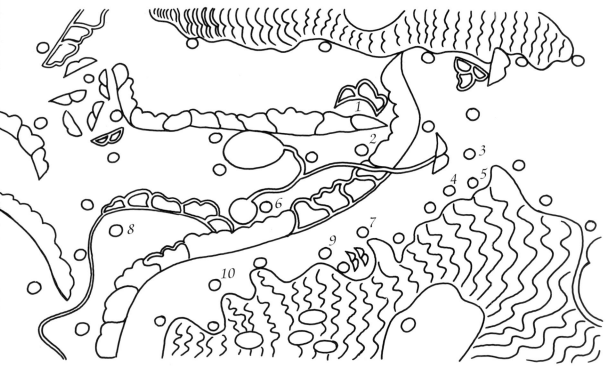

102 On Idrisi's map, cities are shown by yellow circles, principal seas are in blue, while Lake Tiberias, the Jordan and the Dead Sea are in green. The explanatory drawing highlights the principal locations.

1 *Petra*
2 *Jerusalem*
3 *Gaza*
4 *Jaffa*
5 *Ashkelon*
6 *Tiberias*
7 *Acre*
8 *Damascus*
9 *Tyre*
10 *Beirut*

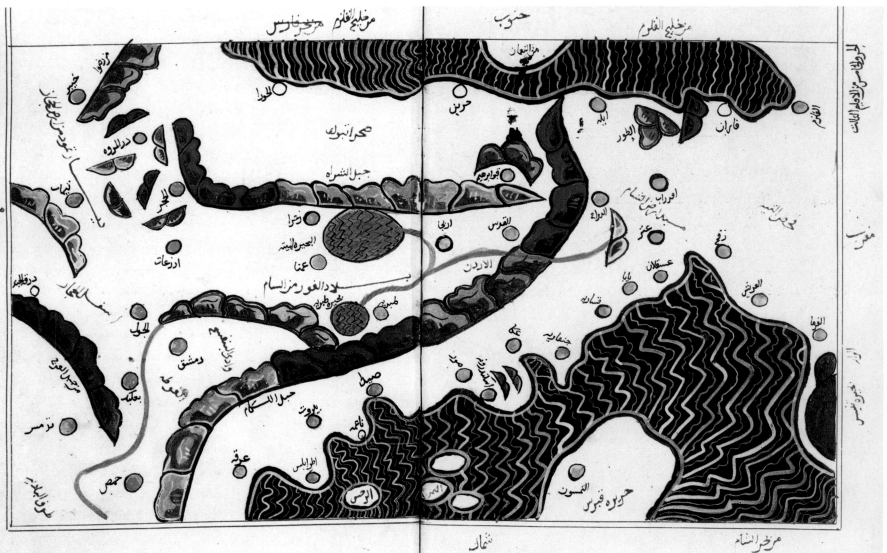

THE *MAPPAEMUNDI* OR WHEEL-MAPS OF THE MIDDLE AGES

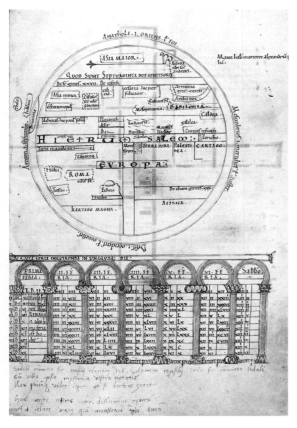

The Middle Ages in Europe saw an interruption in the science of cartography. The more or less accurate maps of the classical world were abandoned in favour of a kind of religious cosmography: the *mappaemundi*. These maps show the Holy Land as envisaged by the medieval monks who drew them.

Described as T-O maps, they are drawn as a circle with a line from left to right through the middle. The upper half of the map is Asia, or Shem. The bottom half-circle is bisected vertically from the middle to the bottom edge: Europe, or Japheth, is in the bottom left-hand quarter and Africa, or Ham, is in the bottom right-hand quarter. The line between the two bottom quarters represents the Mediterranean Sea.

Orientated to the east, Jerusalem is at the centre, or 'navel', of the world. According to the book of Ezekiel (5, 5) 'Thus saith the Lord God: This is Jerusalem: I have set it in the midst of the nations and countries that are round about her.' Places holy to the medieval Christian are also shown: the sacred mountain, Mount Sinai; the River Jordan; and Golgotha. Paradise is at the very top.

There are over 600 known examples of *mappaemundi*. The first was probably that of Isidore of Seville, published in 800 as part of his 'Christian encyclopaedia'. The best known is now in Hereford Cathedral, in England, and was drawn by Richard of Haldingham in about 1285. These maps were used to illustrate religious manuscripts or, in the case of the larger ones, to serve as a backdrop to the altar.

Circular maps of Jerusalem probably all derive from the same map of the Crusader period, the *Situs Hierusalem*. However, most of them date to the fourteenth century and may have been intended for pilgrims to the Holy Land. Besides showing the biblical sites, they also give useful information such as the location of the money exchange.

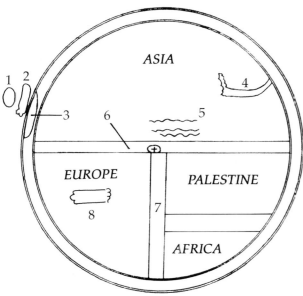

103 (above) Known as Byzantine-Oxford T-O, *this map of the habitable world is a copy of a Byzantine original drawn on parchment in England, c. 1110. Jerusalem is positioned centrally; it divides Asia from Europe and Africa and is flanked on the right by Jericho. The explanatory drawing aids its interpretation.*

1 Iceland
2 Ireland
3 Great Britain
4 Noah's Ark
5 The Jordan
6 Jerusalem
7 Mediterranean Sea
8 Rome

103 (right) This map with Jerusalem as the centre of the world is included in a Latin manuscript version of the Book of Psalms, dating from c. 1250. The Asian continent occupies the upper section, while Europe and Africa are in the lower right and left respectively; the Holy City is indicated by the double circle.

The Portolan Sea Charts

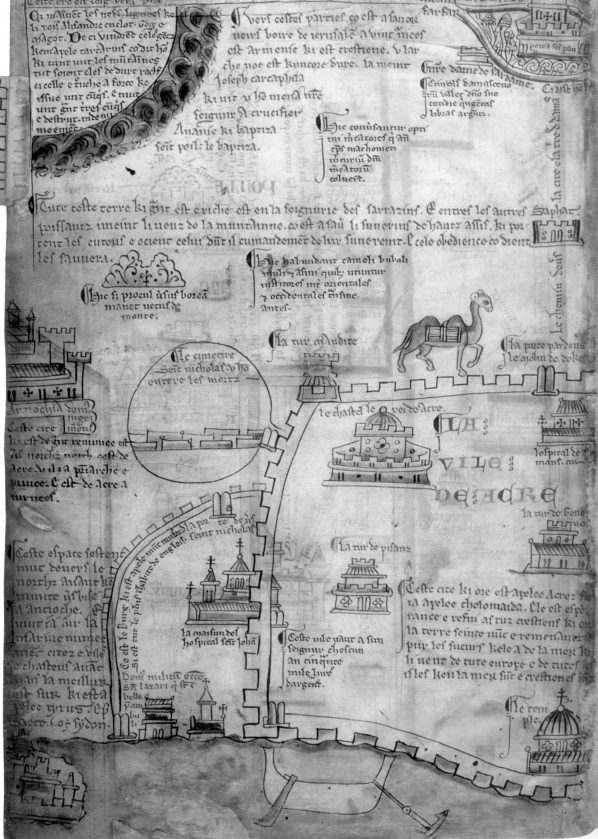

Portolan maps were produced in the late Middle Ages for the use of navigators. Essentially sea charts, they resemble the scientific maps of today. The best known are those by Pietro Vesconte, drawn in the first half of the fourteenth century for Marino Sanuto, a wealthy Venetian merchant interested in promoting another crusade to the Holy Land. The maps were drawn to scale, orientated to the north. Since they were intended for the use of navigators, all the major ports and rivers are shown. Although the interior features of countries were not considered important for navigators, the one exception is the Holy Land, where the major religious sites are represented.

Among those notable for this kind of map were the Jewish cartographers Abraham Cresques and his son, Judah, working on the island of Majorca. They are thought to be the makers of the renowned *Catalan Atlas* (1375) in which the influence of Idrisi and the Arab geographers is visible. Other information came from the accounts of travellers, such as Marco Polo.

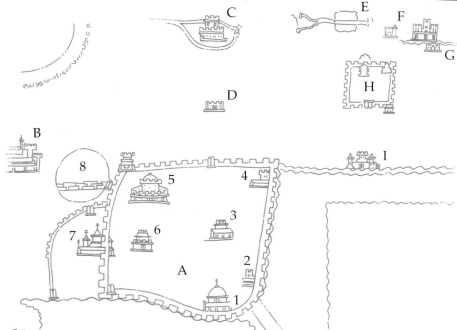

104 (left) Explanatory drawing identifying the buildings and principal cities on the map of Acre by Matthew Paris.

A *Acre*
B *Antioch*
C *Damascus*
D *Safed*
E *The Dead Sea*
F *Bethlehem*
G *Cairo*
H *Jerusalem*
I *Jaffa*

1 *The House of the Order of the Knights Templar*
2 *The Constable's House*
3 *The Genoese Merchants' Tower*
4 *The Teutonic Knights' Hospital*
5 *The Castle of the King of Acre*
6 *The Pisan Merchants' Tower*
7 *The Hospitallers' House*
8 *The Cemetery*

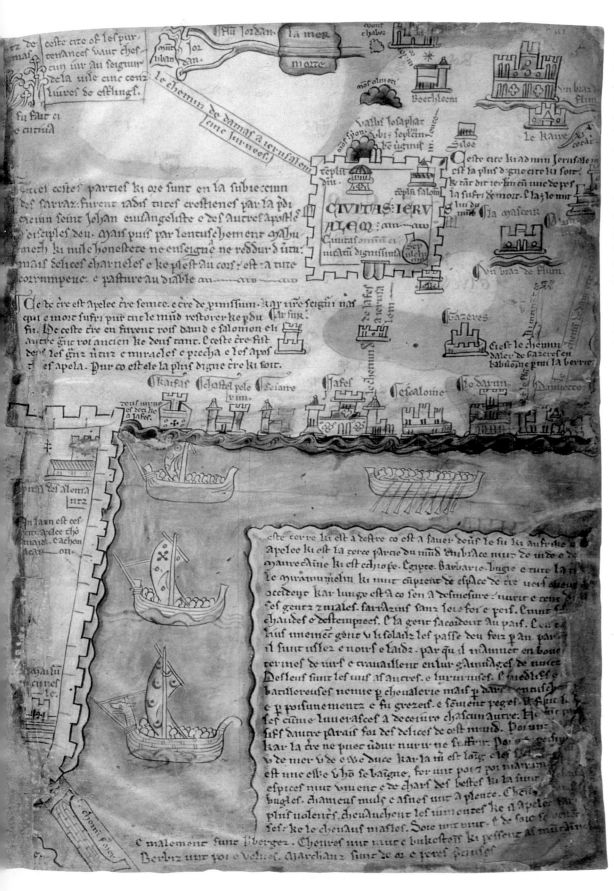

104–105 As well as being the leading chronicler at St Alban's – which in the twelfth and thirteenth centuries was the main cultural centre of England – Matthew Paris was also interested in cartography. His two-sheet manuscript on parchment, from around 1252, depicts Palestine and the principal cities in the region. Acre is much enlarged so as to permit the depiction of the most important buildings.

105 (below) With their Liber Secretorum Fidelibus de Crucis, published in Venice around 1320, Marino Sanuto and Petrus Vesconte revolutionized medieval cartography; this map of Palestine was used as a model for the next three centuries.

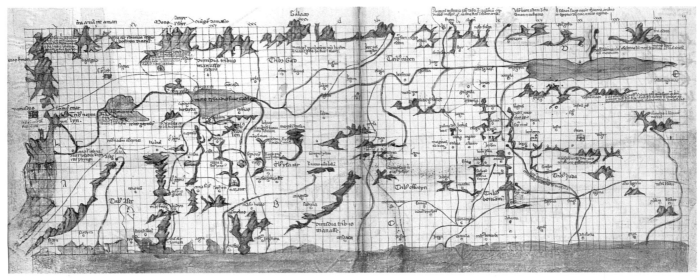

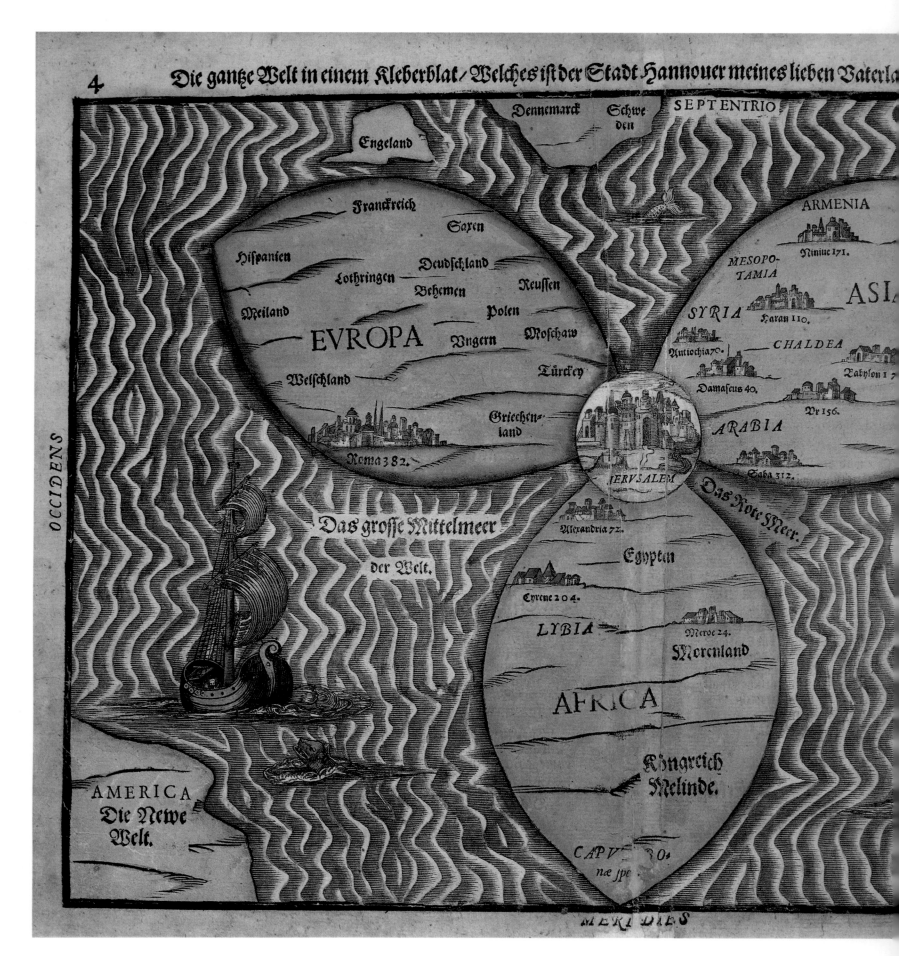

Die gantze Welt in einem Kleberblat/ Welches ist der Stadt Hannouer meines lieben Vaterla

SEPTENTRIO

Dennemarck Schwe den

Engeland

ARMENIA

Franckreich

Saxen

Niniue 171.

Hispanien

Lothringen Deudschland

MESOPO-
TAMIA

Meiland Behemen Reussen

SYRIA

ASIA

Haran 110.

EVROPA Polen

Ungern Moschaw

Antiochia 70.

CHALDEA

Babylon 17

Welschland Türckey

Damascus 40.

Vr 156.

ARABIA

Griechen-
land

Roma 382.

Saba 312.

JERVSALEM

Das grosse Mittelmeer

Alexandria 72.

Das Rote Meer.

der Welt.

Egypten

Cyrene 204.

LYBIA

Meroe 24.

Morenland

AFRICA

AMERICA
Die Newe
Welt.

Königreich
Melinde.

CAPV 30.
næ spe

OCCIDENS

MERIDIES

106–107 In this
celebrated map by
Heinrich Bünting, the
world is represented
as a cloverleaf with
Jerusalem at the
centre. Although
printed in 1581, the
map still relies on
geographical
conceptions typical
of the era of the
Crusades. At the top,
Denmark is depicted
as an island lying
just off Great Britain;
the New World is
shown bottom left.
Note the colouring
of the Red Sea.

FIRST PRINTED MAPS AND GEOGRAPHIES

The invention of printing and especially the publishing of the Bible at the end of the fifteenth century created a new demand for books and maps about the lands of the Bible. Indeed, the first printed map was of the Holy Land, produced in Lübeck in Germany in 1475. Although more pictorial in form, it was based on the now-lost map by the Dominican monk, Burchard of Mount Zion.

The panoramic map of Palestine by Bernhard von Breitenbach, drawn by Utrecht artist Erhard Reuwich, is also very impressive. The two made a pilgrimage to the Holy Land in 1483 and their book, *Peregrinatio in Terram Sanctum*, gives an impression of Jerusalem as it was before the destructions of the Turks in 1517.

It is not surprising that the first map drawn by Gerard Mercator, in 1537, was of Palestine. He is the inventor of the system of map projection still used today.

107 The work of Lucas Brandis, the first printed map was of Palestine. Published in Lübeck in 1475, it was produced on the basis of the information supplied by Burchard of Mount Zion, a thirteenth-century Dominican monk whose story and drawings of a pilgrimage to the Holy Land were widely known in Europe from early in the Renaissance period. Jerusalem is placed centrally while to the left is the city of Acre.

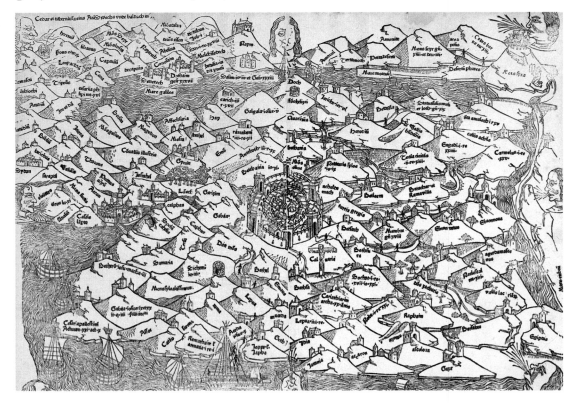

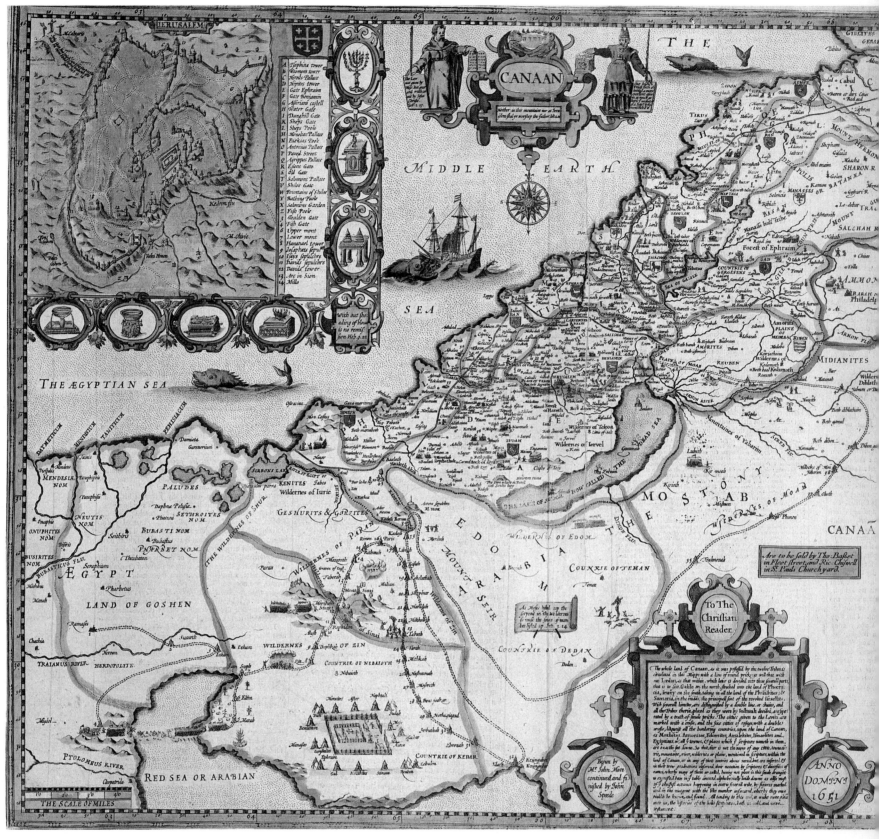

108 (left) A map of Israel, by Nicholas Sanson d'Abbeville in his Sacred Geography of 1662, had a lasting influence on his successors. The same cartographer and, later, his son, published a number of versions of this map, modifying the dedication and scroll ornament.

108–109 (above) This map of the Holy Land printed in London in 1611 is one of John Speed's best works. It shows the route of the Exodus with each of the encampments, the 12 Tribes of Israel, biblical scenes and, top left, a detailed map of Jerusalem. Around this is the equipment used in the Temple.

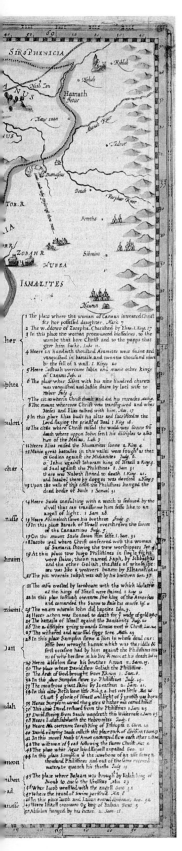

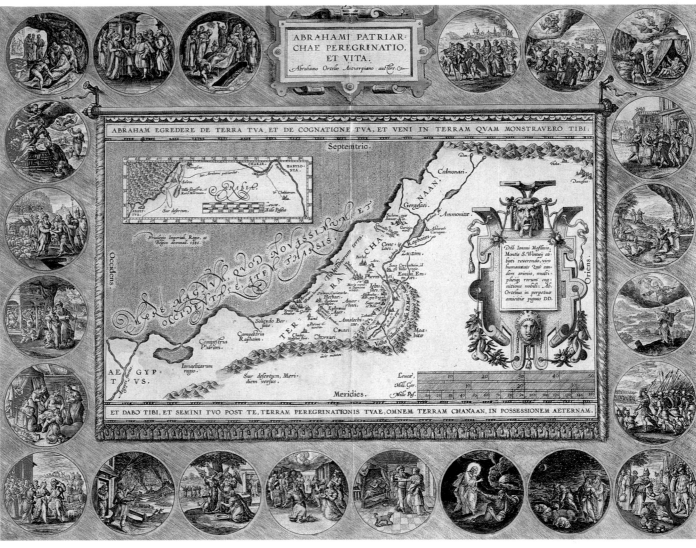

109 (above right) This map, printed in Antwerp in 1586, is considered to be one of the masterpieces of Abraham Ortelius. Conceived as a tapestry, it depicts the land of Canaan divided among the ancient tribes of Israel and is surrounded by 22 magnificent multi-coloured medallions illustrating the life of Abraham, forefather of Israel. The small map inserted in the top left shows the route of the patriarch's journey from the Euphrates Valley to the Promised Land. The two medallions shown above illustrate the sacrifice of Isaac and Abraham setting out from Ur.

Abraham Ortelius is celebrated as the first large-scale publisher of modern atlases, in many editions and in various languages. His first, the *Theatrum Orbis Terrarum*, was a collection of 53 maps, among them two of the Holy Land, one by the cartographer Tilleman Stella and the other derived from the map by Peter Laicksteen and Christian Sgrooten. His maps are notable for their artistic quality and this is especially apparent in his illustrated map of Canaan, with a border of 22 circular illustrations of the life of Abraham.

The English cartographer John Speed also chose to draw the Holy Land as his first map, in 1595. He is best known for his atlas of the British Isles published in 1611, which included yet another map of Palestine. His maps of the Holy Land were also republished in many English Bibles. A second English

map-maker, Thomas Fuller, published his atlas of the Holy Land, *Pisgah-Sight of Palestine*, in 1650.

The first map of the Holy Land printed in Hebrew was by two Jews, Yaaqov Ben Abraham Zaddiq and Abraham Goos. Originally published in 1621, and reprinted in 1633, the map was intended to enable Jews on pilgrimage to Jerusalem, and also the Jewish armchair traveller, to locate all the important sites in the Bible. Later in the seventeenth century, in 1695, Abraham bar Yaaqov of Amsterdam

provided a lavishly illustrated map for his Passover *Haggadah*.

Biblical dictionaries and encyclopaedias were also illustrated with maps. In 1714, the Dutch orientalist Adrian Reland published one of the first biblical geographies, *Palaestina ex Monumentis Veteribus Illustrata*. This was a scholarly piece of work and was often reprinted, well into the nineteenth century. The first Bible Encyclopaedia in France was published by Augustine Antoine Calmet in 1711, and also included maps of the Holy Land.

110 In this map, printed in Amsterdam by Willem Blaeu in 1629, the Promised Land is orientated towards the west, as it appeared to the Israelites from the peak of Mount Pisgah after the Exodus from Egypt. On either side of the title are portraits of Moses, with the Tablets of the Law, and of Aaron.

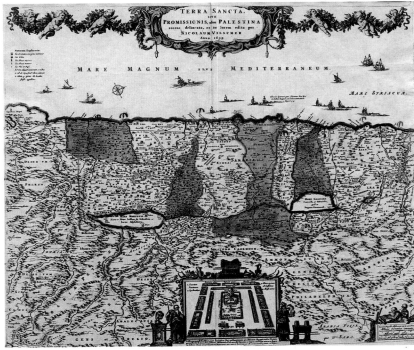

111 (above) This is the first of the many maps of the Holy Land drawn by Abraham Ortelius for his atlas, the celebrated Theatrum Orbis Terrarum, *published in Antwerp in 1570. Considerable importance is given to the route followed by the Israelites during the Exodus, from Egypt to the Promised Land.*

111 (right) Nicholas Visscher the Elder *included this elaborate map of the Holy Land in his atlas published in Amsterdam in 1659. At the bottom is Moses' encampment at the foot of Mount Sinai, with the tabernacle in the centre surrounded by the 12 Tribes of Israel; Aaron is portrayed on the right, Moses on the left.*

112–113 The map drawn by Abraham bar Yaaqov for a Haggadah, printed in Amsterdam between 1695 and 1696, was one of the earliest exclusively in Hebrew. The route of the Exodus and the subdivisions of the tribes of Israel are clearly indicated. Solomon's boats carrying the Cedars of Lebanon used in the construction of the Temple are illustrated at the bottom, along the coast, while on the right a vignette depicts the story of Jonah and the whale. The cartouche contains a list of the Exodus encampments. The woman sitting on a crocodile symbolizes Africa, while to the left the four cows and the beehives under the portico of the farm represent the fertility of the Promised Land. The eagle is a symbol of divine power.

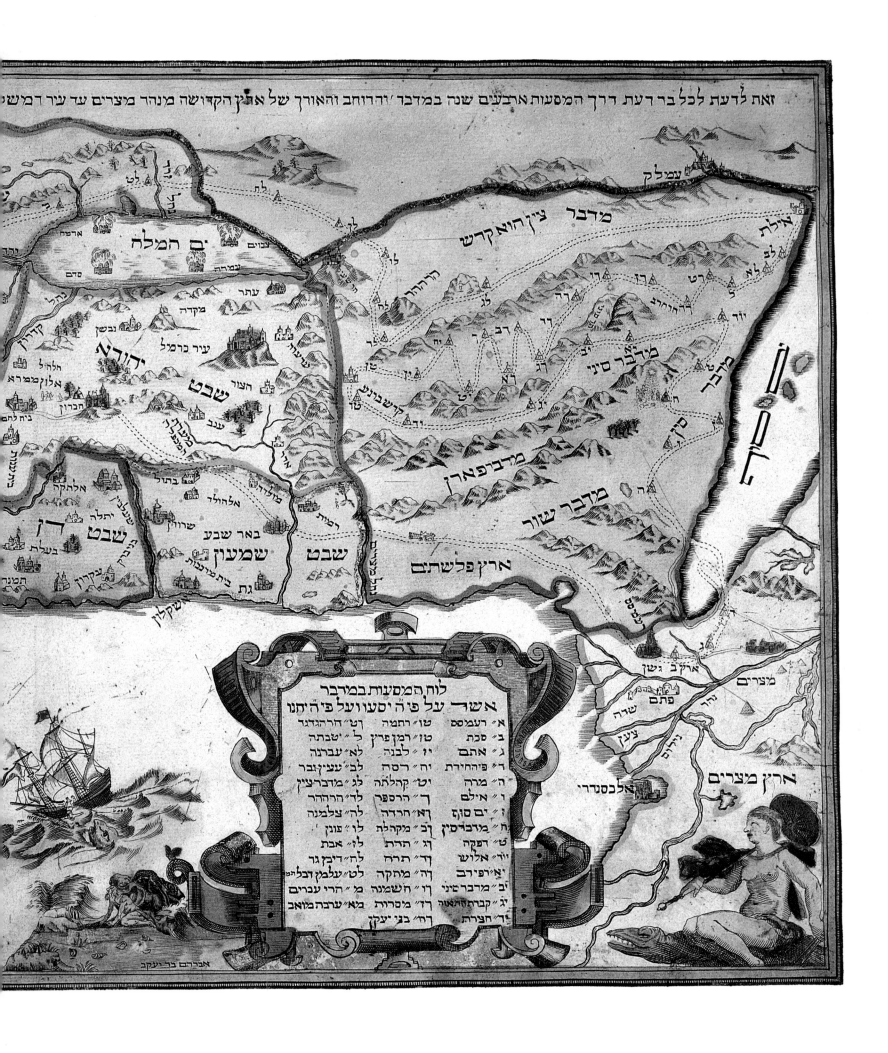

116 (left) The
Christian cavalry
drives off the Saracens
below the walls of
Jerusalem in this
manuscript from the
mid-twelfth century.
The conquest of the
Holy City was to
have enormous
repercussions on
medieval cartography,
which saw it as the
centre of the world.

117 (right) In this
splendid manuscript, a
copy of an original by
Burchard of Mount
Zion, drawn in 1455
for Philip of Burgundy,
the Holy City is
dominated by the
domes of the Mosque
of Omar, centre, the
Mosque of el-Aqsa,
right, and the Holy
Sepulchre, left.

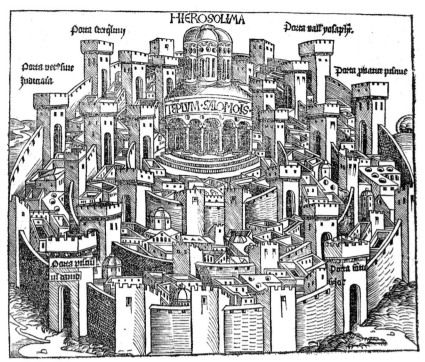

118 Contained in the Nuremberg Chronicle of Hartmann Schedel, published in 1493, this is almost certainly the first printed picture of Jerusalem. Solomon's Temple is placed centrally and dominates all other buildings; the gates in the walls are given their names in Latin.

Jerusalem appears in maps either on its own or as part of a larger map of the Holy Land. It is often drawn out of proportion, larger in scale than other cities in the map. The oldest known representation of Jerusalem is in the Madaba Map, a mosaic made in the sixth century. The circle maps resulting from the Crusades resemble the *mappaemundi* in form, serving as a schematic guide to the Holy City, which is divided into four quarters. The important Christian sites are shown in each quarter. Outside the circle are the major sites of interest to the pilgrim. These circular maps gradually changed as pilgrims brought back more details for the map-makers.

The sixteenth-century depiction of Jerusalem by Christian von Adrichom in his history of the Bible lands became the basis of many other maps in the following two centuries. Jerusalem is shown as it was thought to have been at the time of Jesus and Adrichom marked 14 sites along the Via Dolorosa, the route of Christ to the crucifixion. The principal buildings are drawn with European features, the houses built around neat green squares. While the map is certainly not realistic, the location of the buildings corresponds with travel reports available at the time.

A common concern of many maps of Jerusalem was to locate the northern or 'second' wall of the time of Jesus. Travellers to Jerusalem noted that the Church of the Holy Sepulchre was deep within the city. However, according to the Gospel accounts of the crucifixion, Golgotha was located outside the walls of the city. Furthermore, according to Jewish burial practices, the tomb of Joseph of Arimathea must also have been outside the city. Thus, many map-makers paid close attention to literary sources, such as the writings of Josephus, to determine where the city walls would have stood in New Testament times. In these drawings and maps, the crucifixion is placed outside the city walls. Many of these maps were used to illustrate Bibles and biblical encyclopaedias.

Only at the beginning of the nineteenth century were the first accurate maps of Jerusalem drawn. Muslim authorities and the general population did not allow map-making by western surveyors, and any maps had to be surveyed and drawn surreptitiously. In 1841 a party from the British Corps of Royal Engineers was allowed to survey the city without any interference.

Realistic representations of Jerusalem in paintings and prints also began to appear in the nineteenth century. Earlier images of the Holy City reflected the style and time of the artist. For instance, *The Delivery of the Keys* by Perugino, of 1480-1482, now in the Sistine Chapel in Rome, shows Jerusalem with buildings in Renaissance style. In this painting, as in most other pictures of Jerusalem, the Dome of the Rock has a prominent place. Nineteenth-century artists also emphasized the skyline of the city, with the Dome of the Rock, the dome of the el-Aqsa Mosque, the cupola of the Church of the Holy Sepulchre, and the Tower of David all very prominent.

118–119 Christian von Adrichom's views of Jerusalem as it would have been in the time of Jesus are the most spectacular and influential of the sixteenth century. While imaginative, they display great attention to historical details deriving from the Holy Scriptures. This map, dated 1584, was dedicated to the Archbishop of Cologne.

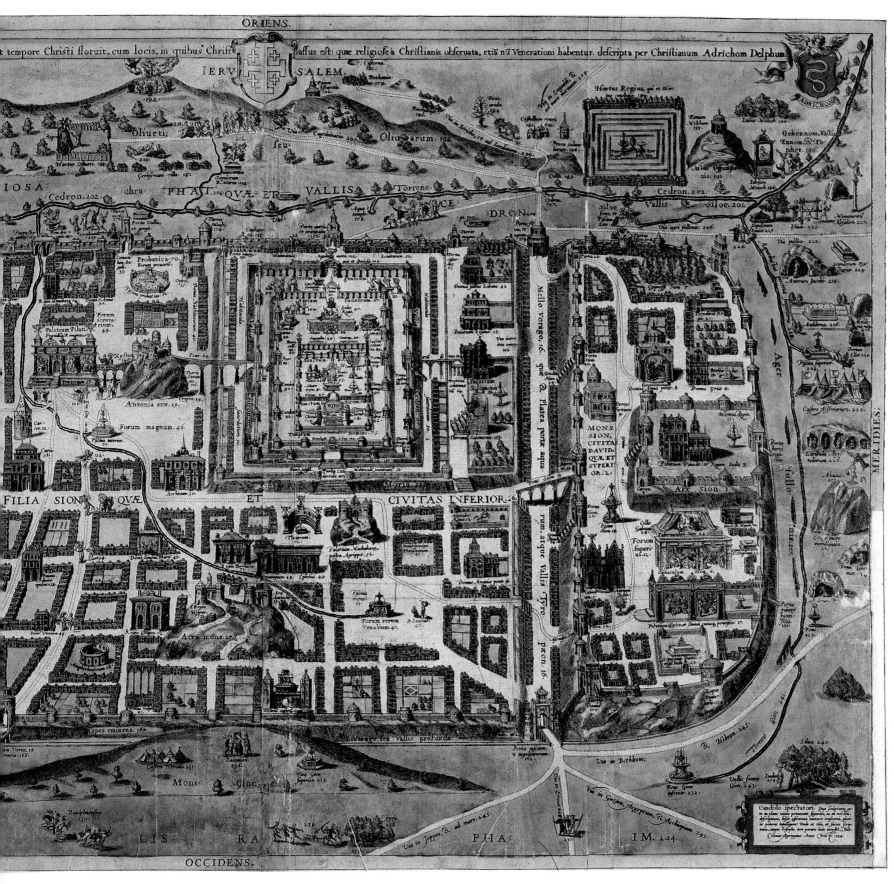

t tempore Christi floruit, cum locis, in quibus Christ passus est: quæ religiosè à Christianis observata, etiã nũ Venerationi habentur. descripta per Christianum Adrichom Delphum.

IERVSALEM.

OCCIDENS.

119 (left) Franz Hogenberg's view of Jerusalem was printed in Cologne in 1575. The city is seen from the east: in the foreground, within the walls, is the Temple area dominated by the Dome of the Rock. Along the city wall can be seen the Golden Gate, the Lions' Gate, the Damascus Gate, the Jaffa or Pisan Gate and the Zion Gate, here called the Judas Gate. Nearby is marked the Tomb of David and the Coenaculum, the site of the Last Supper.

DAVID ROBERTS

The nineteenth-century Scottish painter David Roberts has provided us with perhaps the most famous and enduring pictures of Jerusalem and the Holy Land. His style catches the quality of the light and the colour of the stone unique to Jerusalem.

Roberts was born near Edinburgh in 1796, the son of a shoemaker. He received his early training as a house-painter and decorator, and, later, as a scene-painter in the theatre. After this rather unorthodox training, Roberts became especially well known for his architectural paintings and landscapes of various countries, including England, Scotland, France, Spain and Italy, and in 1841 he was elected a fellow of the Royal Academy.

The great biblical scholar and explorer, Edward Robinson, praised the work of David Roberts as the first to show the landscapes of the Holy Land accurately. However, Roberts himself confessed that he had difficulties in reproducing the rock formations of the Judaean mountains. After a trip to Egypt, Palestine and Syria in 1838 and 1839, Roberts returned to London and published a large, three-volume collection of his work, in the form of lithographs, between 1842 and 1849.

Roberts' background in the theatre is demonstrated in his dramatic views of architectural wonders like Petra, and also of the pomp and splendour of the interior of the Church of the Holy Sepulchre. His paintings also prominently feature the people of Palestine, often in somewhat theatrical poses.

120–121 *David Roberts reached Jerusalem on 29 March, 1839. One of the artist's first views (later transformed into a lithograph by Louis Haghe) was probably this, of the Citadel. This imposing and frequently rebuilt fortress near the Jaffa Gate was established on Roman foundations.*

122 (below) Roberts spent some time in the Kidron Valley, which contains some magnificent funerary monuments carved from solid rock. The so-called Tomb of Absalom, capped by an unusually shaped cupola, dates from the period of the Second Temple.

122 (bottom) This drawing, faithfully depicting the Damascus Gate, is dated 14 April, 1839; on that date Roberts left the city for the north. He arrived in Beirut almost a month later, after visiting and drawing Baalbek.

122–123 (above) This painting, depicting the Pool of Bethesda, is one of the most spectacular and best known of those that Roberts made of the Holy City and its monuments. The complete work of his travels, comprising 123 lithographs, was published in London by Francis Graham Moon between 1842 and 1849.

123 (left) The so-called Tombs of the Kings, located close to the Damascus Gate, were an inspiration to David Roberts. The deluxe colour edition, from which the plates on these pages are taken, was produced at the behest of, and dedicated to, Queen Victoria.

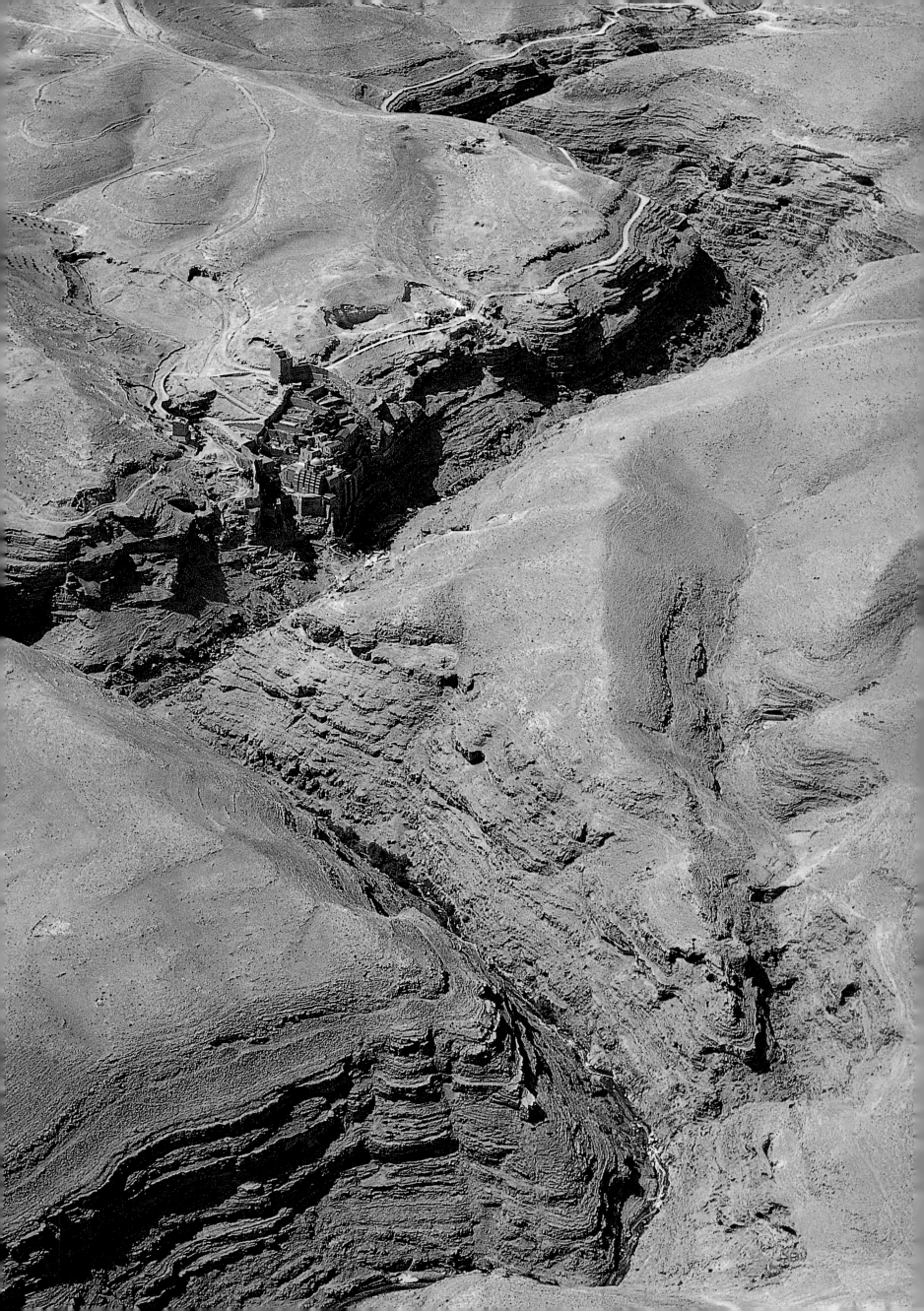

ISRAEL FROM THE SKY

124 (opposite) The monastery of Mar Saba in the Judaean Desert, southeast of Jerusalem overlooks the Kidron River. This desert is on the leeward side of the Judaean Mountains and receives very little rain each year.

125 (above) At the northern end of the Dead Sea is a flat plain that was once underwater. Because there is no outflow from the Dead Sea, the level of salt content of the water can be as high as 33 per cent.

125 (below) In the Judaean Desert, the dry river valleys, or wadis, follow the geological faults. During the sudden rainstorms of autumn and spring, these wadis rapidly fill with torrents flowing at great speed.

Israel's long, narrow shape is a result of the formation of the Great Rift Valley in distant geological eras. Mountain ranges running down the centre of the country rise to over 915 m (3000 ft) above sea level, while the Dead Sea, at 388 m (1275 ft) below sea level is the lowest point on earth. Israel lies in a sub-tropical zone: there is a rainy season in winter and a dry season in summer. However, while it may be raining along the coast, in the mountainous regions it can be snowing, and only a few miles away on the Dead Sea the weather can be fair and the temperatures pleasant.

The elongated form of the country creates a borderland between the humid climate of the Mediterranean and the dry desert to the east. While the winds on the coastal plain blow in from the sea, during a *sharav* or *hamsin* an inversion of this process occurs and very hot, dusty, dry winds blast in from the desert.

The mountains and the highlands that run the length of the country block the passage of warm, humid winds from the Mediterranean and on the lee-side to the east is a semi-arid desert zone. Rain falls quite intensively on a limited number of days in the winter. In the highlands and in the deserts of the Jordan Valley and the Negev rainfall can be quite sudden and intense, filling up the wadis (deep desert canyons) with sudden torrents of gushing water.

Much of the landscape of Israel is manmade and differs considerably from its natural state in prehistoric times. The Bible mentions four forests: in the Negev, or the south; Ephraim, or the Samarian Highlands; Carmel; and the forests of Lebanon.

When these forests were cut down, they were not replaced. The job of reforestation began with the efforts of the Jewish National Fund in the 1920s. Large parts of the coastal plain, the central valleys of Jezreel and the Harod, and the Huleh Basin were malaria-ridden swamps, only drained by the first settlers at the beginning of this century.

126–127 (overleaf) Close to En Gedi, where the Judaean Desert meets the Dead Sea, are several river canyon outflows with alluvial fans spreading out into the sea. Jordan is visible on the opposite shore.

Terraces in the highlands of Judaea and Samaria date in some cases to biblical times, and entire mountains are encircled by stepped rows of low stone walls. As these terraces fall into disuse, they sometimes appear like natural geological formations.

Within a relatively narrow strip of land – about 177 km (110 miles) at its widest – Israel contains a great range of landforms which can be divided into three major regions: the coastal plain; the central mountain range; and the Jordan Valley.

The coastline has few large natural harbours, with the exception of Haifa Bay in the north. In addition to this smooth coast, there are no offshore islands. In many places a high cliff or ridge rises up from a narrow stretch of beach. In other areas, large tracts of shifting sand prevent easy access to the coast. While there have been important harbours in ancient times – at Acre,

The *Via Maris*, a major trade route of ancient times, thus also passed inland. Even the modern city of Tel Aviv was first built facing away from the sea. The southern part of the coastline is almost a straight line, made up of wide beaches of quartz sands brought by currents from the Nile Delta.

The northern section of the coast, beginning at about Tel Aviv–Jaffa, is indented by very small harbours, with the exception of Haifa, where there is a large natural bay. Because of the mild climate and adequate rainfall, the coastal plain has always been well populated. The northern border is determined by the white cliffs of the promontory of Rosh ha-Niqrah or the 'Ladder of Tyre'. To the south is the Zebulun Plain, or Plain of Acco. The coastal plain is the narrow strip of land that extends south from, and is bordered on the east by, the Mount Carmel range.

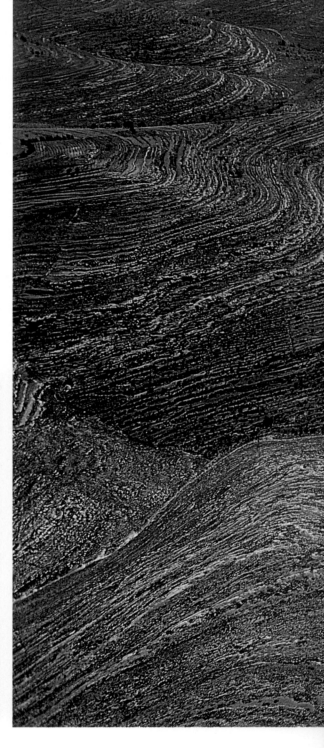

Dor, Jaffa and Ashkelon – many of them are artificially constructed. Only to the north, in Lebanon, is the major port of Tyre, which played such a large part in Israel's history.

Along the coastline are ridges of *kurkar*, fossilized sand dunes, parallel to the coast. Because of sand dunes and *kurkar* ridges, most major cities of Palestine grew up inland.

From the spur of land near the town of Zikhron Ya'akov south to the River Yarkon is one of the most fertile areas of Israel, the Sharon Plain. This receives adequate rain and was once largely forested. Today it is mostly agricultural, although in many places farmland vies for space with the expanding residential areas of Tel Aviv.

128–129 Terraced hillsides in Samaria and Judaea bear evidence of intensive farming techniques that developed over centuries in a semi-arid climate where every drop of water needed to be collected and every piece of land utilized. The technical expertise associated with this kind of agriculture was not easily acquired, and if the terraces are not maintained they quickly fall into disuse, the rock barriers washed away by sudden rains. The stone walls also support vegetation for the raising of sheep. The Roman historian Flavius Josephus described the lands of Judaea and Samaria in this way: 'Both regions consist of hills and plains, yield a light and fertile soil for agriculture, are well wooded, and abound in fruits, both wild and cultivated... But the surest testimony to the virtues and thriving conditions of the two countries is that both have a dense population.'

130–131 (overleaf) A closer view of traditional farming methods in Samaria shows the standard crops of fruit and olive trees, and vines. Stones from the rocky soil have been cleared into small mounds to allow more room for cultivation.

Much of the Sharon is covered by a red sand suitable for the growing of citrus fruits. The wide Judaean Plain extends south from the large metropolitan area of Tel Aviv–Jaffa to the Gaza Strip. Where coast meets sea is a band of sand dunes. This area is also called the Philistine Coast. During biblical times the main port was Ashkelon, where there is a natural break in the dunes.

The central mountain range runs from the border with Lebanon in the north to Eilat in the south. In many places these mountains can only properly be called hills, yet their steepness in comparison with the surrounding plains and valleys makes their elevation more pronounced. The mountains are not continuous since the steep sides of the river canyons, or wadis, cut through them. In ancient times large areas of the hill country were heavily forested. Many of the denuded hills bear the evidence of terracing for agricultural purposes.

The mountains of the Upper Galilee are a continuation of those in Lebanon to the north. The Lower Galilean highlands are centred around the town of Nazareth. Their most prominent feature is Mount Tabor, whose round, domed summit towers over the Jezreel Valley below.

The central mountains are interrupted by a system of large valleys, including the Haifa Plain, the Jezreel Valley and the Harod Valley, which cut across in a northwest–southeast direction. The Harod Valley is an extension of the Beth Shean Valley and runs into the Jordan Valley. The Jezreel Valley is better known to readers of the Bible as the Plain of Armageddon. It was crossed in ancient times by the *Via Maris*, one branch of which travelled north and the other northeast to the vast desert lands. The Jezreel Valley was thus of considerable strategic value. Situated in the Jezreel Valley are Mount Gilboa and the tell of the ancient fortress city of Megiddo.

The Samarian Highlands, which were once well forested, include two holy mountains, Ebal and Gerizim. Nablus, or Shechem, lies in a large flat valley. The Mount Carmel range is the northern extension of the Samarian Highlands. The northernmost point juts into the Mediterranean and this is where the modern city of Haifa is located.

South of the Samarian Highlands are the Judaean Hills, with Jerusalem, Bethlehem and Hebron along the central ridge. On the eastern side is the Wilderness of Judah, an area of desert deprived of the rain-bearing winds from the Mediterranean by the higher Judaean Hills. The ridge gradually decreases in elevation before dropping off sharply to the Jordan Valley and the Dead Sea. The hills and mountains are cut by deep valleys and wadis and many are flat-topped, as seen most graphically at the fortress site of Masada.

On the western side of the lower range of the Judaean Hills is the Shephelah, a band of low hills forming a boundary between the mountains and the coastal plain. It is a fertile area, famous for its wine, and was heavily settled during biblical times, serving as a buffer between Judaea and the land of the Philistines.

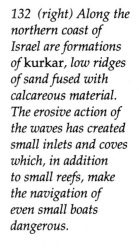

132 (right) Along the northern coast of Israel are formations of kurkar, *low ridges of sand fused with calcareous material. The erosive action of the waves has created small inlets and coves which, in addition to small reefs, make the navigation of even small boats dangerous.*

133 (left) The coast
north of Tel Aviv is
bordered by steep cliffs
formed of kurkar with
often only a narrow
beach. Sand dunes
have developed on the
tops of these cliffs.
Bathing is only
possible where an
artificial breakwater
has encouraged the
deposition of sand.

132–133 (above) The
coast south of Tel Aviv
is relatively straight
and bordered by wide
beaches and areas of
sand dunes. In ancient
times, the latter
formed a barrier to
easy access to the sea
and most habitation,
as well as the coastal
road, tended to be
further inland.

To the south is the Negev Desert, covered by a thick layer of 'loess', a fine soil deposited by the wind. With proper irrigation techniques, such as those developed by the Nabataeans, this soil can be made quite productive. Although the Negev makes up a large proportion of the land area of modern Israel, it is still relatively uninhabited; its chief city is Beersheba.

The Jordan Valley is part of the larger Great Rift Valley that begins in Turkey, runs down the Beq'a Valley in Lebanon, along the Jordan Valley in Israel, and continues south through eastern Africa. In Israel, it begins with the Huleh Basin, travels to the Sea of Galilee, south again along the Jordan Valley to the Dead Sea, the Aravah and the Gulf of Aqaba. The Red Sea is a continuation of this system. About 70 per cent of Israel's runoff rain water empties into the Jordan Valley. It is the deepest depression on the surface of the earth. The Dead Sea is around 388 m (1275 ft) below sea level and the Sea of Galilee is 200 m (660 ft) below sea level. This water drainage system is entirely internal:

it does not empty into an ocean or other large body of water.

The fault line that caused the rift is still active. There have been several catastrophic earthquakes along it. Numerous hot springs that well up from deep under the earth are further evidence of seismic activity.

The basalt rock that forms much of the surrounding landscape is also the result of past volcanic activity. Gigantic lava flows dammed up the lower part of what is now the Huleh Basin, separating it from the Sea of Galilee. In the Middle Pleistocene, a vast lake extended from the Sea of Galilee south to the Aravah. Called the Lashon, it was 215 m (700 ft) higher than the present level of the Dead Sea and its outline can be seen in the terraces that surround the Dead Sea Basin today.

The climate of the Jordan Valley is unique. It receives very little rainfall because any moisture from the Mediterranean is lost over the high mountains of the western side of the valley. Rainfall averages about 30 cm (12 in) a year at the Sea of Galilee, 10 cm (4 in) or less at the Dead Sea and only 2.5 cm (1 in) at Eilat. The temperatures in the Jordan Valley are among the highest in Israel and although it comprises a large catchment area, even under natural conditions the amount of water flowing into the system is matched or exceeded by the amount that naturally evaporates. Recently, the large amounts taken out for agriculture and for the needs of urban Israel have caused the level of the Dead Sea to fall. The allocation of water has become a major political issue in the region.

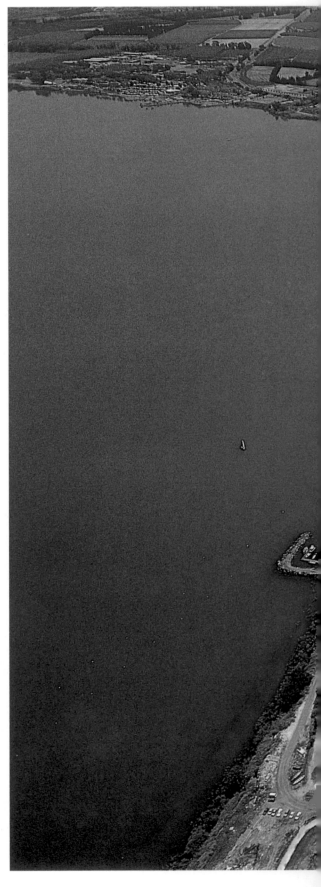

134 (left) The River Jordan, winding its way through a flood plain covered with thick, low forest and lush farmland, follows the depression of the Great Rift Valley.

134–135 (above) Degania, where the River Jordan flows out of the southern end of the Sea of Galilee, was founded in 1909 and was the first Jewish communal settlement.

135 (left) The Jordan Valley provides a strip of well-irrigated farmland, and its high temperatures are suitable for the cultivation of tropical crops like dates and bananas.

136 (left) From the air, different types of farmland form a patchwork of various colours and textures.

136–137 (right) Mount Tabor, with the Basilica of the Transfiguration on its summit, commands a panoramic view of the Jezreel Valley and is itself visible from a long distance.

138–139 (overleaf) The spectacular and wild highlands of the Negev Desert are broken by shallow valleys caused by flash flooding.

140–141 The Underwater Observatory at Eilat allows visitors to view the dazzling array of tropical fish in comfort.

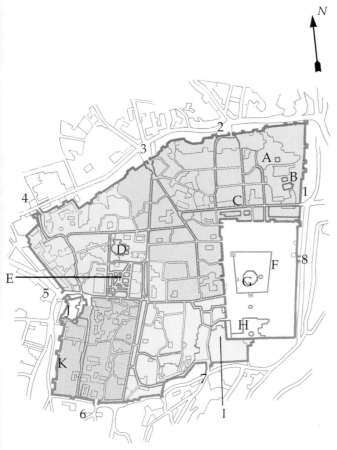

JERUSALEM OF GOLD

WALLS AND GATES OF JERUSALEM AND THE CITADEL

Christian Quarter **Muslim Quarter**

Armenian Quarter **Jewish Quarter**

1 Lions' Gate
  (St Stephen's Gate)
2 Herod's Gate
3 Damascus Gate
4 New Gate
5 Jaffa Gate
6 Zion Gate
7 Dung Gate
8 Golden Gate
  (closed)

A Pool of Bethesda
B Church of St Anne
C Platform of the
  Antonia Fortress
D Holy Sepulchre
E Muristan
F Temple Mount
G Dome of the Rock
H El-Aqsa Mosque
I Western Wall
J Citadel
K Armenian Garden

Jerusalem is situated high in the Judaean mountains and is a holy city of major significance in the three great monotheistic religions of Judaism, Christianity and Islam. Its importance cannot be attributed to a location on a major trade route, to a strategic position or even to its being the centre of a fertile area. The only explanation lies in its holy aspect.

Ancient Jerusalem is buried beneath the city of today and the earliest evidence of settlement must be pieced together from archaeological remains as well as from documentary sources. Since the 1860s, over 100 archaeological expeditions have attempted to discover Jerusalem's secrets.

The city is built on two main ridges, bordered on the east by the Kidron Valley, on the southwest by the Hinnom Valley, and divided by a central valley, the Tyropoeon. This position makes it easily defensible but the city's defences are weakest at the north, where the ridges merge with the surrounding hills and there is no natural boundary.

The four quarters of the city created by Hadrian in the second century AD still influence its plan today. Jerusalem was then divided from north to south by the *Cardo Maximus*, and from east to west

142 (top) The Golden Gate in the eastern wall of the Temple Mount dates from the sixth or seventh century. Since the Crusader period it has been blocked. In Christian tradition Jesus will enter the city through it on the Day of Judgment.

142 (above) The original Jaffa Gate, now used as a pedestrian entrance, was built by Suleiman in 1538. It was widened in 1898 to accommodate the carriage of Kaiser Wilhelm II, during his visit to the Holy City.

142 (left) St Stephen's Gate, also called the Lions' Gate, was constructed in 1538. The two pairs of lions on either side, the symbols of Sultan Baybars, were reused by Suleiman when he built the gate.

143 (opposite) The Citadel of Jerusalem was founded in the Hasmonaean period and much rebuilt by Herod. One of Herod's towers survives and is known as David's Tower. The Citadel today houses the Museum of the History of Jerusalem.

142

by another thoroughfare, called the *Decumanus*.

The surviving walls of the Old City of Jerusalem date from the time of the Ottoman sultan, Suleiman the Magnificent. He began the new fortifications in 1537 and they were finished three years later, using blocks and even sections of previous walls. Seven gates interrupt the walls of Jerusalem. The most impressive, the Damascus Gate, originated in Hadrian's rebuilding of the city in the second century AD and reuses many blocks of earlier Herodian masonry. This was the monumental entrance to the new Roman city, *Aelia Capitolina*. Parts of this original entry have been excavated and can be seen today under the present Damascus Gate.

The New Gate was constructed at the end of the nineteenth century to provide access to the Christian Quarter. The Jaffa Gate, so named because the road to Jaffa ran far west by the time of John Hyrcanus (134–104 BC). Here, Herod built his three towers – Hippicus, Phasael and Mariamne – and a magnificent palace. Although the palace was destroyed during the First Revolt, the ruins of the towers were preserved and the area to the south became the camp of the Roman Tenth Legion. During Byzantine times, pilgrims to the Holy City came to identify these fortifications as David's Palace.

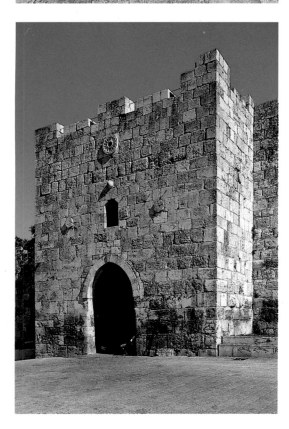

through it, was once an L-shaped gate but was opened up in 1898 for the state visit of Kaiser Wilhelm II. Zion Gate leads out to Mount Zion, now outside the walled city. In Arabic it is called Bab Nabi Daud, or the Gate of the Prophet David.

Further along the walls to the south is the Dung Gate, given its name because rubbish was removed from the city there. In Arabic it is the Bab el-Magharbeh, or Gate of the Moors, since the North African quarter was just inside. To the north of the Temple Mount is St Stephen's Gate where traditionally St Stephen was stoned to death. It is also called the Lions' Gate, after the lions carved on either side of the entrance. Herod's Gate is so named because in medieval times it was thought to be close to the palace of Herod Antipas. The history of the walls of Jerusalem must include the Citadel which has long been a specially fortified area. The city of Jerusalem extended this

144 (above left) Zion Gate, badly scarred from the fighting in 1948, leads from the Old City to Mount Zion. Built by Suleiman in 1540, it is also known as the Gate of the Prophet David.

144 (below left) Herod's Gate is also called the Gate of the Flowers because of its medallions. At one time it was thought that it led directly to a building considered by medieval pilgrims to be the palace of Herod Antipas.

144 (above) The Dung Gate, at one time used for removing rubbish from the city, was also called the Gate of the Moors because the Moorish Quarter was just inside. The entrance was enlarged in 1948 to allow cars to pass through.

145 (opposite) Damascus Gate lies on top of the gate built by Hadrian for Aelia Capitolina *and one of the original entrances can be seen to the left, below the causeway. Veering to the right can be seen the* Cardo Maximus, *while in an almost straight line is another covered street, also dating from the time of Hadrian.*

146–147 The three bazaars of the Old City lie at the eastern end of David Street. The sights and sounds have not changed greatly in hundreds of years. These three parallel streets date from the Crusader period and are built on the same location as the Roman and Byzantine Cardo Maximus, *just north of where it met the* Decumanus. *In a few of the shops the initials SA have been incised on the stone, indicating that this was part of the property of St Anne's Church. The New Bazaar of the Muristan, south of the Church of the Holy Sepulchre, was built in 1901 and caters largely for tourists.*

The City of David

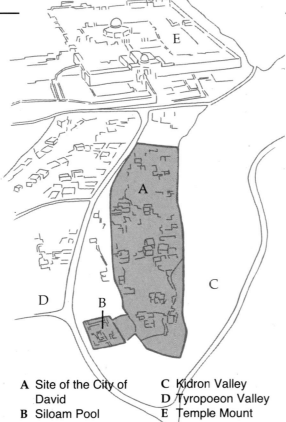

A Site of the City of David
B Siloam Pool
C Kidron Valley
D Tyropoeon Valley
E Temple Mount

Jerusalem was first settled on the ridge south of the present Temple Mount, a site chosen probably because of the presence of the Gihon Spring. Archaeological evidence of occupation dates back to the late Chalcolithic and Early Bronze Age, and by the twentieth and nineteenth centuries BC Jerusalem is found in the Egyptian Execration Texts. It is mentioned also in the Amarna Letters of the fourteenth century BC.

The Canaanites made Jerusalem a fortified city, and remains of this date include sections of wall and possibly a tower. According to biblical evidence, the Jebusites settled in the city for a period of about two hundred years until David captured it from them and made it the capital of his new, united kingdom.

The City of David, as this area is known, was small, but David built a palace and also city walls. Hiram, King of Tyre, provided him with cedar trees, carpenters and masons for the erection of his house (2 Samuel 5, 11). A stepped stone structure consisting of terraces filled with stones is visible in the city today and may have served as the foundation of David's palace. The Ark of the Covenant was brought to Jerusalem, thus establishing the city as the religious capital of Israel also. David bought a threshing floor from the Jebusite Araunah and there he built 'an altar unto the Lord, and offered burnt offerings and peace offerings' (2 Samuel 24, 25).

The building of the first temple, however, was undertaken by David's son, Solomon. He was probably the first to extend the city walls to enclose the Temple Mount area and he also built himself a fine palace and administrative buildings.

At the time of the Divided Monarchy, after the death of Solomon (about 930 BC), Jerusalem was the capital of the southern kingdom of Judah. Several houses dating from the seventh century BC have been excavated, one of which, called 'Ahiel's House', has the typical construction of monolithic stone pillars. In another, called the 'House of the Bullae', many stamped clay seals were found, indicating that the house may have been a sort of registration office for property or taxes. The Babylonian destruction of Jerusalem in 586 BC is graphically demonstrated by a thick layer of burnt debris.

Jerusalem had a very sophisticated system of water supply, part of which is called Warren's Shaft. Discovered by the archaeologist Charles Warren in 1867, the shaft, possibly dates to the tenth century BC. It descends down through natural fissures in the rock and manmade tunnels to the Gihon Spring. In this way, the city's water supply was assured even in times of siege. The Siloam Tunnel brought water from the spring to reservoirs in the valley at the south of the city. Apertures in the walls of the tunnel could be opened to provide water for irrigating fields outside the walls. Another tunnel was built by Hezekiah in 701 BC, and it is still possible today to walk through this tunnel, 485 m (1600 ft) in length, from the Gihon Spring, under what was the old City of David, to the Pool of Siloam. This is where Jesus performed the miracle of curing the blind man (John 9, 1–12).

148–149 (above) The City of David extends south along a ridge from the walls of the Temple Mount.

149 (right) The Siloam Pool is fed by a tunnel bringing water from the Gihon Spring, the primary source of water for the City of David.

THE CITY OF DAVID

The first city of Jerusalem was built on a narrow and steep-sided spur of land, south of what is now the Temple Mount. The Jebusites built fortifications around the city which were enlarged by Solomon. The key to the defence of the city lay in its water-supply systems. The principal source of water was the Gihon Spring, outside the city. Warren's Shaft provided access to a tunnel leading under the city walls to the spring. Later, the Siloam Tunnel was built to supply water to the reservoirs to the south of the city and during the reign of King Hezekiah another tunnel was dug to a reservoir within the city walls.

1 The Temple of Solomon, or the First Temple, was divided into the Ulam, or portico in front, the Hekhal, or central hall, and the Debir, or inner sanctuary. In front of the temple were two columns called Jachin and Boaz.

2 Solomon's Palace and administrative complex.

3 The stepped-stone structure, possibly 'the Millo', supported the citadel enclosing the administrative buildings.

4 Evidence of the East or Water Gate has been discovered by archaeologists excavating the City of David.

5 The entrance to Warren's Shaft. As it lay outside the city walls, access was gained to the Gihon Spring through a tunnel leading from what is now called Warren's Shaft.

6 The Gihon Spring. The early city depended on this spring for its water.

7 The Siloam Tunnel brought water from the Gihon Spring to the reservoirs south of the city (underground).

8 Apertures in the walls of the Siloam Tunnel could be opened to let water out into the Kidron Valley for irrigating the fields.

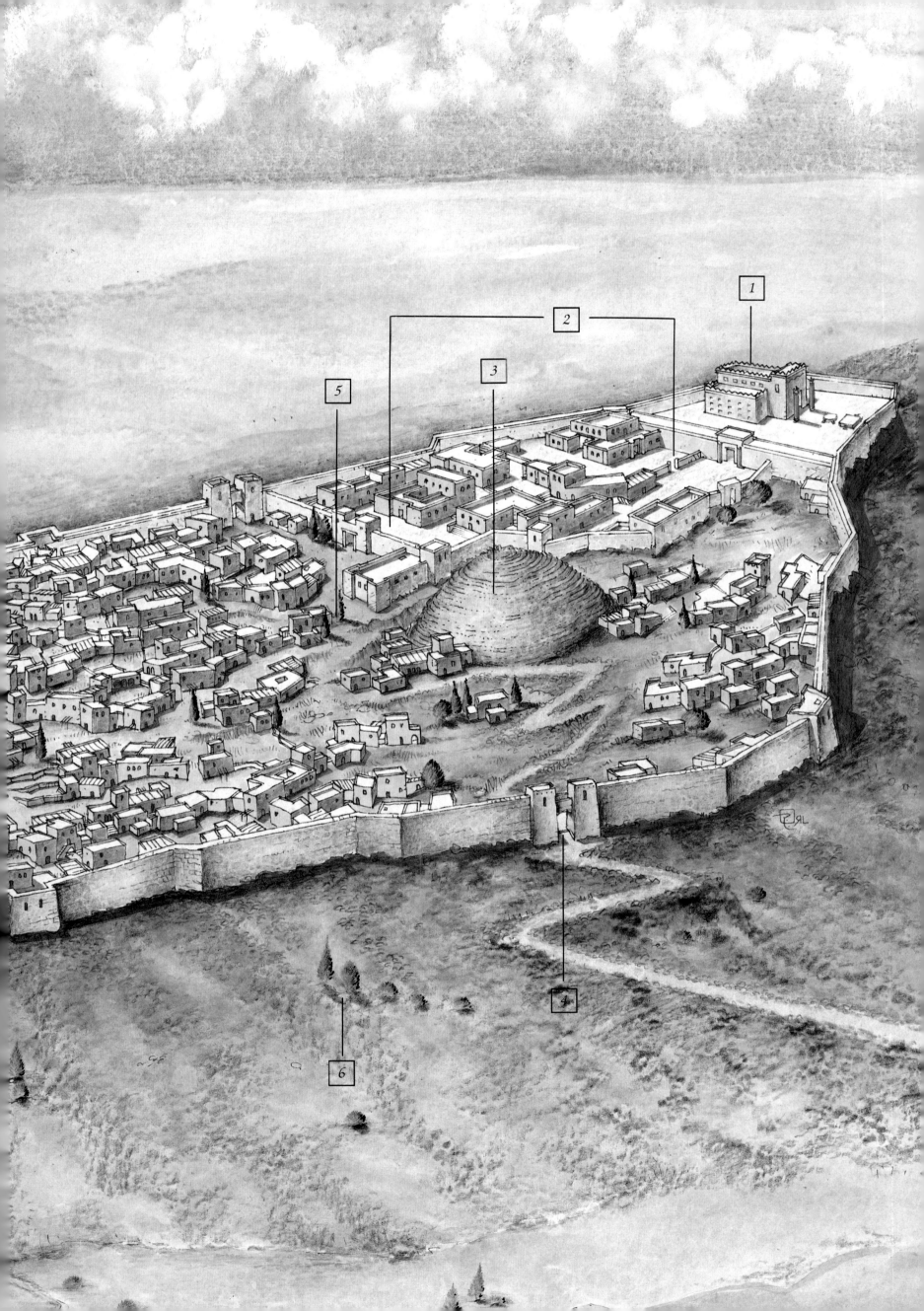

THE TEMPLE MOUNT

In the three great monotheistic religions, Jerusalem is regarded as the centre of the world. In Judaism, the image of Jerusalem was closely linked to the Temple. Bar Kokhba used the image of the façade of the Temple on the coins he struck during the Second Jewish Revolt, 60 years after its destruction in AD 70. Islamic Jerusalem is most often represented by the Dome of the Rock. This image was also adopted by the Crusaders and became the most common universal symbol for Jerusalem. Because of its prominent position on the skyline, nearly all panoramic illustrations of the city feature the majestic golden dome at their centre. The Haram al-Sharif in Arabic, Har ha-Bayit in Hebrew, or the Temple Mount as it is commonly called in English, is the focal point of the Old City. It was probably Solomon who first extended the area enclosed by the city walls to include the Temple Mount. According to the Bible, this area was bought by Solomon for the construction of a temple to house the Ark of the Covenant. Although no physical remains of the First Temple have been found, it is described in detail in the Bible and was probably similar to other temples at Israelite sites like Hazor. The temple was completely destroyed by the Babylonians in 586 BC, and the Ark of the Covenant disappeared. After the return from exile, the temple was rebuilt by Zerubbabel, presumably along its previous lines, though the Bible suggests it was more modest.

152 (above) A small ivory pomegranate, perhaps a sceptre-head, is the only object that can possibly be associated with Solomon's Temple. (Israel Museum)

152 (centre) A silver coin minted during the Second Jewish Revolt, depicting what may be the façade of the Temple in Jerusalem.

152 (below) A pottery jug inscribed with the name of its owner, '(Belongs) to Eliyahu'.

152–153 (right) The excavations outside the southwestern corner of the Temple Mount with the remains of Robinson's Arch projecting from the wall.

154–155 (above) The
excavations at the
southeast corner of the
Temple Mount. At the
centre, under the el-
Aqsa Mosque, are the
reconstructed steps
leading to the Double
Gate of the Second
Temple.

154 (left) Secondary
burial in limestone
ossuaries, sometimes
beautifully carved,
became a common
custom among the
Jews during the late
Second Temple period.

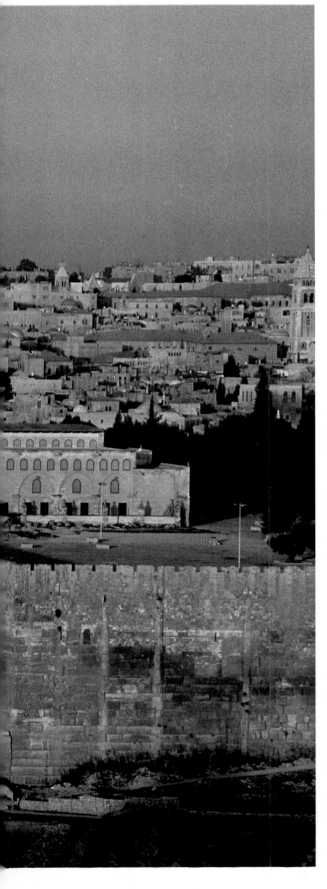

Herod the Great rebuilt the Temple on a truly magnificent scale and expanded the Temple platform to reach monumental proportions – virtually the same as today. The Second Temple was the focus of pilgrimage for thousands of Jews every year, many of them from distant parts of the Jewish Diaspora.

It was in this Temple that Jesus argued with the priests and overthrew the tables of the money-changers. In AD 70 it was stormed and destroyed by the Romans, as Josephus describes in vivid detail. The platform lay in ruins for more than a century, until the reign of Hadrian, when a temple to Jupiter may have been built there.

Only with the Arab conquest of 638 did the Temple Mount regain its importance. The Dome of the Rock was completed in 691/692 and the Dome of the Chain several years later. The el-Aqsa Mosque was constructed in several stages, at first as a large wooden building that could accommodate 3000 worshippers and later as an immense stone building composed of 15 prayer aisles. To the south were several large palaces connected with the Temple Mount via the gates constructed during Herod's time. The palaces themselves were destroyed in the earthquake of 1033 and never rebuilt, although evidence has been discovered in excavations.

With the taking of Jerusalem by the Crusaders in 1099, the Dome of the Rock became a Christian Church but was not destroyed. The el-Aqsa Mosque was first the palace of the Crusader king of Jerusalem and later became the headquarters of the Order of Knights Templar. Details of Crusader architecture still remain; for example, the Dome of the Ascension, where traditionally Muhammad prayed before rising to heaven, was rebuilt by the Crusaders.

Under the Mamelukes the northern and western sides of the Temple Mount were enclosed by buildings that still exist today; especially notable is the al-Madrasa al-Ashrafiyya, rebuilt 1479–1482 by Sultan Qa'itbay with an impressive façade including an elaborate arched doorway. Also named after this sultan is the Fountain, or Sabil, of Qa'itbay.

During the Ottoman period, further renovations were undertaken on the buildings on the Temple Mount. Until 1856, and the Russian-Turkish treaty, non-Muslims were forbidden to enter the area, although some westerners in oriental disguise did manage clandestine visits.

155 (above)
Excavations of the remains of the monumental buildings to the south of the Temple Mount. Much of this debris was thrown from the Temple Mount after its destruction.

156–157 (above)
Mount Zion, with
the Church of the
Dormition in the
centre and the tall
tower of the Abbey of
the Dormition to the
left, bordered by
Christian cemeteries.

157 (opposite above)
The Coenaculum,
or Cenacle, was built
in the twelfth century
on the traditional site
of the Last Supper of
Jesus and his disciples.

157 (opposite centre)
The Church of the
Holy Saviour, or the
House of Caiaphas,
where Jesus was
imprisoned the night
before the crucifixion.

157 (opposite below)
In the fifteenth
century the site of the
Tomb of David was a
Muslim shrine; in
1948 it came under
Jewish control.

Mount zion

Mount Zion now lies outside the old walls of Jerusalem, to the south of the Zion Gate. The exact location and significance of Zion changed with the history of Jerusalem. In the Old Testament, the city is the 'stronghold of Zion'– the Jebusite fortress – and later, after its capture by David, it became the 'City of David'. By the fourth century, Zion was on the opposite, western, hill and in tradition is connected with the last days of Jesus. The area was enclosed in the second century BC and so, at the time of Jesus, Mount Zion lay within the city walls. The Last Supper is believed to have taken place on Mount Zion, though the tradition seems to be a late one. The site is now the Room of the Last Supper, or Cenacle, which dates from the fourteenth century. By the eleventh century, there was a Jewish belief that Mount Zion was the site of the Tomb of David, and this was continued by the Muslims who built a mosque to 'the prophet David' in 1524. The Tomb of David became an important place of pilgrimage after 1948, when it was the only place in east Jerusalem under the control of Israel. The Tomb of David and the Room of the Last Supper now share the same building.

Today the Armenian Church of the Holy Saviour commemorates the story of Jesus' imprisonment in the house of the High Priest, Caiaphas. Also on Mount Zion is the Church of St Peter, built by the Augustine Assumptionist Fathers to mark the house of Caiaphas and the spot where Peter denied Jesus three times before the crowing of the cock.

THE MOUNT OF OLIVES

The Mount of Olives lies across the Kidron Valley from the Old City of Jerusalem. The Old Testament (Ezekiel 11, 23) recounts how 'the glory of the Lord went up from the midst of the city, and stood upon the mountain which is on the east side of the city'. This echoes Zechariah 14, 4, which says that the Lord will stand upon the Mount of Olives, which will cleave in half. Not only is it the site of a large Jewish cemetery, but also of many events in the last week of the life of Jesus. At the summit of the Mount of Olives the Crusaders built a chapel, now a mosque, to commemorate the traditional place of the Ascension of Jesus. Nearby is the Church of Pater Noster, marking the spot where Christ instructed his disciples. Bethphage, also on the Mount of Olives, was the small village where Jesus made his preparations before his entry into Jerusalem. The place where Jesus wept over Jerusalem is marked by the Franciscan Church of Dominus Flevit. The most picturesque of the churches on the Mount of Olives is the Russian Orthodox Church of St Mary Magdalene at Gethsemane, with its seven golden domes. The site of Jesus' betrayal by Judas is marked by the Franciscan Garden of Gethsemane, with its modern Church of All Nations. The Church of the Tomb of the Virgin is traditionally the site of the tomb of Mary, her parents Anne and Joachim, as well as of Joseph. Nearby is the Cave of Gethsemane, where the disciples rested while Jesus was arrested after being betrayed by Judas.

On the northern ridge, Mount Scopus, is the Hebrew University. This was established in 1925 and has buildings dating from that period as well as a new campus built in 1981.

158–159 (opposite) A tombstone in the Jewish cemetery on the Mount of Olives. It is customary for visitors to place small stones on the graves.

158 (opposite, below left) The Mount of Olives has served as a cemetery for the Jews of Jerusalem since the times of the City of David.

158 (opposite, below right) The Tomb of the Bene Hezir, a priestly family, and the Tomb of Zechariah both demonstrate Hellenistic influence.

159 (below left) The Garden of Gethsemane is the place where Jesus was betrayed by Judas. Today the Church of All Nations stands on the site of a fourth-century basilica.

159 (below right) The misnamed Tomb or Pillar of Absalom was built in the later part of the first century BC and probably served as part of the burial complex of a wealthy family.

Jewish Jerusalem

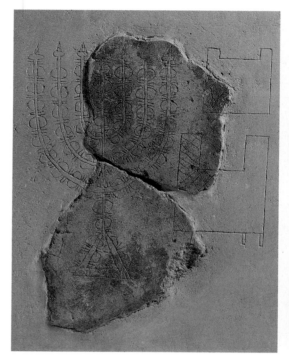

For Jews, Jerusalem is not only the capital of Israel, it is also home for all the Jews of the world. A verse from Psalms (137, 5) reads 'If I forget thee, O Jerusalem, let my right hand forget her cunning'. Each Passover *Seder* meal ends with the injunction not to forget Jerusalem. A Jew at prayer should face towards Jerusalem and there is an obligation to go on pilgrimage to Jerusalem, especially on the festivals of the Feast of Tabernacles, Passover and *Shavuot*. The ninth day of the Hebrew month of Av is a day of

mourning and fasting for the destruction of the Temple.

The Jews of Jerusalem represent all the ethnic groups and strands of belief that make up the Jewish people today. For many, the return to Zion is not just the return to the land of Israel, but is a return to Jerusalem in particular. Religious Jews have special influence in Jerusalem but they, too, are not one homogeneous group. Although they look very similar at first glance, with their black coats, black hats and beards, ultra-orthodox Jews belong to many different sects originating in central Europe in the sixteenth century. The ultra-orthodox Naturie Karta refuses to recognize the State of Israel. Other orthodox groups, however, especially the 'modern-orthodox', are active in the political life of modern Israel.

Matters of family law are under the direction of the rabbinical courts and the Chief Rabbinate. The day-to-day matters of religious life are under the jurisdiction of the Religious Council of Jerusalem. State education is provided in religious schools, while the ultra-orthodox generally educate their children privately in special schools. Other streams of Judaism are still not accepted by religious authorities, although their numbers are growing every year.

160 (opposite above) A partially preserved plaster graffito of the seven-branched menorah in the Temple, together with depictions of the showbread table and the altar.
(Israel Museum)

160 (opposite centre) A mosaic 'carpet' from a Herodian mansion, excavated in the Jewish Quarter of Jerusalem. This was the home of a wealthy family, perhaps high priests in the Temple.

160 (opposite below) The Burnt House still shows signs of the conflagration that destroyed the City of Jerusalem in AD 70. The stoneware and pottery were left in their original positions.

160–161 (above) The Batei Machaseh Square is situated at the centre of the restored Jewish Quarter. The apartment houses combine both new and old architectural styles.

162 (left) The
commemorative arch
on the ruins of the
Hurva Synagogue,
originally built next
to that of the Jewish
sage, the Ramban, in
the thirteenth century.

162–163 (above) The
old and the new: the
Jewish Quarter of
Jerusalem viewed from
the north, with the
reconstructed arch of
the Hurva Synagogue
at the centre right.

163 (above) The original columns and capitals of the Byzantine Cardo Maximus *excavated in 1967 and restored to their original positions during the renovations of the Jewish Quarter.*

163 (below) The steps leading away from the wide plaza in front of the Western Wall. This area is crowded with Jewish worshippers on the Jewish holidays.

The Jewish Quarter is today the area close to the Western Wall of the Temple Mount. This is a section of the Herodian platform supporting the Second Temple, the destruction of which marks the beginning of the dispersal of Jewish people. Every year on the ninth day of the Jewish month of Av, the destruction of the Temple is commemorated and the wall is also called the 'Wailing Wall' from those who come to mourn its loss. The Wall is now crowded on Friday evenings and on Saturday during the Sabbath prayers. On the left of the Wailing Wall is Wilson's Arch, the remains of part of an elaborate causeway that went from the Temple Mount to the other side of the Tyropoeon Valley. Forming the other boundary of the Western Wall area is a ramp leading to the Gate of the Moors, one entrance to the Temple Mount. It is forbidden for Orthodox Jews to enter the Temple Mount for fear they might walk on the Holy of Holies.

The rebuilding of the Jewish Quarter, begun in 1967, provided the opportunity for archaeological excavations. What is now called the Broad Wall was excavated in 1969; it is thought that it was constructed in 701 BC by Hezekiah, in the face of invasion by the Assyrian forces of Sennacherib. While the exact size of the city at this time is much debated, the discovery of this wall shows that it had expanded to the western hill opposite the Temple Mount by the eighth century BC. Slightly further to the north, a defensive tower was discovered, probably built by the Hasmonaeans in the second century BC, and joined to an earlier Israelite tower.

The remains preserved in the Burnt House, now a museum, are very graphic illustrations of the destruction of Jerusalem by the Romans in AD 70. It is very possible that this house belonged to the priestly family of Katros since a weight bearing that name was found in the ruins.

Evidence of what life was like for the wealthy during the first century AD was found in the excavations of one of the Herodian Mansions, now the Wohl Archaeological Museum. The interior of these mansions was particularly luxurious: many of the walls are decorated with brightly coloured frescoes; the floors are paved with elaborate mosaics; luxury items like carved stone table-tops have survived the destruction; and in the basements are elaborate baths and *mikvehs* for ritual purity. Because of the wealth of one house, and the bathing facilities, it has been suggested that it may have belonged to the High Priest of the Temple.

The Byzantine *Cardo Maximus* was
uncovered during the post-1967
excavations and has been restored as
an open-air museum and shopping
area for tourists. The east side of this
monumental street was covered by
an arcade supported on huge pillars.
The *Cardo Maximus* was continued
southwards in the Byzantine period
to the Nea Church, the largest
basilica in Jerusalem at the time,
built by Emperor Justinian and
consecrated in 543. The ruins of the
twelfth-century church of St Mary's
of the Germans have been conserved
as an archaeological garden.

Also preserved are the ruins of the
Hurva and Ramban synagogues,
built in the thirteenth century, when
the Jewish population of Jerusalem
stood at only 2000. The famous
Jewish scholar, Moses ben
Nachmanides, also known as the
Ramban, built the synagogue which
bears his name. Destroyed more
than once, the synagogue served the
small population of Jewish residents
and pilgrims. Only in 1856 was a
larger synagogue, the Hurva, built
on the site. It was destroyed in 1948
and left in ruins as a memorial after
the reuniting of Jerusalem in 1967.

A complex of four synagogues,
restored after 1967, still serves the
Sephardic Jewish community as it
has done since the seventeenth
century. The synagogues were built
below ground level, in part to be
inconspicuous in what was a
Muslim city. The Old Yishuv
Museum shows what domestic and
religious life was like for the Jewish
inhabitants of Jerusalem a century
ago, with a house and synagogue
reconstructed from that period.

164 (left) Wilson's
Arch, to the north of
the Western Wall, was
one of the arches under
the great causeway
that crossed the
Tyropoeon Valley from
the Temple Mount to

the Western Hill. The
great blocks that made
up the walls of
Herod's Temple
Mount are still visible
and look very new. It
is now used as a men's
prayer hall.

164–165 The Western
or Wailing Wall of the
Temple Mount is part
of the original wall of
the Temple Mount
platform built by
Herod and destroyed
in AD 70. The area is
divided into two: to the
north is the section for
male worshippers,
while women are
allotted the smaller
area to the south.

166–167 A Jewish man at prayer wearing the prayer shawl, the tallit, *with tassels at each of the four corners and the phylacteries or* tefillin. *The two black leather boxes of the* tefillin *contain scriptural passages and are worn for the morning services, with the exception of the Sabbath. The* tefillin *are put on after the* tallit, *with straps wrapped around the head and arm in a symbolic order. The duty of wearing* tefillin *begins when a boy reaches his* bar-mitzvah *on his thirteenth birthday.*

168–169 The midday meal at a school in Jerusalem. At this Talmud Torah, or ultra-orthodox school, boys are taught only religious subjects, including the Torah and the Talmud. The language of instruction is usually Yiddish, with Hebrew used only for the study of sacred texts. Studies generally begin at the age of three, with the learning of the Hebrew alphabet, and continue until the age of the bar-mitzvah, at 13. Afterwards, the boys continue on to yeshiva, the religious secondary school. This type of school is usually not funded by the government and children are taught few secular subjects.

*170–171 (left)
A Jewish scribe
painstakingly checking
a religious text. From
biblical times it has
been the job of the
scribe to copy religious
texts, according to a
certain set of laws.*

*Only a feather quill
and a special indelible
ink may be used on
specially prepared
parchment. The
scribe must be
ritually clean and
wear a particular
ritual garment.*

*171 (above) A man
engrossed in study
and prayer at a shul,
or neighbourhood
synagogue. Men
gather in the
synagogue twice a*

*day for the early
morning and evening
prayers. Before prayers
can begin a minyan,
or quorum, of ten
adult males, must be
present.*

CHRISTIAN JERUSALEM

Almost every known denomination of Christians is represented in the population of Jerusalem. Each is in charge of marriage, divorce and many other matters of family law relating to their congregation.

The majority of the Christian population is Arab and speaks Arabic, although a sizeable number of Christians live in Israel as foreign residents. Altogether Christians constitute little more than two per cent of the population. The Greek Orthodox make up the largest group in Jerusalem and although mainly Arab, many of the priests and most of the senior hierarchy, including the Patriarch, are Greek. Many of the most splendid churches in the Holy Land are under the control of the Greek Patriarchy. There are also small communities of Russian Orthodox and Romanian Orthodox clergy.

The Armenian Church is another Christian group with ancient roots in Jerusalem; much smaller congregations are served by the Syrian Orthodox Church, also called the Jacobites, and by the Copts. The Ethiopian Church is a small community of monks and nuns.

The Catholic Church has several communities in Jerusalem, the largest being the Roman Catholics, while others, such as the Chaldeans, Melkites, Maronites, Coptic Catholics, Syrian Catholics and Armenian Catholics are found there also. The Latin community also supports many monastic orders, the Franciscans being the longest serving in the Holy Land.

Protestant activity in the Holy Land dates back to the nineteenth century and the formation of the joint English Anglican and Prussian Bishopric. This formed the basis of the largely Arabic-speaking Evangelical Episcopal Church of Jerusalem today. Many American Protestant groups also arrived in the nineteenth century. Nearly every Protestant denomination now has some representative institution in Jerusalem. During the Feast of Tabernacles, several thousand Christians come on pilgrimage to the city, sponsored by the International Christian Embassy.

The Church of the Holy Sepulchre lies almost hidden within the Christian Quarter, only its dome rising above the buildings that encompass it. Construction on the church was begun in 326 by Emperor Constantine, to mark the site of the crucifixion, tomb and resurrection of Jesus. The original church was larger and was laid out on an east–west plan. The tomb was covered by a great circular building, the Anastasis, crowned with a golden dome. The rock of Golgotha lay in the Holy Garden, a large colonnaded courtyard. The Basilica marked the place of the crucifixion and was a large five-aisled hall which opened on to the Atrium, or entrance hall, where wide steps descended to the *Cardo Maximus*.

172 (above) The Parvis, or forecourt, of the Church of the Holy Sepulchre. The double-arched entry is from the Crusader period. Originally there was a third door.

172 (below) A clerical procession in Jerusalem. Each of the major Christian denominations has its own religious representatives in Jerusalem.

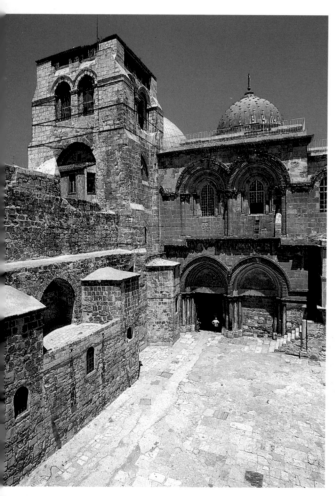

172 (above right) The Stone of Unction, where Nicodemus anointed the body of Jesus after it was removed from the cross, stands close to the entrance of the Holy Sepulchre.

173 (opposite) The Church of the Holy Sepulchre with the large grey Rotunda over the tomb of Jesus and the smaller dome over the Catholicon.

The church was almost levelled to the ground several times in the tumultuous history of Jerusalem and its architecture reflects this. While some basic components of the church of Constantine have been retained, various structures have been added on and the church now blends into the surrounding city. As a result, it is beautiful in its parts but difficult to consider as a whole, unlike most other great churches.

By the fourteenth century, the keys to the church were held by a Muslim

174 (opposite) The Edicule, built over the tomb and the place of the resurrection of Christ. This chapel was rebuilt in 1808 after a fire destroyed much of the church.

175 (right) The ownership of the Church of the Holy Sepulchre is divided among many different denominations of the Christian faith. During the major Christian holy days, and especially at Easter, it is possible to celebrate a wide range of services. The rights to various parts of the church – chapels and even small ornaments – were disputed over the course of many centuries and now a status quo has been arrived at. This diversity in both devotional and architectural forms creates the unique atmosphere of this international meeting place, the most sacred place for Christians.

watchman, to ensure access for the Latins, Greeks, Georgians, Copts, Syrians and Ethiopians, all of whom claimed rights. Today, a careful *status quo* is maintained.

Directly to the south of the Church of the Holy Sepulchre, the Muristan occupies a large square that was once the Roman forum and later became the property of the Crusader Knights of St John, the Hospitallers. In twelfth-century Jerusalem, the Knights maintained a hospice and hospital, housing up to 400 knights of the Order and caring for as many as 900 patients. The hospital was closed when the Christians were forced to leave the city by Saladin in 1187. Part of the building continued as a hospital but it gradually fell into disuse, becoming a wasteland by the nineteenth century.

176–177 (overleaf) The view from the steps leading down into the Chapel of St Helena, the mother of Constantine, who found the True Cross.

THE CHURCH OF THE HOLY SEPULCHRE

The Crusader Church of the Holy Sepulchre was rebuilt on the same spot as the fourth-century Church of Constantine. In 938, the Muslims had destroyed much of the Byzantine Church and built a mosque over part of the entrance. In 1009, the church was almost entirely demolished on the orders of the Fatimid caliph al-Hakim. Although the Rotunda was restored in 1048 by the Byzantine emperor Constantine Monomachus, the remainder of the church lay in ruins. After the Crusader conquest of the city in 1099, the church was rebuilt and dedicated in 1149. Its architecture resembles the contemporary Romanesque churches of France. Much of the interior decoration of the church has changed, but it retains a basilical plan.

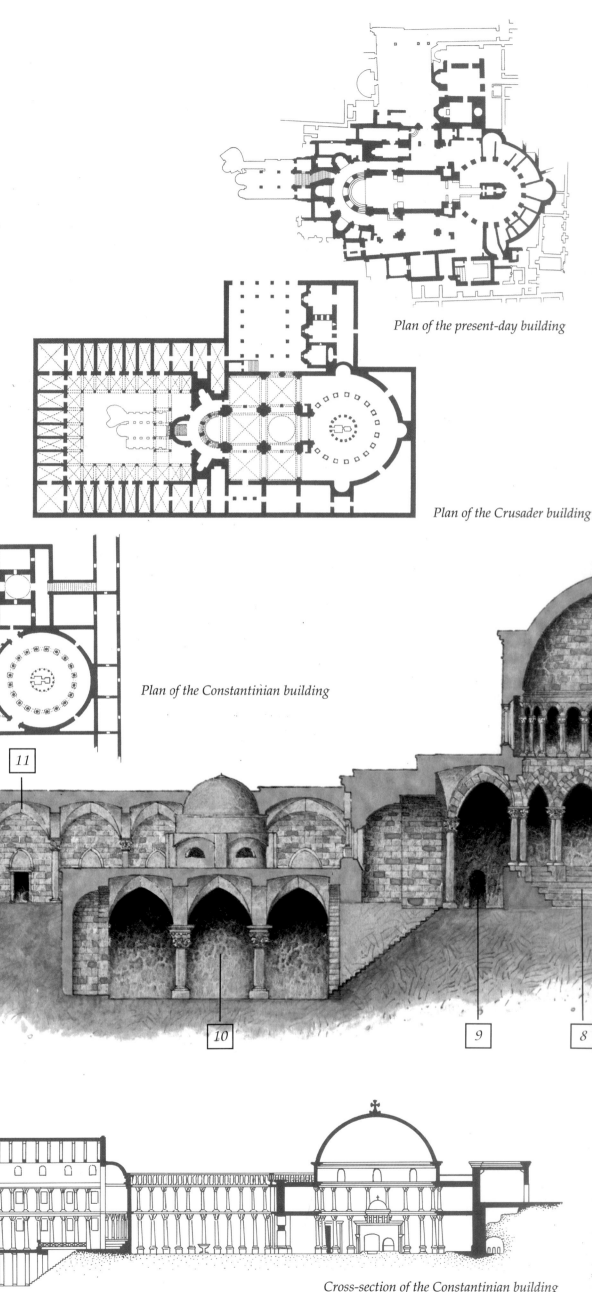

Plan of the present-day building

Plan of the Crusader building

Plan of the Constantinian building

Cross-section of the Constantinian building

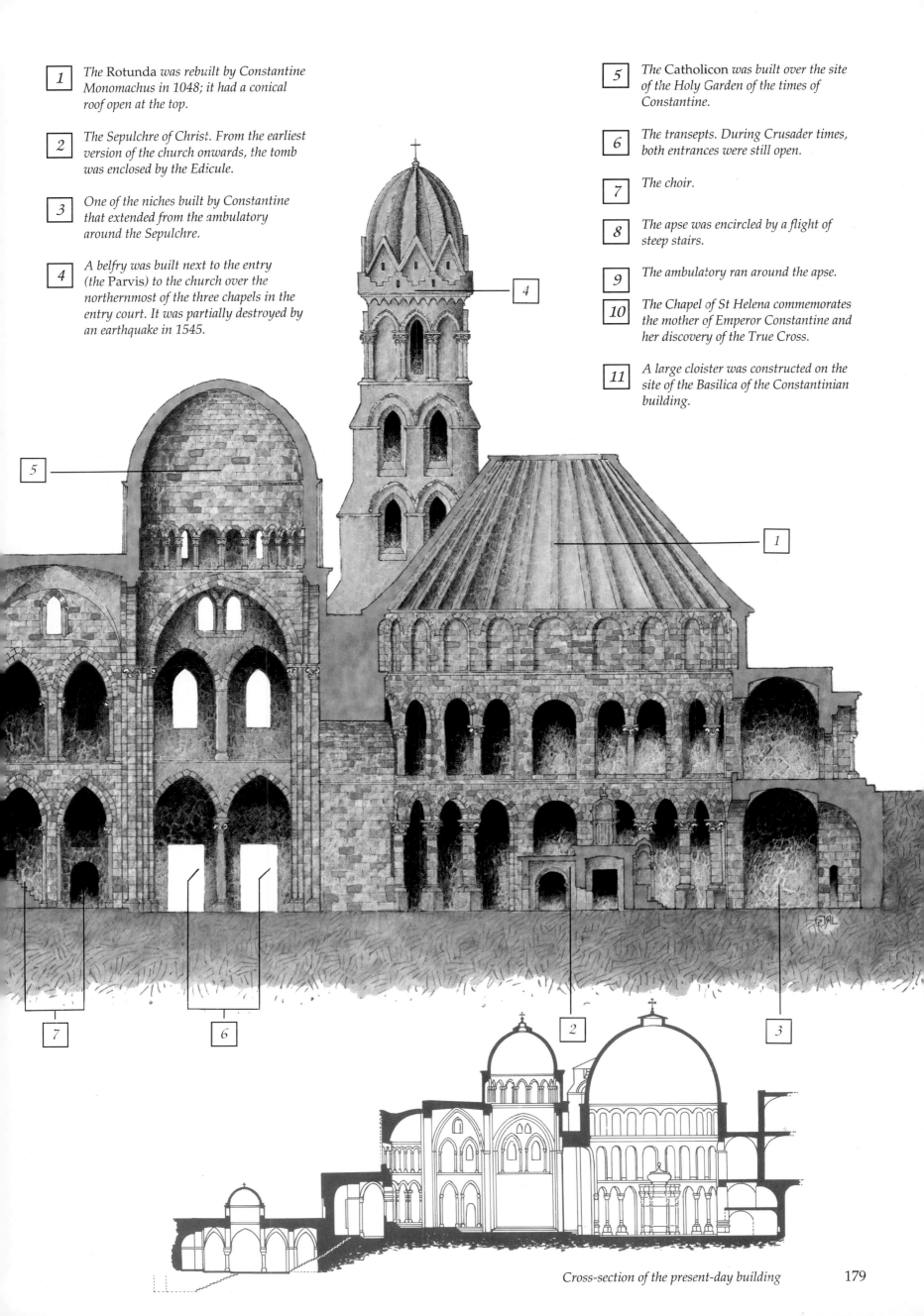

1 The Rotunda was rebuilt by Constantine Monomachus in 1048; it had a conical roof open at the top.

2 The Sepulchre of Christ. From the earliest version of the church onwards, the tomb was enclosed by the Edicule.

3 One of the niches built by Constantine that extended from the ambulatory around the Sepulchre.

4 A belfry was built next to the entry (the Parvis) to the church over the northernmost of the three chapels in the entry court. It was partially destroyed by an earthquake in 1545.

5 The Catholicon was built over the site of the Holy Garden of the times of Constantine.

6 The transepts. During Crusader times, both entrances were still open.

7 The choir.

8 The apse was encircled by a flight of steep stairs.

9 The ambulatory ran around the apse.

10 The Chapel of St Helena commemorates the mother of Emperor Constantine and her discovery of the True Cross.

11 A large cloister was constructed on the site of the Basilica of the Constantinian building.

Cross-section of the present-day building

Crown Prince Frederick William of Prussia visited the Holy Land in 1869 and was given part of the area as a gift. The German Protestant Church of the Redeemer was built in the northeast corner of the square and consecrated during the visit of Emperor Wilhelm II and Empress Augusta Victoria in 1898. The church was designed to follow the outline of the Crusader Church of St Mary of the Latin; one of the best views of Jerusalem can be obtained from its bell tower. One of the most pleasant spots

in the city is the Crusader church of St Anne, which, along with the monastery of the White Fathers and a Greek Catholic seminary lies to the north of the Temple Mount. Excavations have shown that this was site of the Bethesda Pool, where Jesus healed the crippled man. In the middle of the fifth century a church was built on the spot and devoted to Mary, mother of Jesus. By Crusader times it came to be associated with Mary's birthplace and derived its name from her mother, St Anne. After the Muslim conquest in 1187, the church became a religious school (*madrasa*), and later still it fell into disuse until given to Napoleon III by the Ottoman Sultan, in 1856.

The site of the Antonia Fortress built by Herod the Great is now the Umariyya Boys' School. This forms

the traditional site of the *Praetorium*, where Pontius Pilate condemned Jesus to death. It is considered by some to be the First Station on the Via Dolorosa, the route Jesus took on the way to his crucifixion. The First Station of the Franciscans is now at the Chapel of the Condemnation and the Second Station, where Jesus took up the cross, is at the entrance to the courtyard of the Monastery of the Flagellation. Nearby is the Convent of the Sisters of Zion, with the ruins of the Struthion Pool.

180 (above left) In the Treasury of the Orthodox Patriarchate innumerable sacred objects of great value are preserved, such as this carved wooden pendant representing the Virgin with Infant Jesus, surrounded by saints, dating from the seventeenth century. (Museum of the Greek Orthodox Patriarchate)

180 (below left) A unique reliquary dating from the Crusader period. It was carved from a piece of rock crystal, encased in gold, set with precious stones.

180 (centre left) A gilded cover of a Book of Gospels, decorated in gold relief with cabochons and pearls. The reliefs are scenes from the life of Christ. (Museum of the Greek Orthodox Patriarchate)

181 (opposite) A detail of the gilded cover of the Book of Gospels from the Museum of the Greek Orthodox Patriarchate. This precious object dates from the seventeenth century.

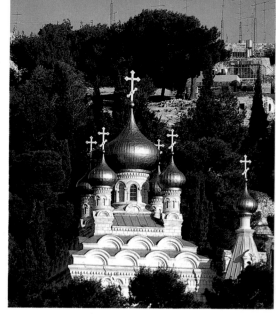

182 (left) The Russian Orthodox Church of St Mary Magdalene at Gethsemane, with its seven golden domes, was erected in 1888 by Czar Alexander III.

182 (right) Services in the Church of St Mary Magdalene. The Russian Orthodox congregation is one of the smallest Christian communities in Jerusalem.

PRECES SVPPLICATIONESQVE CVM CLAMORE VALIDO ET LACRYMIS OFFERENS EXAVDITVS EST PRO SVA REVERENTIA

182–183 (below) The Church of All Nations (Church of the Agony), built by the Franciscans in 1924. The mosaic on the façade shows scenes from the life of Christ.

183 (below right) The Cathedral of St James of the Armenian Christian community is decorated with eighteenth-century Kutahya tiles and paintings on canvas.

The Ecce Homo Arch emerges from the outer wall of the convent. 'Ecce Homo', meaning 'Behold the Man', is the traditional place where Pilate showed Jesus to the Jews. A recent study has proposed that the arch dates from the time of Herod Agrippa, although this is not certain.

The Third Station of the cross, outside the Polish Catholic Chapel, marks the place where Jesus stumbled and fell. South of this is the entrance to the Armenian Catholic Patriarchate and the Church of Our Lady of the Spasm, marking the Fourth Station, where Jesus met Mary. The Fifth Station is where Simon of Cyrene took the weight of the cross from Jesus. The Church of the Holy Face and St Veronica, the Sixth Station, marks the spot where Veronica gave Jesus her handkerchief. Further along, the Seventh Station is where the sentence of death was posted. The Eighth Station, where Jesus told the women accompanying him not to weep, is at the Monastery of St Caralambos. At the Ninth Station Christ fell for the third time. The remaining stations of the cross are within the Church of the Holy Sepulchre. Hezekiah's Pool is hidden behind buildings on the north side of David Street. Also called the Pool of the Patriarch, it is very beautiful when filled with water after the winter rains.

Between the Jaffa and Zion gates lies the Armenian Quarter. Armenians were some of the first converts to Christianity. In the twelfth century they bought the Church of St James, which is still the centre of their community and of the Armenian diaspora today. The complex built around what is now the Cathedral of St James is entered by a single gate through a wall. It now encompasses not only the cathedral, but also two other churches, the Armenian Patriarch's residence, a seminary and library, the residences of Armenian monks, nuns and pilgrims, a museum, a school and accommodation for families. Close to the Armenian compound and opposite the Citadel is the complex of Christ Church, consecrated in 1849 and still a centre of evangelical Protestantism.

The Syrian Church of St Mark is also worth a visit. Syrian Orthodox Christians, also called Jacobite or Assyrian Christians, separated from other orthodox Christians in 451 and ancient Syriac is still used in the liturgy of the Church.

MUSLIM JERUSALEM

184 (below left) The architecture of the buildings around the Temple Mount dates mostly from the Mameluke period. However, there is also some influence and reuse of materials from the Crusader period.

184 (below) The entrance to al-Madrasa al-Ashrafiyya on the western side of the Temple Mount was built in 1465 and then rebuilt by the sultan Qa'itbay in 1482. Its decorations are typical of the Mameluke period.

The Qoran relates the Night Journey of Muhammad, when he was taken by angel Gabriel to Jerusalem, from where they rose to Paradise. During this voyage they saw Abraham, Moses and Jesus. The Muslim holiday of al-Isra Wal-Mi'raj celebrates this event. Jerusalem was recognized as a holy city very early in the preaching of Muhammad and initially he turned towards it during his prayers. Only later did he pray instead towards Mecca.

Jerusalem was first conquered in the name of Islam by the second caliph, Omar, in 638. The completion of the Dome of the Rock little more than half a century later confirmed the central position of Jerusalem in Islamic theology. The rock in the middle of the mosque is thought to be the centre of the universe. On the Day of Judgment, the angel of death will stand on the holy rock and blow a ram's horn. At that time a bridge will be suspended from the Mount of Olives and the dead will have to cross over, passing through seven arches. At each arch, every person will have to explain his life.

Today, the Arab residents of Jerusalem are mostly Muslim. Religious matters are under the supervision of the Supreme Muslim Council, with the Mufti as its chief official. It also presides over the *shari'a,* or religious courts, and administers the *waqf,* a property-holding trust that supports Islamic religious institutions and supervises Muslim holy places. Each year several thousand Israeli Muslims make the *haj* pilgrimage to Mecca.

The Muslim Quarter of Jerusalem is both the largest and most

184 (left) The Gate of the Chain fountain was built by Suleiman the Magnificent. The trough below may be a Crusader period sarcophagus and the rosette above is reused from a Crusader church. The inscription gives the date of construction: 1537.

185 (opposite) The magnificent Gate of the Cotton Merchants, or Bab al-Qattanin, built in 1336–1337, leads from the market, or Suq, of the Cotton Merchants, built at the same time. The suq is made up of 30 bays, containing shops and the entrances to other buildings.

populous quarter in the Old City, and is also the least open to the public eye. It includes part of the city incorporated by Herod the Great and the northern section of the city enclosed by Herod Agrippa. During the Fatimid period it housed the Jewish Quarter and in Crusader times it contained many churches, some of which are now Muslim educational institutions.

In the area close to the Temple Mount are several interesting Mameluke buildings. It was during the Mameluke period, beginning in 1291 and ending with incorporation into the Ottoman Empire in 1517, that Jerusalem assumed much of the architectural character that it has today. Although the country as a whole experienced a period of economic decline, Jerusalem became a centre for Islam and many religious institutions were built: hostels for pilgrims, Islamic seminaries (*madrasas*) and tombs.

The Palace of Sitt Tunshuq was built at the end of the fourteenth century as a hostel for Dervishes. This building displays many of the characteristics of Mameluke architecture, including the use of black, white and red stonework. Most of the decorative emphasis is placed on the entrance, which is composed of a square door with a single, flat lintel on top. Above is an arch, about twice the height of the door and decorated with carved and inlaid stone in geometric and floral designs. Often an inscription lists the benefactor or builder of the edifice, the date of construction, the purpose of the building and includes passages from the Qoran.

186 (top) The black dome of the el-Aqsa Mosque, the centre for Muslim prayer and devotions in Jerusalem. The first building was a wooden structure and was probably begun in AD 638. It can now contain around 5000 worshippers. On the western side of the mosque is a smaller hall called the Women's Mosque.

186 (centre) A Muslim kneeling in prayer. The area of the Haram al-Sharif, or Temple Mount, is crowded with worshippers every Friday for midday prayers.

186 (below) The vast interior of the el-Aqsa Mosque has seven aisles made up of 75 columns and 33 piers. Light is provided by 155 windows, many of them with coloured glass.

187 (opposite) The platform between the el-Aqsa Mosque and the Dome of the Rock during prayers. The arcade, known as the 'scales', at the top of the flight of stairs leads to a central fountain, al-Kas, for ritual ablutions.

The Suq al-Qattanin, or Market of the Cotton Merchants, is a long market street with two rows of shops. It leads from Haggai Street to the Temple Mount, which is entered through a large, impressive gate.

The Dome of the Rock is the third holiest place in Islam after the Qaa'ba in Mecca and the Mosque of the Prophet in Medina. It is important as a place of pilgrimage and is a shrine rather than a mosque. The four-sided platform on which it is built lies over the highest point of the rocky ridge underlying the Temple Mount. On each side is a set of steps, at the top of which are the 'scales', graceful arches from which the scales for the weighing of souls will be hung at the Last Judgment. The building is in the shape of an octagon topped by a gilded dome. The lower walls are covered with coloured marble, and the upper walls with tiles from Kashan, Persia, in geometric and floral designs.

In the centre is the Holy Rock, an outcrop of natural rock, connected in tradition with Judgment Day. An indentation in the rock is believed by Muslims to be the footprint of Muhammad, left when he ascended to Paradise. Underneath the rock is a cave with two small shrines, one to Elijah and the other to Abraham.

The el-Aqsa Mosque is a centre of prayer and can hold up to 5000 worshippers. Its black dome is another familiar feature of the Jerusalem skyline. A modest mosque was built in 709, but this has been greatly enlarged. Architectural features recovered from renovations of the Dome of the Rock and the el-Aqsa Mosque are on display in the Islamic Museum next to the mosque.

Under the southeast corner is an area of supporting arches, called Solomon's Stables, although they date not from the time of Solomon but rather to Herod. The Crusaders stabled their war-horses in them.

188 (above) The Haram al-Sharif, the 'Noble Sanctuary', essentially covers the same area as the platform built by Herod for the Second Temple, which in turn was built on the same location as the First Temple of Solomon. The Dome of the Rock lies off-centre on top of a smaller platform, while the el-Aqsa Mosque lies at the south of the Haram. The eastern and northern sections are laid out in gardens.

188–189 (right) The Dome of the Rock from the southwest. Three smaller domed buildings immediately adjacent to the Dome of the Rock serve to complement its structure. To the northwest the eight-sided building is the Dome of the Ascension of the Prophet; by its side is the smaller, open Dome of the Prophet, and on the eastern side of the Dome of the Rock is the Dome of the Chain.

192–193 The dome is
supported by a drum
which in turn rests on
a circle of columns.
The interior of the
dome rises above a
wooden gallery and is
painted in a gold, red,
white and green
arabesque design,
decreasing in size
from bottom to top,
giving the illusion of
added height. The
circular band at the
top is the passage from
the Qoran beginning
with, '… there is no
God but He, the
Living, the Eternal…'
The dome rests over
the Holy Rock.

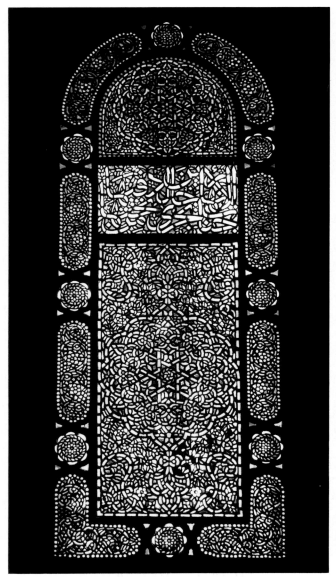

194 The interior of the Dome of the Rock has three ambulatories separated by two sets of columns. The arches above are covered with glass mosaics which belonged to the original structure. Coloured glass windows decorate the outer wall. The arcade of the inner ambulatory is made up of four piers and 12 columns. This supports the drum, which in turn supports the dome over the Holy Rock. A tall, four-sided shrine with gilded grilles contains holy relics of the Prophet.

195 (opposite) The outer ambulatory is separated from the middle ambulatory by eight piers and 16 columns made of beautifully veined marble. The floors of the Dome are entirely covered with precious handmade carpets.

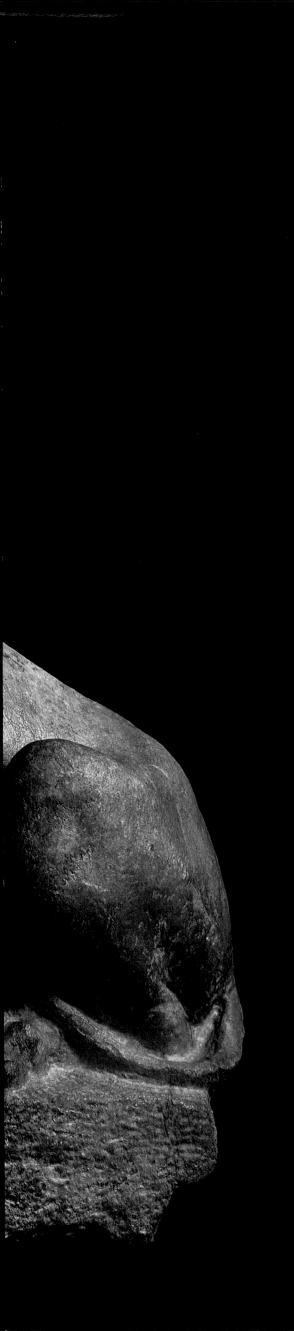

A HISTORICAL TOUR THROUGH THE HOLY LAND

196–197 (opposite) A marble statue of the winged Griffin of Nemesis with the Wheel of Fate, found at Erez. The Greek inscription reads: 'In the year 522 [of the Seleucid Era] I, Mercury [son] of Alexander, set up [this statue] while priest.' (Israel Museum)

OLD ACRE, AN OTTOMAN CITY ON CRUSADER FOUNDATIONS

The port of Acre in Ottoman times, as shown here, was built on the foundations or ruins of buildings dating from the Crusader period. Acre was taken by the Crusaders after a siege of 20 days in May 1104. It fell to Saladin in 1187 and was held by him until 1191. Crusader Acre was divided into different quarters among the various orders of knights who had come to conquer the Holy Land, as well as among the merchants of the Italian city-states of Venice, Genoa and Pisa. The city was retaken by the Mamelukes in 1291 and systematically destroyed to prevent its reoccupation by the Crusaders. Acre lay largely in ruins until it was rebuilt in the middle of the eighteenth century by Dhaher al-'Amir and Jazzar Pasha.

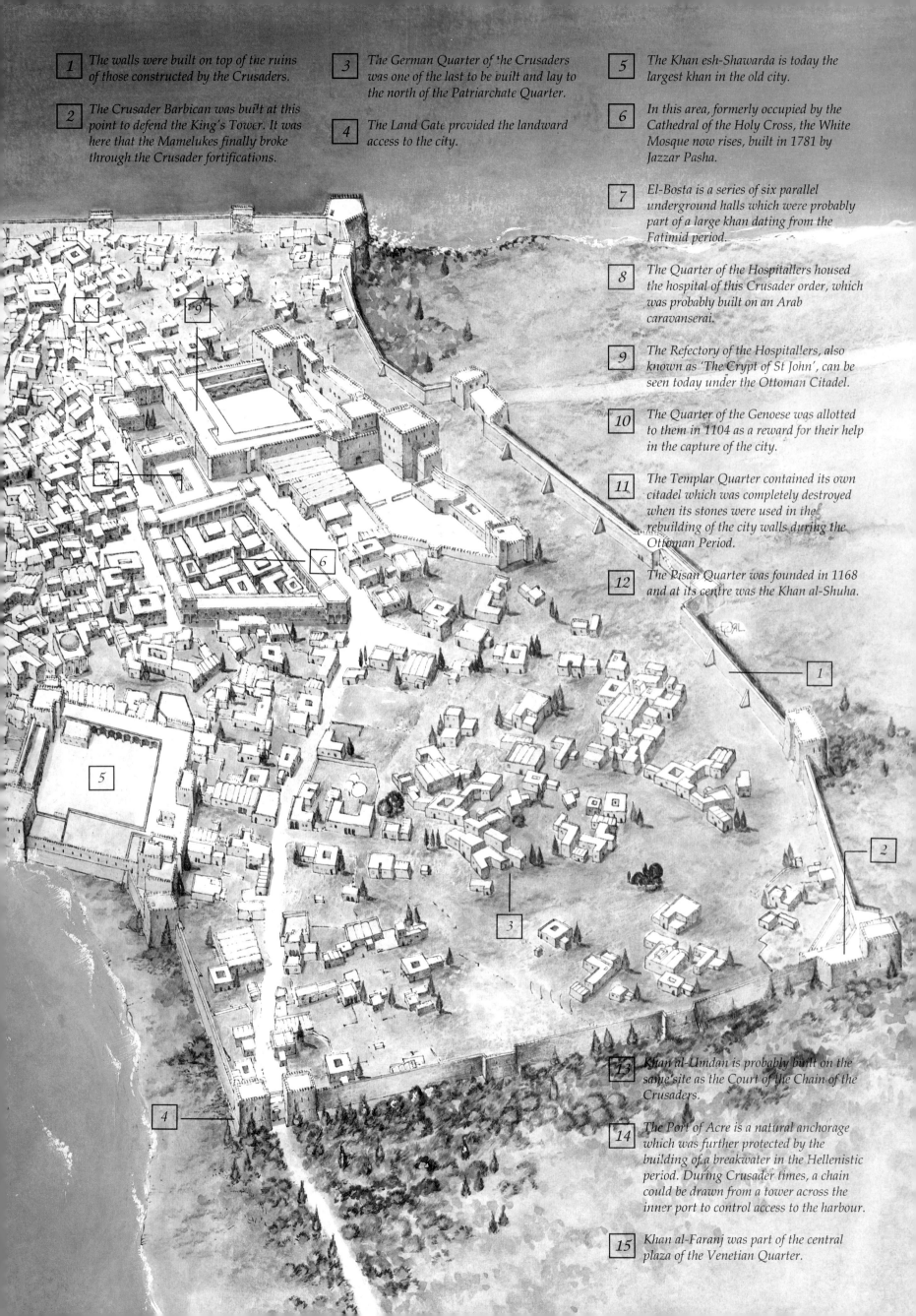

1 The walls were built on top of the ruins of those constructed by the Crusaders.

2 The Crusader Barbican was built at this point to defend the King's Tower. It was here that the Mamelukes finally broke through the Crusader fortifications.

3 The German Quarter of the Crusaders was one of the last to be built and lay to the north of the Patriarchate Quarter.

4 The Land Gate provided the landward access to the city.

5 The Khan esh-Shawarda is today the largest khan in the old city.

6 In this area, formerly occupied by the Cathedral of the Holy Cross, the White Mosque now rises, built in 1781 by Jazzar Pasha.

7 El-Bosta is a series of six parallel underground halls which were probably part of a large khan dating from the Fatimid period.

8 The Quarter of the Hospitallers housed the hospital of this Crusader order, which was probably built on an Arab caravanserai.

9 The Refectory of the Hospitallers, also known as 'The Crypt of St John', can be seen today under the Ottoman Citadel.

10 The Quarter of the Genoese was allotted to them in 1104 as a reward for their help in the capture of the city.

11 The Templar Quarter contained its own citadel which was completely destroyed when its stones were used in the rebuilding of the city walls during the Ottoman Period.

12 The Pisan Quarter was founded in 1168 and at its centre was the Khan al-Shuha.

13 Khan al-Umdan is probably built on the same site as the Court of the Chain of the Crusaders.

14 The Port of Acre is a natural anchorage which was further protected by the building of a breakwater in the Hellenistic period. During Crusader times, a chain could be drawn from a tower across the inner port to control access to the harbour.

15 Khan al-Faranj was part of the central plaza of the Venetian Quarter.

208–209 Some of the most important Crusader buildings of Acre were discovered under what used to be a government hospital. The Refectory of the Order of St John dates from about 1148. At the beginning of excavations it was full of earth and debris to a level above the stone columns supporting the roof. The Crusader buildings were filled in to provide support for the structures built on top during Ottoman times. They are now part of a museum open to the public.

Crusader Acre was divided into various quarters assigned to the military orders: in the centre were the Hospitallers, of the Order of St John; at the south were the Knights Templar; at the east were the Teutonic Knights; and to the north was the Order of St Lazarus. Along the southern coast were the Italian colonies of traders from Venice, Genoa and Pisa. At this period the city was considerably larger than the old city of today.

The Crusader walls have been largely covered by the new city and the present walls to the north and east were built by Jazzar Pasha. The Turkish citadel is now the most prominent building in the old city. Under the British Mandate it was used as a prison and the room where some of the Jewish

leading north to the city walls and south to the port, have also come to light.

Close to the refectory are six parallel underground halls, of the eleventh or twelfth centuries. Called el-Bosta, these halls are probably the remains of a Fatimid period khan (inn) reused by the Crusaders as an infirmary, with the ceiling rebuilt in a European style.

The Great Mosque was erected in 1781 by Jazzar Pasha and probably lies on top of the foundations of the Crusader Cathedral of the Holy Cross. The Roman columns in the courtyard are from the ruins of Caesarea. The municipal baths, the Hamman al-Basha, also built by Jazzar Pasha, are now a museum.

Acre was the major entry into Palestine until the beginning of this century, and several khans were built close to the harbour to house the traders and their animals. The Khan esh-Shawarda contains a tower dating from the thirteenth century. To the south is Khan al-Faranj, centre of the Venetian quarter in Crusader times, with the eighteenth-century church of the Franciscans at its northeast corner. Khan al-Umdan, with its Turkish clock tower of 1906, was part of the Genoese quarter and most of the buildings to the south date from Crusader times. The Abu Christo café was the location of the port of the Pisan community. To the east is the Tower of the Flies, partly visible above the water. Protected by a recently constructed breakwater, the harbour that was once the main port of the Holy Land is now used only by small fishing boats.

209 (above right) A fleur-de-lys is just visible on a corbel in the refectory of the Hospitallers. This heraldic lily, composed of three long petals, was part of France's royal arms.

underground fighters were executed by the British is still preserved.

Many Crusader buildings were filled in during Ottoman times to strengthen the foundations of buildings erected above. The refectory of the Order of St John, dating from about 1148, was found below what was once a government hospital. Subterranean passages dating from pre-Crusader times and

210 (below) The exterior of the White Mosque at Acre, built by Jazzar Pasha. Now the third largest mosque in Israel and the most important after el-Aqsa, it is the spiritual centre for the entire north of the country.

210 (right) This fine inlaid marble work is characteristic of late Ottoman architecture. During this period only geometrical forms were used for decoration.

210–211 (right) The interior of the White Mosque is made light and spacious by both the white interior and the ample light provided by the dome windows.

211 (right) The Khan al-Umdan was once part of the Genoese quarter in Crusader Acre. The Turkish clock tower was built in 1906 and is similar to many others built at this time throughout the Ottoman Empire.

SAFED AND MERON OF THE MYSTICS

212 (below) At Meron only the three doorways of the façade of the late third-century synagogue built on the basilical plan still stand.

212 (below centre) The interior of the synagogue named after Rabbi Joseph Caro, the author of the book of Jewish ritual and law, the Shulchan Arukh.

A Portico
B Main entrance
C Prayer hall

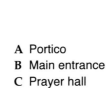

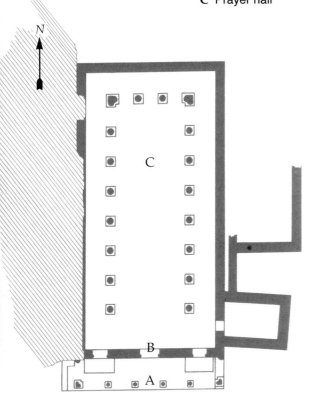

Safed is one of four ancient sacred cities of the Holy Land for the Jewish people, the others being Tiberias, Hebron and Jerusalem. In the Jerusalem Talmud (the Jewish book of law), Safed is named as one of the mountain peaks where, during the Second Temple period, fires were lit to announce the beginning of each month and the start of festivals.

Although Safed was settled by priestly families fleeing from the destruction of Jerusalem in AD 70, it became an important site only when a Crusader fortress, Saphet, was built there in 1140. Saladin conquered Safed in 1188, but it was restored to the Crusaders in 1240. In 1266 the Mamelukes took the fortress and reinforced it. From this period, Safed became a centre of Jewish learning and by the late fifteenth century, after a large influx of Jewish refugees from the Spanish inquisition, Safed became a trading centre.

Safed was then, and still is, a centre of Jewish mysticism. It was the home of Rabbi Joseph Caro, the sixteenth-century author of the *Shulchan Arukh*, a compilation of Jewish ritual and law. Rabbi Isaac Luria, Ha-Ari or the 'Lion', the leading interpreter of Jewish mysticism, the Kabbalah, lived and taught in Safed, and his disciples can be found among the Jews of Safed today. Safed was also the home of the first Hebrew printing press in the Holy Land, set up by the brothers Ashkenazi in 1563.

Seventeenth-century Safed had 300 rabbinical scholars, 18 religious schools and 21 synagogues, as well as 1200 poor living off charity. A decline at the end of the seventeenth century was followed by an epidemic

in 1747 and a severe earthquake in 1759. Safed enjoyed new prosperity at the end of the eighteenth century with the settlement of 300 Hassidim (orthodox Jews), followers of Rabbi Israel ben Eliezer – the Ba'al Shem Tov – and later the followers of Rabbi Elijah Ben Solomon Zalman – the Gaon of Vilna. However, Safed was decimated by another earthquake in 1837, when the houses collapsed on each other down the steep slopes and 4000 people died.

At the festival of Lag ba-Omer, Safed is the start of a procession carrying the Torah scroll to Meron, 9 km (5.5 miles) away. Meron was the home of Rabbi Simeon bar Yochai, author of the mystical book, the *Zohar*, and his son Eliezer. Their place of burial has become an important centre of Jewish pilgrimage. The earliest traces of settlement date from 200 BC and Meron is mentioned by Josephus as one of the villages fortified by him in AD 66. It became a significant settlement only in the third century AD when it was a centre for olive oil. Wooden barrels for the transport of oil, a famous product of Upper Galilee, were made in a cooperage. The ruins of a late third-century synagogue built on the basilical plan stand at Meron. The façade still survives, although the lintel over the central door is cracked and looks as if it might fall at any time. There is a belief that its fall is a sign of the coming of the Messiah.

212 (right) The elaborate ark in the Ashkenazi Ari Synagogue in Safed. First built at the end of the sixteenth century, the synagogue was reconstructed after the disastrous earthquake of 1837.

213 (opposite) The Rabbi Isaac Aboab Synagogue, Safed. When the Jews were expelled from Spain in 1492, the city became a prominent cultural centre of the Holy Land and offered refuge to many scholars.

CAPERNAUM, WITNESS OF THE GOSPELS

215 A small five-branched menorah was carved on one of the Corinthian capitals found in the excavations of the synagogue.

Capernaum was the centre of the Galilean ministry of Jesus. Kefar Nahum, as it is called in Hebrew, also contains the ruins of an impressive synagogue. Situated on the northwestern shore of the Sea of Galilee, the village dates back at least to the thirteenth century BC and was always unfortified. Peter and Andrew, disciples of Jesus, made their home in Capernaum.

The site of a large village has been partially excavated. To the south the remains of a fifth-century octagonal basilica were found, built on the ruins of a house dating from the first century. This is traditionally believed to be St Peter's house. The spacious house was built close to the shore of the lake and within a few decades after the death of Christ a room had been set aside for special veneration.

By the late fourth century it had become a place of pilgrimage, a *domus ecclesia* or house-church, decorated with finely plastered lime pavements and coloured plaster walls. During the next century, an octagonal church was built over the house-church. It was constructed on the plan of two concentric octagons surrounded by a portico on all but three sides. The eight square pillars making up the inner octagon supported a domed roof, a common architectural feature at sites of special veneration in the Holy Land.

The synagogue at Capernaum was probably built at the end of the fourth century, although the original building may date from the second or third century. In the gospel of Luke (7, 5) a synagogue built by a Roman centurion is mentioned, and this was perhaps at the same location. The synagogue was built in three sections, with a portico or porch at the front, a large central basilica with three entrances, and on the east side another room served as a study hall. Built of white limestone, the synagogue was no doubt an imposing structure in a village where the houses were made of the local black basalt.

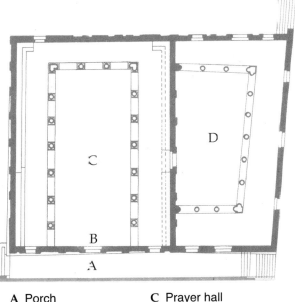

A Porch
B Main entrance
C Prayer hall
D Court

N

214–215 (opposite above) The synagogue at Capernaum next to the octagonal roof covering the excavations of the Byzantine church built over the House of St Peter.

214 (opposite below) A stone block from the synagogue is carved in relief in the form of the Ark of the Covenant on a wheeled base. The shell motif is common in ancient Jewish ceremonial art.

TIBERIAS, A CENTRE OF THE TALMUD

Tiberias is an important city for the Jewish people, for it was here that much of the Talmud, the book of Jewish laws and customs, was written. It was also a significant city at the time of Jesus: the New Testament calls the Sea of Galilee the Sea of Tiberias in the gospel of John (6, 1; 21, 1). The city is situated only 14 km (8.5 miles) from Capernaum and it is likely that Jesus frequently passed through.

Tiberias was founded by Herod Antipas, the son of Herod the Great, when he moved the capital of the Galilee from Sepphoris. Closely connected to the main centre of Tiberias was Hammath-Tiberias, the hot springs that served as a place of leisure. Below sea level, Tiberias is humid and hot in summer, while in winter it enjoys pleasant temperatures in contrast to other, cooler areas of the country.

The Roman city of Tiberias ranged from the royal palace of Antipas, built on Mount Berenice, 198 m (650 ft) above the lake, to a narrow strip of land along the shore. On the south side of the city was an impressive gate made of two circular towers. From the gate the *Cardo* traversed the entire length of

the city, north to south. Excavations have uncovered part of the original *Cardo*, the remains of a bathhouse decorated with fish mosaics, a roofed market and a Roman basilica.

Tiberias is known from Jewish sources to have had 13 synagogues and the ruins of one were discovered on the *Cardo* at the north of the ancient city. At the foot of Mount Berenice were found the remains of a large house built in AD 200 and occupied until at least the mid-eighth century. It has been suggested that this could be the *beth midrash*, or seminary, of Rabbi Jochanan, one of the chief authors of the Palestinian Talmud. Two synagogues have been discovered and one of them, to the south, has a spectacular mosaic floor.

216 (opposite above, left) The town of Tiberias on the western shores of the Sea of Galilee is popular as a resort during the winter and spring months.

216 (opposite above, right) The walls of Tiberias were rebuilt during the rule of Ottoman Governor Ibrahim Pasha, in 1833.

216–217 (opposite) The archaeological gardens in the town of Tiberias, built to display finds from the excavations and as a base for educational field trips.

217 (left) A carved stone seven-branched menorah *found in excavations at Hammath-Tiberias, dating from the third century AD. Indentations on top may have held small oil lamps. (Israel Museum)*

Sepphoris, the Capital of the Galilee

Sepphoris has provided some of the most beautiful examples of mosaic floors found in recent excavations. The first habitation dates from the eighth or seventh centuries BC and the town later rose to prominence because of its location overlooking two of the major highways of ancient times: one ran from the coast at Acre east through Tiberias, and the other south to Nablus, Jerusalem and Hebron.

In the Hasmonaean and Herodian periods, Sepphoris was the capital of the Galilee. Only during the reign of Herod Antipas (4 BC to AD 39) was the capital moved to Tiberias. As the major urban centre of the Galilee, it was no doubt well known to Jesus.

After the destruction of the Second Temple and the exile of the Jews from Jerusalem in AD 70, many Jews fled to the Galilee. For a period of 17 years Sepphoris was the seat of the Sanhedrin, the high court of the Jews, and only after the death of its leader, Rabbi Judah ha-Nasi, did the court move to Tiberias. The *Mishnah*, the first version of Jewish oral law, was codified at Sepphoris by Judah ha-Nasi. In 363, the town was demolished by an earthquake and was later only partially restored, continuing as a centre of Jewish population until the fifth century. By the sixth century there was also a significant Christian population presided over by a bishop. The Crusaders built a fortress, Le Sephorie, the remains of which are still standing. Later, in the eighteenth century, the town was refortified by the Ottoman governor of the Galilee.

The civic centre of Sepphoris was on the summit of the hill. Today, the Roman theatre is especially noteworthy. Apparently dating from the early first century AD, it seated approximately 4500 spectators. South of the theatre is a palatial mansion, probably built in the third century AD. A large building, it had a stately hall at its centre, with living quarters on three sides and a courtyard with a pool on the fourth. The most impressive discovery was the mosaic floor found in the grand hall. This has a Dionysian theme showing scenes from the life of the Greek god and recording the various forms of worship in the cult. At the centre is the portrait of a beautiful woman. After the earthquake of 363, the building was abandoned.

Further west, a residential area has been partially excavated. The houses, orientated on a main street running in a southeast–northwest direction, often consisted of two storeys, with living rooms, storerooms and kitchens as well as a cistern under the ground floor. Many *mikvehs* (Jewish ritual baths) were also discovered.

At the foot of the hill was a large building, built of ashlar stone blocks and measuring over 60 m (195 ft) each side. It contained an impressive mosaic with various scenes from the River Nile, dating from the Byzantine period. The river flows horizontally through the picture and along its banks are a fisherman and a variety of wildlife, such as fish and birds. A nilometer, a column for measuring the height of the water level, is also depicted. In the upper left corner is a reclining female figure with a basket laden with fruits, representing Egypt. In the

opposite corner a male figure personifies the Nile. In the middle is a parade of people marching to the city of Alexandria, represented by two tall towers on either side of the city gates. The lower portion of the mosaic shows various hunting scenes, including the realistic depiction of a ferocious lion pouncing on the back of a bull.

220 (opposite) The Roman theatre, one of the most complete found in Israel, dates from the first century AD and could seat about 4500 spectators.

220–221 (left) The 'Mona Lisa of the Galilee', from the palace at Sepphoris, is part of a larger mosaic on a Dionysian theme.

A Roman theatre
B Crusader tower
C Palace
D Residential area

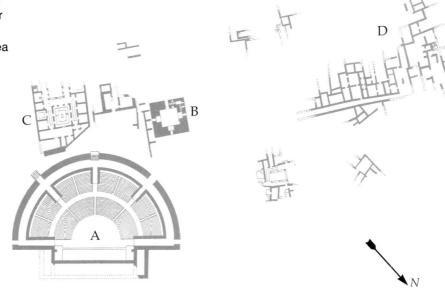

Nazareth, Mount Tabor, Cana and Tabgha: Places of the Spirit

222 (below) The mosaic of the miracle of the Loaves and the Fishes at Tabgha, on the shores of the Sea of Galilee, is preserved in a modern sanctuary built on the site of a Byzantine church.

222–223 (opposite) Nazareth, with the Basilica of the Annunciation in the centre. The rounded summit of Mount Tabor can be seen in the background.

The town of Nazareth, where Jesus spent his boyhood, is dominated by the Basilica of the Annunciation. Consecrated in 1968, the modern church covers the excavated ruins of previous churches. The pilgrim nun Egeria, in the record of her travels of AD 384, tells how she was shown the cave where Mary lived. The original church of the Annunciation was small, only 18m (60 ft) in length, and was built over another structure which may have been a synagogue. Tancred, the Crusader prince, built a Church of the Annunciation in 1099. This church covered most of the site of the Byzantine church, including

223 (opposite, below left) The grotto of Virgin Mary in the Basilica of the Annunciation. A succession of five churches has been built over this place, beginning in 365.

the Grotto of the Annunciation. The present church incorporates five delicately carved capitals made by French artists for the Crusader church and hidden from Saladin.

Other churches in Nazareth include the Church of St Joseph, where a seventeenth-century tradition identified a cave as Joseph's workshop. The Greek Orthodox Church of St Gabriel is built on the ruins of the springs of the Annunciation.

Two places in the Galilee have been identified as the village of Cana where Jesus performed the miracles of turning water into wine at the wedding feast and healing the son of a nobleman. An archaeological survey of the ruins of Khirbet Qana has shown that it was a significant village in Roman times. The village of Kefar Kana, only 6.5 km (4 miles) from Nazareth, is more established as the site of the miracles of Jesus, though with no certainty. There is mention of a church at Kefar Kana from the sixth century, which, in the seventeenth century, was in use as a mosque. In 1641, the Franciscans bought the house next to the mosque and in 1879 they acquired the entire property and built a small church. Later, during the rebuilding of the church, excavations revealed a mosaic floor from a synagogue dating from the third or fourth century AD. A Greek Orthodox church was built nearby in 1885.

Mount Tabor is first mentioned in the Bible as the place where the forces of Deborah and Barak defeated the Canaanite king of Hazor. It was also a Jewish stronghold during the First Jewish Revolt. Although the exact place is not named in the Bible, Mount Tabor has been identified as the site of the Transfiguration of Jesus. A modern basilica, covering the ruins of a Byzantine church, was built in 1924. Spectacular views can be obtained from this site – to Mount Hermon and to Nazareth, the Jezreel Valley and the Samarian mountains.

BETH SHE'ARIM, A MAZE OF CATACOMBS

The catacombs at Beth She'arim provide an insight into the cultural life of the Jews after their expulsion from Jerusalem in AD 70, when many of them settled in the Galilee. The town of Beth She'arim, on the northwestern edge of the Jezreel Valley, became famous in the second century because the eminent Rabbi Judah ha-Nasi lived there and the town was the seat of the Sanhedrin.

Excavations in the town have revealed a synagogue built on the standard basilical plan. Attached to the walls were marble tablets with Greek inscriptions naming the contributors to the building of the synagogue. A large edifice, named the 'Basilica' by archaeologists, is thought to have been a public building, although its exact function is unknown.

What makes Beth She'arim so fascinating is the information that we can glean from its necropolis: the tombs, their inscriptions and their decoration. The figures engraved on the stone sarcophagi supply vital clues to the religious practices of the Jews. The necropolis was important not only for the Jews of the Galilee, but also for those in the Jewish Diaspora who wished their final resting place to be the Holy Land. Beth She'arim was destroyed as the result of the Jewish revolt against the Roman ruler Gallus in 352 and the necropolis fell into disuse.

Burial chambers at Beth She'arim are mostly underground catacombs, cut out of the soft limestone. These catacombs are located on the slopes of a hill descending from the town, and on other nearby hills. It is clear

A Synagogue
B Basilica
C Catacombs
D Reservoir

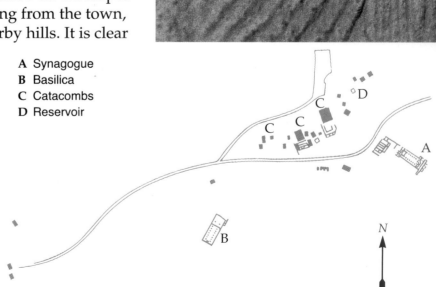

224 (opposite) The main catacomb at Beth She'arim (above). The imposing entrance with three arched doors is reminiscent of synagogue architecture of the period. A seven-branched menorah on a long base (below) is one of the carved designs found in the catacombs.

224–225 (above) Several sarcophagi have survived intact and are lined up along the long corridors tunnelled through the soft stone of the hillsides.

225 (right) An eagle carved in relief in stone, one of the borrowed pagan motifs common in Jewish symbolism of the third and fourth centuries.

that the economy of the town was based largely on the provision of tombs and burial services. Judah ha-Nasi was buried there, as were other members of his family and important judges of the Sanhedrin.

Since entry to Jerusalem was forbidden to the Jews after AD 70, Beth She'arim became the substitute place of burial in the Holy Land. There is evidence that the dead were brought from as far away as Antioch, southern Babylonia, and southern Arabia. Because of the huge transport expenses, only the very wealthy or those very important to their communities could afford the journey.

The most impressive burial halls

are more than one storey high. Access was usually through an elaborate entrance and, in some cases, the doors have survived to the present day. Fashioned in stone to imitate wooden doors, some of them still turn on their stone hinges. The doorways lead to large and ornate courtyards that were probably used by mourners during funeral or memorial services.

Some of the catacombs, the long underground corridors and chambers holding the tombs, were very large. For instance, what has been named Catacomb 1 was a public burial hall holding at least 400 places for graves. Catacomb 20 is the most impressive so far excavated at Beth She'arim. Lined along its corridors and in its many rooms are the remains of over 130 sarcophagi, many decorated with designs typical of Jewish art of the period, especially the seven-branched *menorah* and the Ark, usually in the form of double doors flanked by columns. Other common motifs are the *shofar* or ram's horn trumpet, pairs of lions and forms from nature such as shells and vines. Architectural features such as columns and arches are also frequent.

Perhaps surprisingly, Hellenistic influences are found, and even representations like an eagle or the head of a bull were allowed. Apparently the Jewish injunction against iconographic representations was relaxed at the time. A similar style of decoration was found also in synagogues of the period, for instance at Beth Alpha, where the same charming, naive and primitive style is apparent.

226–227 *Decorative motifs on the sarcophagi in Beth She'arim fall into certain categories. Jewish symbols are common, such as the* menorah, *the* shofar, *the* lulav, *the* etrog, *and the incense shovel, and two columns symbolized the Ark of the Covenant. These are often executed in a primitive, folk-art style. Others are decorated not only in the Hellenistic style but also with apparently pagan symbols, such as the head of a bull. The injunctions against graven images were fairly relaxed at the time and figures like two lions growling on either side of a bull's head seem to have been tolerated.*

MEGIDDO, THE FORTRESS OF ARMAGEDDON

228 (above) The sacred area at Megiddo with a raised circular platform and three temple buildings was in use for a period of over two thousand years. Through decades of peace and years of war and destruction, people returned time and time again to this sacred place.

228 (below) The large public grain silo, dating from the eighth or seventh century BC, was probably covered with a protective roof. Two spiral staircases may have facilitated faster distribution of grain.

Megiddo occupies a strategic position on the *Via Maris*, one of the major trade routes of ancient times. The site also has an important place in the Book of Revelation (16, 16) in the New Testament: at the end of days, the forces of Satan will meet the forces of Good at Armageddon in the ultimate battle. Armageddon is derived from the Hebrew, Har Megiddo, or the Mount of Megiddo.

From the summit of Megiddo the Jezreel Valley, Mount Tabor, Mount Gilboa and Nazareth to the east and the Carmel range to the northwest are all visible. This strategic position is illustrated in an account of Tuthmosis III's victory at the battle of Megiddo in 1479 BC in an inscription at the Temple of Amun at Karnak in Egypt. Coming from the south, Tuthmosis and his generals argued about which route to take over the hills separating Megiddo from the coastal plain. On the more difficult middle route they could have been ambushed in the narrow pass now called Wadi 'Ara. The easier routes were either to the north or to the south. Tuthmosis took a gamble and decided that the Canaanites would be waiting for him on the easier routes and so

228–229 (above) A plaque found in the cache of Canaanite ivories at Megiddo. A ruler is depicted receiving tribute and a procession of prisoners after battle. The holes indicate that the plaque was fixed to a piece of furniture as a decorative element. (Rockefeller Museum)

229 (opposite) The head of a young woman found in the ivory hoard at Megiddo. These ivories had been traded over long distances since the collection includes items that came from Egypt, Greece and Anatolia. (Rockefeller Museum)

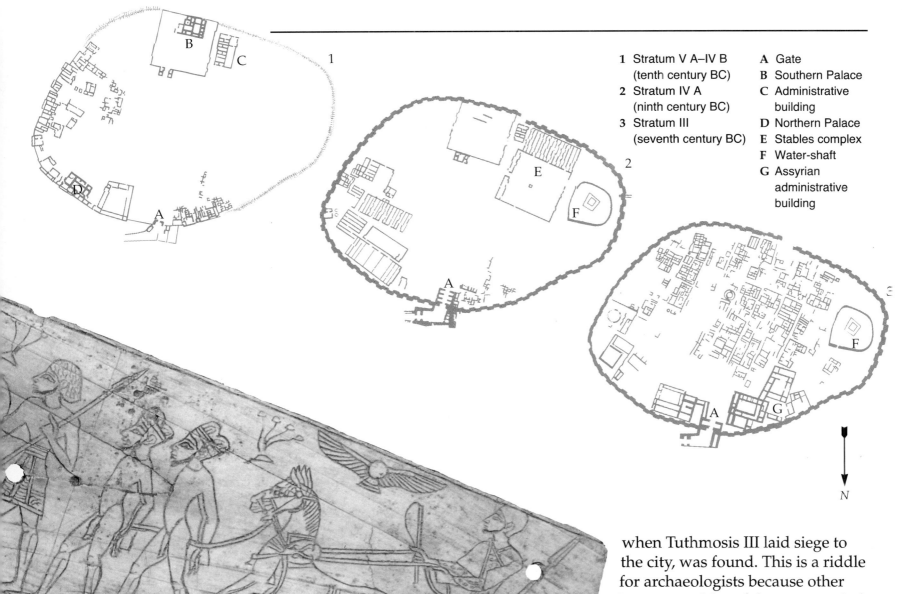

1 Stratum V A–IV B
  (tenth century BC)
2 Stratum IV A
  (ninth century BC)
3 Stratum III
  (seventh century BC)

A Gate
B Southern Palace
C Administrative
  building
D Northern Palace
E Stables complex
F Water-shaft
G Assyrian
  administrative
  building

N

chose the more difficult way. He won the battle and then inexplicably allowed the Canaanites to flee back into the fortress of Megiddo. Only after a seven-month siege was Tuthmosis able to capture the city. Archaeologists have found remains dating before 3300 BC which demonstrate that Megiddo was an important religious centre. On the eastern slope of the mound were traces of a large sacred area that had been in use for a period of two thousand years. Its focus was a *bamah*, or raised circular altar, 8 m (26 ft) in diameter and 1.5 m (5 ft) high with seven steps leading to the top. Nearby were the remains of three rectangular temples. The city was surrounded by a thick defensive wall dating from at least 2000 BC and was entered by a formidable gate. Surprisingly, no evidence of a wall dating from around 1479 BC,

when Tuthmosis III laid siege to the city, was found. This is a riddle for archaeologists because other important cities of the same period (Late Bronze Age) like Hazor, Shechem and Lachish were also unfortified.

The importance of Megiddo as a trading centre is demonstrated by the cache of Canaanite ivories found in a palace dating from around 1550–1150 BC. The 382 ivories from Egypt, Assyria, Canaan and Anatolia probably belonged to a royal prince. Many were small plaques to decorate furniture; others were cosmetic items like combs and small boxes and still others were apparently pieces for board games.

Megiddo was one of the imperial cities of King Solomon and 1 Kings 9, 15 tells how a levy was raised to build the walls of the city. Archaeological evidence points to several grand palaces of the time of Solomon, built of large rectangular ashlar blocks and with columns graced by Proto-Ionic capitals. There is much debate as to the exact form of the fortification wall around Solomon's city. Some scholars believe it was a casemate wall, but not all agree.

The city gate consisted of six chambers, three on each side, closed by a series of wooden doors during times of war. Similar gates have been found elsewhere, including Gezer and Hazor. Later, during the Divided Monarchy, an L-shaped gate was built.

One of the longest running debates among archaeologists concerns the function and date of what are known as 'Solomon's Stables'. According to the Bible, Solomon built 'cities for his chariots and cities for his horsemen'. At Megiddo, 12 elongated buildings were excavated at the north of the site. At the south of the site, five buildings opened up on to a large courtyard, in the centre of which was a large square structure that could have been used as a water basin for horses. Each building consists of long rooms, divided down the centre by two

rows of pillars. Between the pillars are large blocks with carved basins that resemble horse-troughs. In some cases, holes suitable for tying up an animal have been cut in the pillars. However, a significant number of archaeologists argue that these elongated structures are too small for the stabling of horses and that, because of their similarity to other such structures at sites like Beersheba, they were probably storehouses instead. Others have proposed that they could be markets or even barracks for soldiers.

Megiddo became a military stronghold during the period of the Divided Monarchy and was surrounded by a wall 3.6 m (12 ft) thick in an alternating inset–offset construction. To defend the water supply of the city more effectively, a tunnel was built to the spring lying to the southwest of the city. A square, vertical shaft was sunk to the bedrock and a tunnel dug, extending 70 m (228 ft) to the spring. The spring itself was concealed. Also during this period a large public grain silo with a capacity of up to 12,800 bushels was built. Two staircases spiralled down the opposite sides of the silo and the entire structure was probably enclosed by a domed roof to protect the grain.

When King Josiah was killed by Egyptian King Necho at Megiddo (2 Kings, 23, 29–35; 2 Chronicles 35, 20–24), the city at last began to decline and lose its importance. By the end of the Persian period (332 BC), it lay deserted and in ruins, after 3000 years of eminence.

230 (top) Troughs like these discovered at Megiddo have puzzled archaeologists. If they were used for watering horses, as some believe, then the buildings nearby may have been stables.

230 (centre) A water tunnel was dug from the end of a deep vertical shaft within the city to a spring lying outside the fortifications. The location of the spring was disguised so that it would not be discovered by an enemy during a siege.

230 (left) The god Bes, from the cache of Canaanite ivories found in excavations of a Late Bronze Age or Early Iron age palace. Many of the ivories were used as decorative plaques on furniture.
(Rockefeller Museum)

231 (above) This exceptional ivory box, decorated in high relief with sphinxes and lions, is carved from a single piece of ivory, probably the end of an elephant's tusk. From the Megiddo ivory cache, it shows Hittite or Syrian influence. (Rockefeller Museum)

231 (right) An Israelite limestone horned altar found at Megiddo in one of the two impressive sanctuaries built during the times of Solomon. These were well built of ashlar masonry and involved the use of proto-Ionic capitals.

232–233 (overleaf) Tell Megiddo viewed from the east. In the foreground is the circular raised platform of the sacred area. Centre left is the granary and in the background is the large round entrance to the shaft leading to the water tunnel.

THE FORTRESS CITY OF MEGIDDO

Megiddo is a tell made up of 20 strata, or layers, representing at least 14 different cities or levels of occupation. Because Megiddo was one of the earliest sites excavated in the Holy Land, beginning in 1903, and because techniques and theories of archaeology have changed, there is much debate as to the exact structures which made up each stratum. This drawing represents several different periods in Megiddo's history in order to show the richness of the different structures and people represented in the archaeological record.

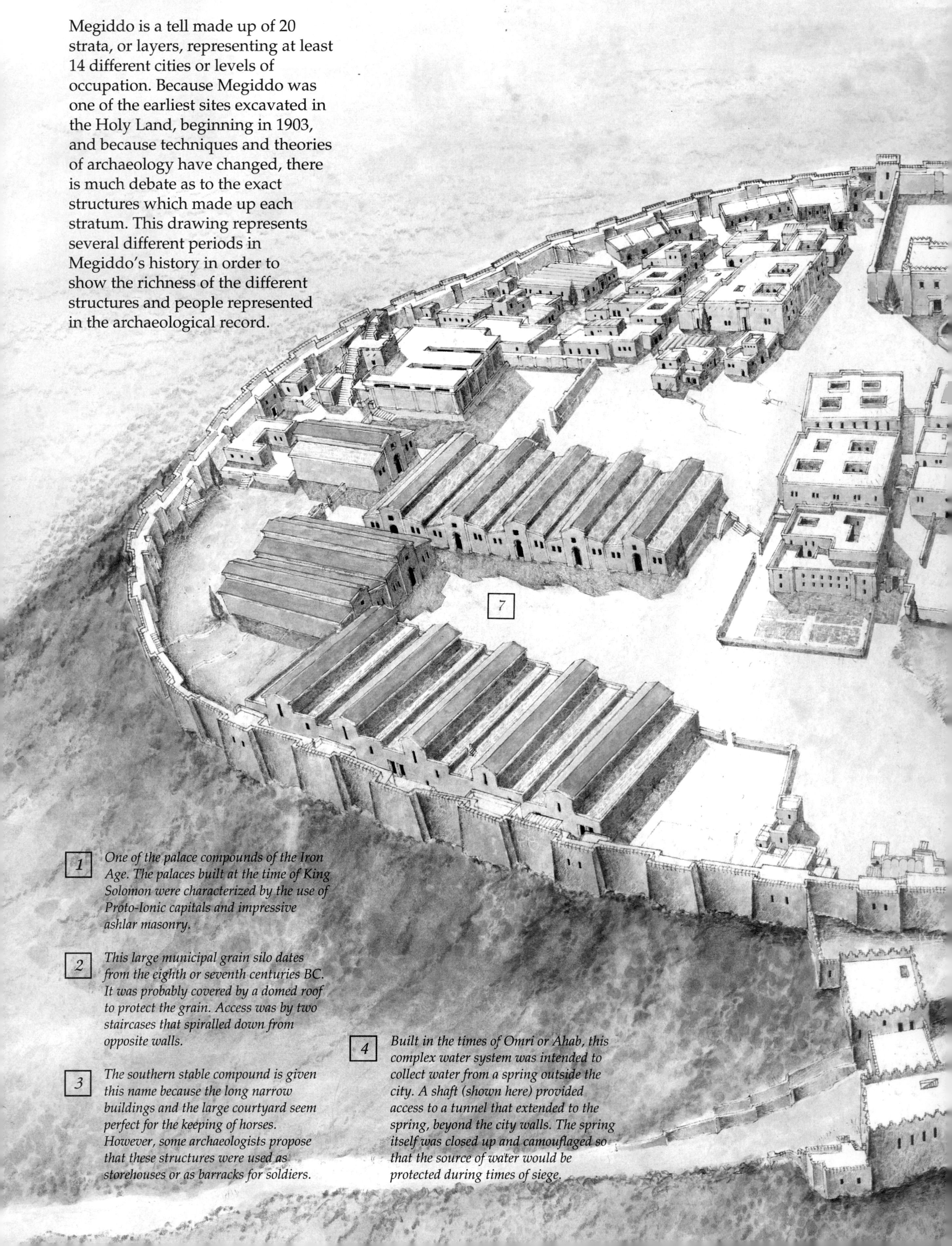

7

1   *One of the palace compounds of the Iron Age. The palaces built at the time of King Solomon were characterized by the use of Proto-Ionic capitals and impressive ashlar masonry.*

2   *This large municipal grain silo dates from the eighth or seventh centuries BC. It was probably covered by a domed roof to protect the grain. Access was by two staircases that spiralled down from opposite walls.*

3   *The southern stable compound is given this name because the long narrow buildings and the large courtyard seem perfect for the keeping of horses. However, some archaeologists propose that these structures were used as storehouses or as barracks for soldiers.*

4   *Built in the times of Omri or Ahab, this complex water system was intended to collect water from a spring outside the city. A shaft (shown here) provided access to a tunnel that extended to the spring, beyond the city walls. The spring itself was closed up and camouflaged so that the source of water would be protected during times of siege.*

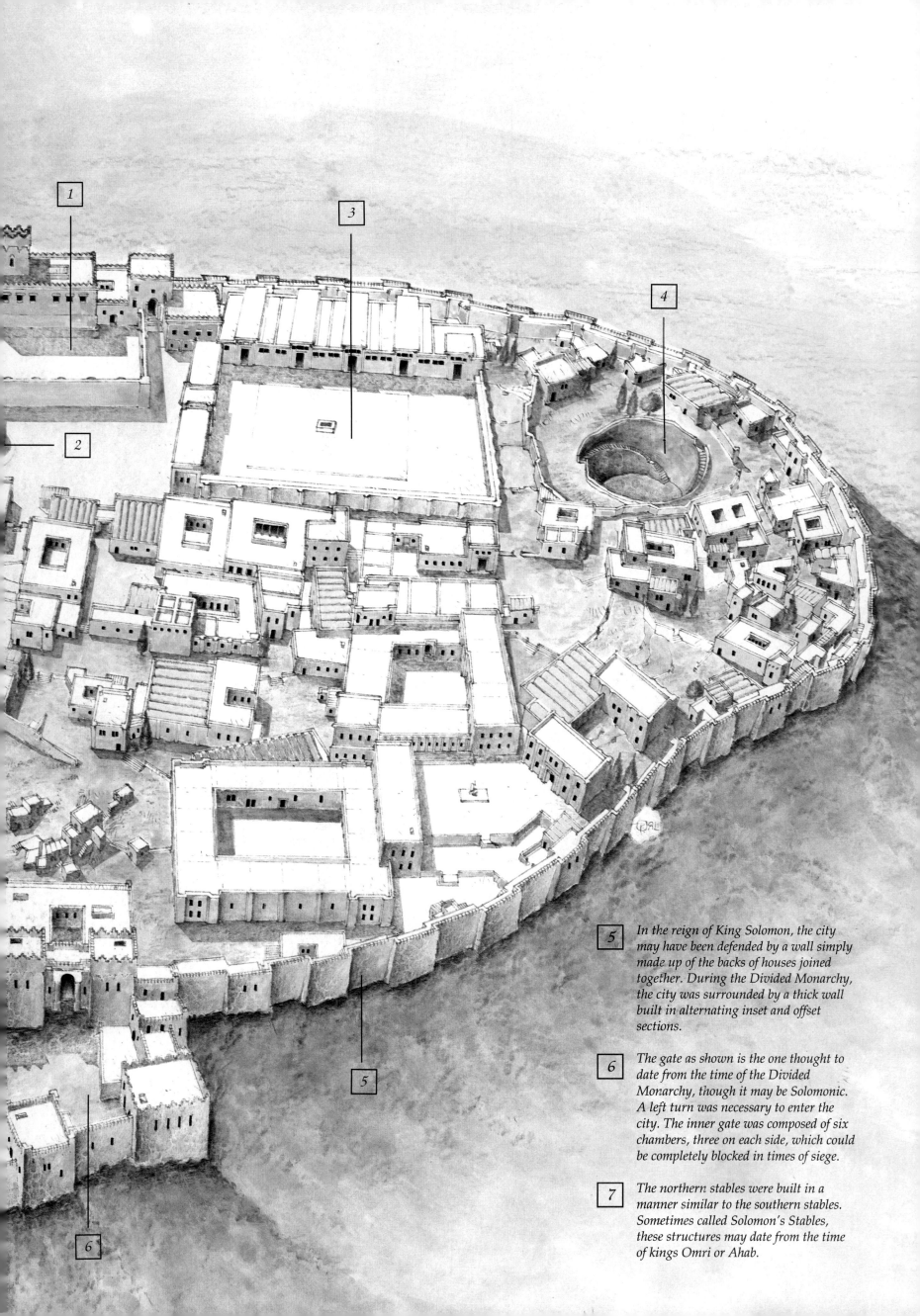

5 In the reign of King Solomon, the city may have been defended by a wall simply made up of the backs of houses joined together. During the Divided Monarchy, the city was surrounded by a thick wall built in alternating inset and offset sections.

6 The gate as shown is the one thought to date from the time of the Divided Monarchy, though it may be Solomonic. A left turn was necessary to enter the city. The inner gate was composed of six chambers, three on each side, which could be completely blocked in times of siege.

7 The northern stables were built in a manner similar to the southern stables. Sometimes called Solomon's Stables, these structures may date from the time of kings Omri or Ahab.

DOR,
THE PHOENICIAN PORT

A Residences   E Shipyard
B Gate   F Temples
C Residences   G Residences
D Harbour storehouses   H Theatre

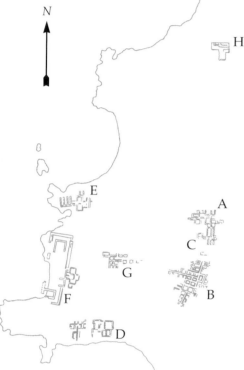

236 (above) Extensive marine archaeology at Dor has revealed various harbour installations constructed over a long period of time. Several quays were built, as well as dry-docks for the repair of boats. Fish pools were also cut into the rock at the edge of the shore.

236 (right) Gold rings, dating from the Roman period, discovered at Dor. The red intaglio gem has been engraved with a picture of a winged figure under a tree. This may have been the personal symbol of its owner. The stone in the second ring is set in a simple bezel.

The seaport of Dor is situated on a small promontory jutting into the Mediterranean Sea which forms a natural harbour. Archaeological evidence has shown that the site was occupied from the early second millennium BC, as a Canaanite or Phoenician settlement. It was also mentioned in an Egyptian inscription of Ramesses II, in the thirteenth century BC.

In about 1200 BC, Dor was conquered by the Shiqlaya, one of the groups of Sea Peoples that also included the Philistines. A deep conflagration layer dated to 1050 BC suggests that the city was violently

destroyed and archaeologists have proposed that it was retaken by the Phoenicians.

Dor was conquered by David when he extended his kingdom up the coast as far as Tyre and Sidon (2 Samuel 24, 6–7). It continued to be an important port and its people and culture were predominantly Phoenician, notwithstanding the powers – Israelite, Assyrian, Babylonian and Persian – that came to govern over it.

Only during the reign of Ptolemy II Philadelphus (283–246 BC), was the Phoenician character of the city lost when it was rebuilt on the Greek model. Dor's importance as a port must have been eclipsed when Herod built his harbour at Caesarea.

The huge mound at Tell Dor is 14 m (45 ft) high and graphically demonstrates the complex history of this long occupied site. Remains of an impressive inset–offset wall and four-chambered gate probably date from the time of King Ahab during the Divided Monarchy. Evidence of Phoenician crafts was found, especially the making of purple dye and the weaving of fine cloth. The Phoenicians were famous all over the Mediterranean for the production of their dye from the murex snail and it appears to have been a major industry throughout Dor's history.

The erosive power of the sea has removed perhaps 15 per cent of the site, so important evidence has been lost. At the north of the site is a natural bay formed by a reef, but it is so shallow that it could only be used by small boats. The main anchorage was to the south in a larger, unprotected bay. As early as the nineteenth century BC, stone structures were built on the natural rock formations under the water to protect the harbour. Another artificial harbour was built between the two bays. It was here that three slipways were found, probably used as drydocks for the repair of boats up to 24 m (80 ft) long.

Dor continued to be an active port well into Byzantine times. The remains of a large number of amphorae – ceramic jars used as containers for foodstuffs – indicate that the port was part of a trade network that stretched from Egypt

to the Black Sea and to the south of France. Although the port was used only on a small scale after the mid-seventh century, it was occupied during Crusader times and renamed Merle. Given the name Tantura, the port was in use in 1664 when a Greek ship was wrecked on its shores. Marine archaeologists have found its remains, along with its cargo of white cheese, preserved in crushed wooden barrels under the sand. On the sea bed have also been found the weapons – cannons, rifles and daggers – abandoned by the troops of Napoleon as they retreated from their defeat at Acre in 1799.

237 (above) A limestone head, of the Persian period, of Tyche, the goddess of fortune, wearing a mural crown. Every city had its own Tyche since she was the guardian of cities. Many other sacred artifacts were found in the private dwellings at Dor.

237 (left) A faience amulet in the image of the Egyptian deity, the hippopotamus goddess Taweret, dating from the Hellenistic period. Believed to protect their bearer, these objects indicate the many influences that wide trade links had on the culture of the Phoenicians.

Caesarea,
PRIDE OF THE ROMAN EMPIRE

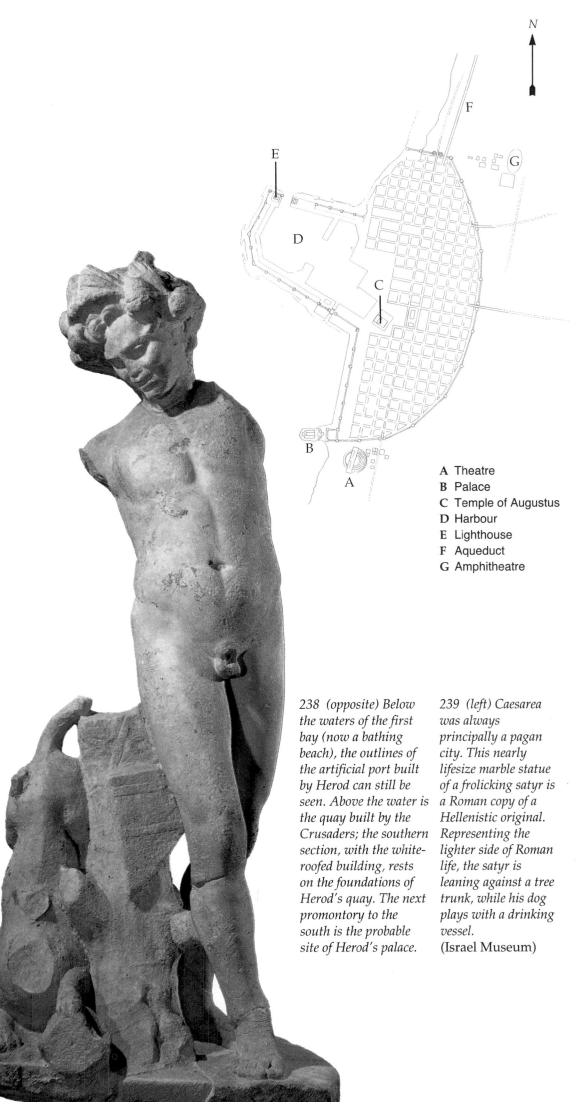

Caesarea still retains much of the splendour it displayed two thousand years ago. Named Caesarea to flatter his patron the Roman emperor Caesar Augustus, Herod the Great built a model seaport larger than Piraeus, the port of ancient Athens. It also served as a monument to himself. The artificial harbour was named Sebastos, the Greek for 'Augustus'. The city boasted a theatre, an amphitheatre, a marketplace (*agora*) and streets laid out on a grid plan, with sewage pipes laid underneath.

On the very edge of the sea, on a high platform facing the port, was a temple dedicated to Roma and Augustus. Ships entering the harbour passed between two massive platforms supporting columns topped by statues of Herod's family. The harbour was guarded by a lighthouse named after Herod's friend, Drusus. Herod further emphasized his sovereignty with a grand palace, built on a promontory jutting out into the sea.

Caesarea was constructed between 22 and 9 BC on the site of a former Phoenician port, Strato's Tower, of the third century BC. Herod may have intended the port and its city to counter the political importance of Jewish Jerusalem and it was run along the lines of a Hellenistic city-state or *polis*.

After Herod's death, Caesarea became the headquarters of the provincial governor of Judaea. An engraved stone excavated at Caesarea shows that one of these governors was Pontius Pilate, who condemned Jesus to death.

A Theatre
B Palace
C Temple of Augustus
D Harbour
E Lighthouse
F Aqueduct
G Amphitheatre

238 (opposite) Below the waters of the first bay (now a bathing beach), the outlines of the artificial port built by Herod can still be seen. Above the water is the quay built by the Crusaders; the southern section, with the white-roofed building, rests on the foundations of Herod's quay. The next promontory to the south is the probable site of Herod's palace.

239 (left) Caesarea was always principally a pagan city. This nearly lifesize marble statue of a frolicking satyr is a Roman copy of a Hellenistic original. Representing the lighter side of Roman life, the satyr is leaning against a tree trunk, while his dog plays with a drinking vessel. (Israel Museum)

Almost the entire Jewish population of the city was massacred in AD 66 in the First Jewish Revolt. Caesarea is named in Acts 10 as the place where Peter converted the centurion Cornelius. By the middle of the third century, it was home to Origen, the great Christian scholar. The Jewish population returned and established a rabbinical academy.

When the Roman Empire became Christian in the fourth century, Caesarea reached its largest size. New fortifications were built as well as a Christian church on the temple platform. Caesarea was also the home of Eusebius, the author of the history of the early church. It was conquered in 627 by the forces of the Byzantine Emperor Heraclius, but was soon taken by Arab forces, in 640 or 641. The town fell into

241 The water supply system of Caesarea, with two aqueducts, was one of the best conceived in Palestine. The high-level aqueduct was around 9.6 km (6 miles) long and brought water from springs in the Carmel range north of the city. It dates from the reign of Herod.

240 (opposite below) An inscription inserted in the main aqueduct of Caesarea reads: Imp. Traiano Hadriano Aug. Vexillatio Leg. X Fre. It shows that the structure was repaired by units of the Tenth legion Fretensis during Hadrian's reign, at the beginning of the Bar Kokhba revolt.

240–241 (above) The Roman theatre has been reconstructed and is now used for open-air concerts. During the Crusader period it was made into a small fortress enclosed by a wall. Jutting into the water are the remains of what is thought to be the palace of Herod. The large rectangular pool is part filled with water from the sea.

disrepair and it did not become an important port again until 1101, when it was won by the Crusaders. Today, the Crusader ramparts are the most outstanding feature for visitors, though they enclose a much smaller area than in Byzantine times.

A system of aqueducts brought water to the city from springs on Mount Carmel and the remains of this feat of engineering still traverse the countryside north of Caesarea. The theatre to the south of the city

has been excavated and restored to its former glory, and is today used for open-air concerts.

To the northeast an oval-shaped amphitheatre catered for Roman popular entertainment, such as gladiatorial contests. Measuring 60 by 95 m (195 by 310 ft), it was larger than the Colosseum, built in Rome a century later. The focal point of Herod's city was, of course, the grand temple to Roma and Augustus.

CAESAREA, HEROD'S PORT

Herod built Caesarea as a Roman city, to serve as his administrative headquarters away from Jerusalem. The new city was built on the site of a Phoenician port, Strato's Tower, and was named after Herod's patron, the Roman emperor Augustus. The artificial harbour, called Sebastos, was very imposing, enclosed by a quay lined with storehouses and guarded by large columns supporting statues of members of Herod's family. Overlooking the harbour on a high platform was a large temple dedicated to the goddess Roma and to Emperor Augustus.

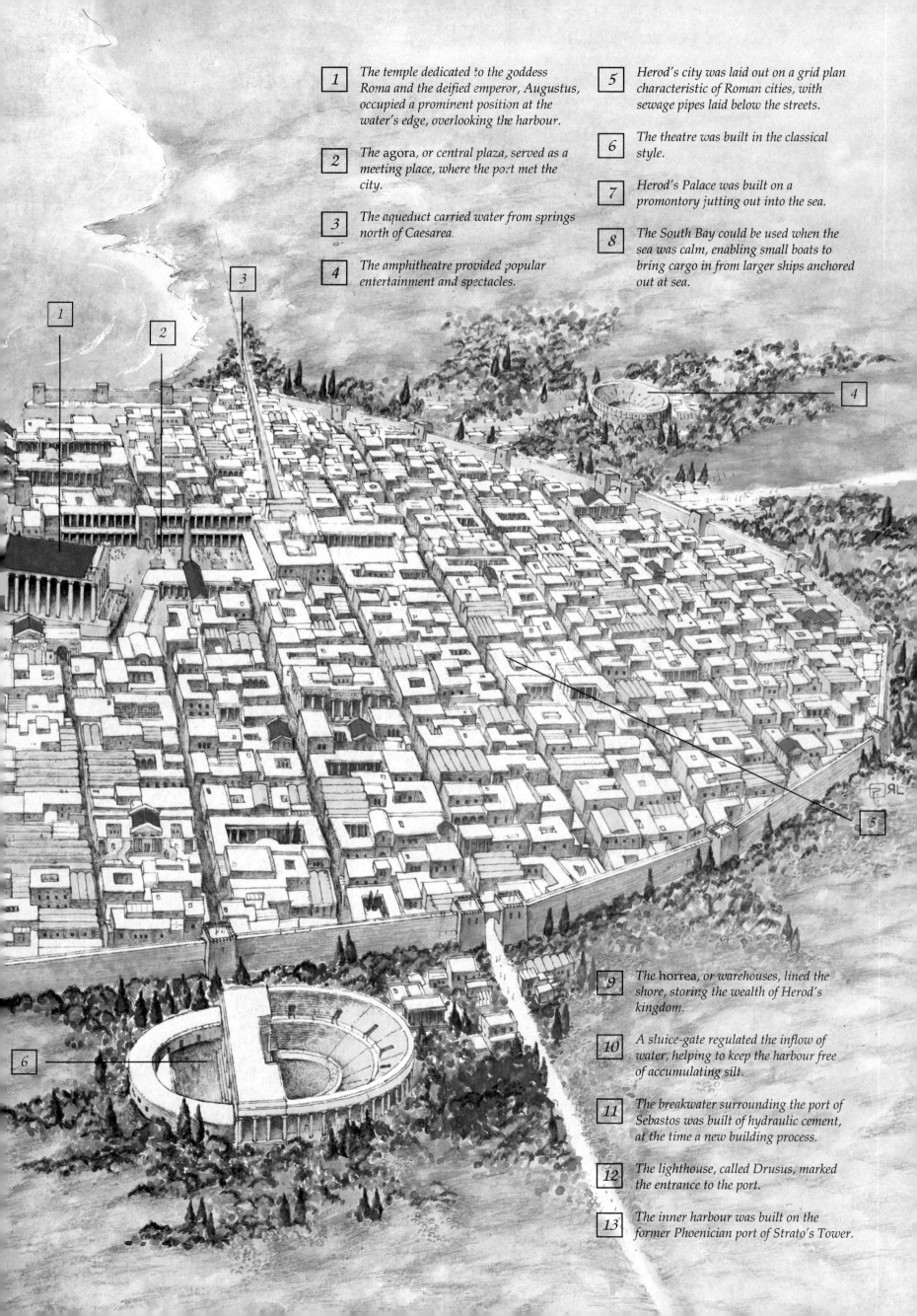

1. The temple dedicated to the goddess Roma and the deified emperor, Augustus, occupied a prominent position at the water's edge, overlooking the harbour.

2. The agora, or central plaza, served as a meeting place, where the port met the city.

3. The aqueduct carried water from springs north of Caesarea.

4. The amphitheatre provided popular entertainment and spectacles.

5. Herod's city was laid out on a grid plan characteristic of Roman cities, with sewage pipes laid below the streets.

6. The theatre was built in the classical style.

7. Herod's Palace was built on a promontory jutting out into the sea.

8. The South Bay could be used when the sea was calm, enabling small boats to bring cargo in from larger ships anchored out at sea.

9. The horrea, or warehouses, lined the shore, storing the wealth of Herod's kingdom.

10. A sluice-gate regulated the inflow of water, helping to keep the harbour free of accumulating silt.

11. The breakwater surrounding the port of Sebastos was built of hydraulic cement, at the time a new building process.

12. The lighthouse, called Drusus, marked the entrance to the port.

13. The inner harbour was built on the former Phoenician port of Strato's Tower.

Inside the temple were gigantic statues of Caesar Augustus, Herod's patron, and Roma, the goddess of the city of Rome. The temple could be seen from the sea and marked the meeting point of city and harbour.

Josephus describes how Herod built this important seaport on a coastline with strong currents and few natural bays. His impressive harbour had three parts: the inner basin probably encompassed the earlier Phoenician harbour. The middle basin was the main harbour, and the entrance of water was regulated by a system of sluices designed to force through a current of water to wash away the sediment silting up the harbour. A huge breakwater made a large curve enclosing a vast area from the south and west. This was built of conglomerate hydraulic cement poured into wooden frameworks built in the water, and was protected from winter storms by another, parallel wall.

The crowning statement of Herod's power was the spectacular palace he built for himself. Its probable location has been identified by archaeologists on a natural point projecting out into the sea just south of the artificial harbour. At the centre of this palace was a large freshwater pool with a pedestal for a statue in the middle. Opening on to the pool was a dining room with a multicoloured mosaic floor and walls painted in marbled designs. During Herod's lifetime, Caesarea was the grand entrance to his kingdom, and it still retains some of this glory.

245 Architecturally, Caesarea was comparable to other cities of the Roman empire. These details – the elaborate, carved stone lintel, the stone foot of a monumental statue and the Corinthian capital – were all small statements of the cultural domination of Rome. On a large scale, most Roman towns and cities were constructed according to the same general plan: a colonnaded main street, the Cardo Maximus, traversed the city, meeting at right angles with the Decumanus, another colonnaded street. Every city of any size could count a forum, an agora, or market, a hippodrome for sports, an amphitheatre, a theatre and a bathhouse, or thermae, among its major buildings. Roman religion was encouraged by the provision of large, spectacular temples. The water supply was provided by aqueducts and the drainage by a well conceived sewage system.

244 (opposite) A statue sculpted from red porphyry, a stone imported from Egypt and reserved for the most important monuments. It may have been a portrait of Hadrian, who visited Palestine in 129–130. The Roman emperors were keen to promote the Romanization of their far-flung colonies by financing both large and small building projects. The Hadrianeum, a temple, was one of Hadrian's benefactions, as well as the second course of the aqueduct bringing water to the city.

BELVOIR,
A CASTLE HIGH
ABOVE THE JORDAN

Belvoir Castle certainly lives up to its name, 'Fair View', with its splendid outlook over the Jordan Valley and Samaria to the southwest, Mount Tabor to the northwest, and the Yarmuk Valley and Mount Hermon on the Golan. This Crusader fortress is also known as Kochav ha-Yarden, 'Star of the Jordan', in Hebrew. It began as a fortified farm in 1140 and in 1168 was sold to the Knights Hospitaller.

It withstood attacks by the forces of Saladin twice in 1183, but one month after his victory at the Horns of Hattin in 1187, Saladin laid siege to it again. The Crusaders held out until January 1189, when the outer tower, or barbican, guarding the entrance to the fortress was undermined. Tunnels dug by Saladin's forces caused it to collapse and the defenders, realizing they would ultimately lose, negotiated a surrender and were permitted to retreat to Tyre. The castle was destroyed in 1217–1218, when all the abandoned fortresses in the Holy Land were dismantled to prevent their reoccupation.

In 1241, a treaty with the Muslim rulers of Palestine enabled the Crusaders to return for a short time, but the extent of the destruction prevented them rebuilding the fortress. However, the ruins of the castle are in a good state of preservation as they were never permanently reoccupied or reused for construction material.

Measuring 111 by 99 m (365 by 325 ft), Belvoir is a good example of a concentric castle with three levels or lines of defence.

246–247 The Crusader fortress of Belvoir commanded a view over the entire Jordan Valley. It was surrounded on three sides by a dry moat and on the fourth by a massively built tower.

A Gate
B Outer tower (barbican)
C Outer towers
D Cistern
E Courtyard
F Inner towers
G Kitchen
H Inner courtyard
I Refectory
J Main tower (keep)
K Second gate
L Drawbridge
M Moat

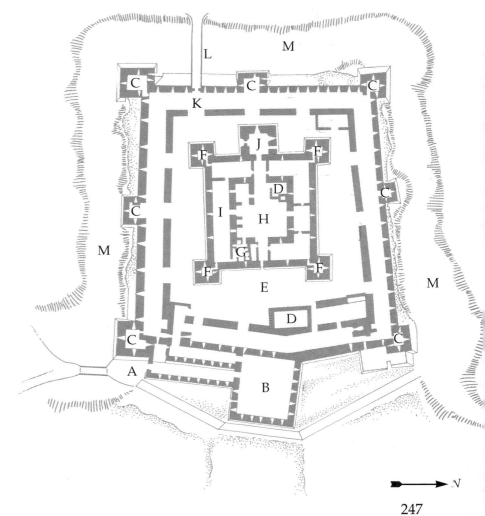

BELVOIR CASTLE

Built in the form of a pentagon, Belvoir Castle had three lines of defence. At the centre was the inner keep, which formed a self-contained fortress in itself, with its own cistern, food supplies and a church. It was further protected by a second line of fortifications, the outer walls, with seven guard towers, and by a dry moat on three sides. The fourth side was guarded by the barbican: a massive tower with narrow doors that could be blocked. It could accommodate the entire forces of the castle and serve as a last line of defence, being a small fortress in itself. Nevertheless, the castle fell to the forces of Saladin when the tower was undermined. Tunnels were built under the barbican and caused its collapse, leaving the Crusader forces with no choice but to surrender.

1   The drawbridge and secondary entrance to the castle. This would be entirely blocked during a siege.

2   A dry moat or fosse surrounded the castle on three sides.

3   The inner keep, or donjon, consisted of four barrel-shaped vaults that formed a square around the central courtyard.

4   The church on the second floor of the eastern vault.

5   The outer tower or barbican.

6   The main entrance to the fortress. Access was via a long walkway that first entered the barbican and then doubled back on itself before entering the castle.

250 (left) The view from the inner keep, the innermost defence at Belvoir. If the outer walls were breached, the defending force could retreat either to the outer tower or to the central keep.

250 (below) A cornice from the church at Belvoir with a carved stone head. It was executed by a European stonemason brought to Palestine by the Crusaders.

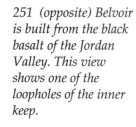

The innermost fortification was the keep – a quadrangle with a tower at each corner. The inner courtyard was surrounded by the kitchens and refectory, while the living quarters were upstairs, as was the chapel. The inner keep was a fortress in itself since the rooms opened only on to the centre and the outer walls had small loopholes instead of windows. In the centre of the western wall was an L-shaped gate leading to the outer bailey, or courtyard, between the walls.

As a second line of defence, the outer walls were built in the shape of a pentagon, with the two eastern walls meeting at a great outside tower. There was a tower at each corner and in the centre of the other walls. Four of these had hidden posterns, small concealed doorways, allowing the castle's defenders to exit secretly and attack siege engines trying to undermine the walls.

A dry moat or fosse, 10.6 m (35 ft) deep and almost 21 m (70 ft) wide, also protected the outer walls. The slope on the eastern side was sufficiently steep not to need a moat. There were only two entrances into the castle. On the eastern side a bridge crossed the fosse, followed by a long corridor that crossed back on itself at the barbican. The bridge was probably wooden and could be removed or burned under threat of war. On the western side of the castle, a drawbridge allowed entry via a small gate. Vaults in the outer walls served as workshops, storehouses and stables.

The entire defence of the castle was reliant on the great outer tower, or barbican, built on a steep slope overlooking the Jordan Valley far below. The tower was protected by a thick glacis, or artificial mound, at its base. It was intended as the place of last retreat since it could hold a large number of soldiers if both the inner and outer walls of the castle were breached. Narrow staircases connecting the barbican with the main castle could be blocked to prevent access. Ironically, this was the first line of attack by the forces of Saladin and as it was almost completely destroyed, there is little evidence of its structure.

251 (opposite) Belvoir is built from the black basalt of the Jordan Valley. This view shows one of the loopholes of the inner keep.

BETH SHEAN, A REMINDER OF IMPERIAL MAGNIFICENCE

252–253 (left) The rows of columns at Beth Shean, some of them restored with their original Corinthian capitals, give a hint of how the city must have looked during the Roman and Byzantine periods. The Roman theatre, to the south of the city, was remarkably well preserved and originally could hold up to 5000 spectators.

254–255 (overleaf) The view of Beth Shean from the east. The city began on the tell and only in Hellenistic times did it expand to the area below. One long colonnaded street began at the theatre and met another street at an intersection. A temple and other important civic structures were built on this plaza at the foot of the mound.

Beth Shean is one of the longest occupied sites in Israel, inhabited for around 6000 years. The city is strategically situated at a point where the Jordan Valley meets the southern end of the Jezreel Valley and is thus on an important east–west route. The earliest remains at Beth Shean are on the tell above the later city and date from the fifth millennium BC.

In the Late Bronze Age, Beth Shean was under Egyptian control and its importance as an administrative centre in the thirteenth century was confirmed by the discovery of three Egyptian stelae. Also from that period are several anthropoid coffins, their lids decorated with realistic, grimacing faces and small hands clasped across the chest. Beth Shean was a Philistine city in the early Iron Age and the Bible has a graphic description of how the bodies of Saul and his sons were hung from the walls of Beth Shean after defeat by the Philistines. Later, it became an Israelite city and is listed as one of the administrative districts established by Solomon.

On top of the tell were the remains of a series of three-chambered temples in use for at least 500 years. Only during the Hellenistic period did the civic part of the city move to the foot of the mound. Beth Shean was renamed Scythopolis when it became one of the ten city-states, the Decapolis, created by the Roman general Pompey in 63 BC. A temple, probably dedicated to Zeus of the 'high mountain', was built on the acropolis above the town. At the base of the tell were structures including a Roman temple, a basilica, a fountain and a columnar monument at the street junction.

A Bathhouse
B Theatre
C Semicircular public area
D Colonnaded street
E Temple
F Nymphaeum
G Monument at the street junction
H Basilica
I Colonnaded street with shops
J Area of early temples
K Gate

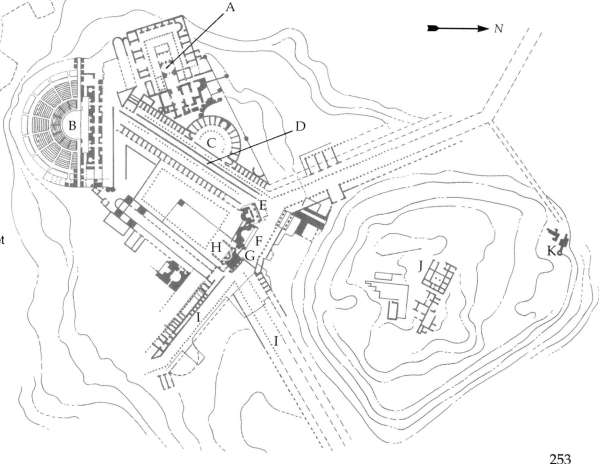

THE ROMAN-BYZANTINE CITY OF BETH SHEAN

Beth Shean is one of the longest occupied sites in Israel, with the earliest remains on the tell dating from the fifth millennium BC. The city is mentioned in Egyptian sources and also features prominently in the Bible. In the Hellenistic period, the city moved to the foot of the mound. Beth Shean was known as Nisa-Scythopolis, and was one of the cities of the Decapolis. The lower city was built on the classic Roman plan, though the topography of the land did not permit the construction of a *cardo*, crossed at right angles by a *decumanus*. Instead, the four main colonnaded streets met at a central plaza. Much of the city was destroyed by an earthquake in AD 749.

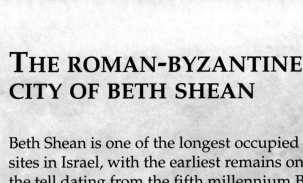

N

9

8

7

7

3

10

1 The ancient tell overlooking the city. The acropolis was built here, with a temple to the god Zeus.

2 A colonnaded street, with a covered walkway, or stoa, along one side. A pool with a marble statue of the young Dionysus was excavated in this area.

3 The basilica, where a Dionysian hexagonal altar was discovered.

4 A monument with columns was built at the front of the basilica. Constructed of elaborately carved marble, its niches probably held statues.

5 The nymphaeum, with a semicircular apse at its centre.

6 At the centre of the city was a temple on a podium with a broad flight of stairs to a porch supported by four columns.

7 The main colonnaded street, with a row of elegant shops on one side, connected the theatre with the foot of the mound.

8 A semicircular public area of the Byzantine period.

9 The public baths were in an ornate building with eight halls. This is the largest baths complex excavated in Israel.

10 The theatre was located at the end of the most prominent street in the city. The stage, or scenae frons, was elaborately decorated with carved marble and granite.

1

6

5

4

2

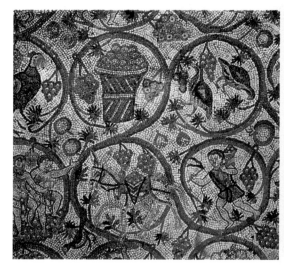

An oval amphitheatre was built outside the town. Later, during Byzantine times, a large bathhouse was constructed. The Roman temple was built on a high podium located at the plaza where the two main colonnaded streets met.

An impressive set of white limestone steps led up to a colonnaded prostyle, or porch, over 20 m (65 ft) wide. Four large limestone columns supported a triangular pediment and a gabled

roof. The square in front of the temple contained several six-sided holes in the pavement, apparently the settings for small altars. The pedestal of a statue, but not the statue itself, honouring the emperor Marcus Aurelius, who reigned from AD 161 to 180, was also discovered.

Directly to the direct east of this temple was a nymphaeum, an elaborate monument with a semi-circular apse which, at least by

Byzantine times, had a decorative fountain. On the other side of the nymphaeum was a basilica, over 45 m (150 ft) in length with an apse at one end. A six-sided altar was found inside the basilica, decorated with various Dionysian scenes. Later, another monumental structure was built on the plaza side of the basilica. Its walls contained a series of niches, probably for statues.

From the central plaza two streets ran southeast and southwest. One had a covered walkway, or *stoa*, along one side, with a long pool where a marble statue of Dionysus was found. The other had a *stoa* and a row of shops on one side. This street led to the Roman theatre, one of the best preserved in Israel. At the other end of the city was a large amphitheatre, holding as many as 7000 people to watch games and gladiatorial contests.

The city was further embellished with a bathhouse – an elaborate building with eight halls. It was provided with hot air by furnaces and was surrounded by pools and recreational rooms as well as a colonnaded *palaestra* for exercise.

Close to the entrance to the baths was an odeon, a small theatre that may date from Roman times. Part of this building was converted in the Byzantine period into another public building that contained a beautiful mosaic floor with the portrait of the goddess of good fortune, Tyche. On one side of the street was a raised portico protecting the entrances to a row of shops, luxuriously decorated with marble façades and mosaic floors. The Byzantine city was enclosed within walls though it is not certain when they were built; it seems that for much of the Roman period the city was unfortified.

BETH ALPHA
AND ITS SPECTACULAR MOSAIC

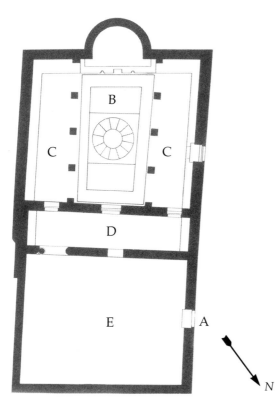

A **Main entrance**
B **Mosaic floor**
C **Prayer hall**
D **Vestibule**
E **Courtyard**

Beth Alpha is an ancient synagogue with one of the most spectacular mosaic floors in Israel. Built among the houses of a village northwest of Beth Shean in the late fifth century AD, the synagogue consists of three parts: the outer courtyard; the vestibule; and the basilica or main hall, with its apse orientated south towards Jerusalem.

The courtyard was decorated with a geometric patterned mosaic of poor quality and in the vestibule the remains of another geometric mosaic floor were uncovered. There were three doorways into the main hall but as the façade has not survived their configuration is uncertain.

The hall is divided into three aisles by two rows of plastered stone columns. A curved recess in the south wall housed the ark of the law on a low platform with three steps. Stone benches lined the walls.

On the western wall was a doorway that may have led to stairs up to a women's gallery on the second storey. The centre aisle is paved with a well-preserved mosaic laid out in a charming, primitive style and divided into three panels. Looking at the mosaic from directly in front of the apse, the first panel shows the door of the Temple or of the Holy of Holies inside, with columns on the right and left sides, extending up to a curtain that is drawn aside. Above is a gable-roof with an eternal light hanging from the top and two birds. On each side is a snarling lion guarding the double doors. Behind the lions are

two lighted *menorahs*, surrounded by ritual objects.

The middle panel is a circular zodiac. The 12 signs, with their names in Hebrew, are arranged around a depiction of the sun god, Helios, in a chariot drawn by four horses. At the four corners of the mosaic panel are winged female figures representing the four seasons of the year and surrounded by seasonal fruits and wildlife.

The third mosaic panel, closest to the door, shows the Sacrifice of Isaac. The picture is presented, like Hebrew, from right to left. The child Isaac is depicted with his hands bound, held by Abraham over the sacrificial fire. A ram is caught up in a bush and a hand emerges from a cloud at the top of the panel, next to the words 'Lay not thine hand upon the lad' from Genesis 22, 12. On the left side of the mosaic are the two boys who accompanied Abraham, leading an ass.

A border encloses the entire mosaic, decorated with various geometric patterns and designs from nature. The entrance to the synagogue is guarded by two mosaic figures, a lion on one side and a buffalo on the other.

An inscription in the centre tells of the donations that were collected to pay for the floor. Unfortunately, the date has been obliterated. A Greek inscription names Marianos and his son Hanina as the creators of the mosaic. Another example of their work has also been found in the synagogue floor at Beth Shean.

260–261 The zodiac mosaic floor of the synagogue at Beth Alpha has close stylistic parallels with other synagogues, for instance Beth Shean, and with some of the ceremonial art found at Beth She'arim. The zodiac theme itself was common in Jewish art of the Byzantine period, as for example at Hammath-Tiberias.

BETHLEHEM, THE BIRTHPLACE OF JESUS

Every Christmas, Christians from all over the world gather in Bethlehem to celebrate the birth of Jesus in the Church of the Nativity. Bethlehem first enters the biblical record as the birthplace of David. The Book of Micah (5, 2) names the town as the place where the Messiah will be born. According to the Bible, Joseph returned with Mary to his home in Bethlehem for the census ordered by Caesar Augustus. It was there, according to Luke, that Jesus was born in a cave and laid in a manger.

During the reign of Constantine, the Christian holy sites were reclaimed and, in 339, Queen Helena dedicated the first church, built over the cave. This church had a large atrium and a basilica with two rows of columns on each side of the nave. An octagon was built over the Grotto of the Nativity, allowing a view of the cave underneath. The town was further sanctified when St Jerome made it his home. In the sixth century, the church was altered and embellished by Emperor Justinian.

The Church of the Nativity is still largely the Justinian church, with some alterations. Tradition has it that it was spared destruction by the Persians in 614 because the three Magi portrayed on the façade were dressed in the Persian style. In 1169 the church was restored by the Crusaders and never completely destroyed in subsequent Muslim occupations. However, much of the rich interior decoration was plundered and the marble facing used in Muslim holy sites, such as the Dome of the Rock. In 1934, the original mosaic floor was excavated and parts can be viewed today.

262 (top) The nave of the Church of the Nativity. Most of the ceremonial decoration was plundered after the Crusader period and was restored only at the end of the nineteenth century.

262 The Altar of the Birth of Christ. Fifteen lamps, representing many of the different Christian denominations, are hung here.

262–263 The Chapel of the Nativity is under Greek Orthodox jurisdiction. The altar celebrating the Birth of Christ is on the left and the Altars of the Crib and of the Magi are on the right.

263 (right) The Church of the Nativity in the town of Bethlehem. This building, dating from the time of Emperor Justinian, has remained largely unchanged in its structure. It was built over the earlier church of Constantine.

HERODIUM,
THE PALACE-FORTRESS
OF KING HEROD

Herodium is one of the most remarkable architectural structures in the western world. From a distance, across the barren landscape of the hills to the south of Jerusalem, it looks like a volcanic cone. At its base are the ruins of a large palace, an enormous pool, storehouses and baths. The fortress became a stronghold of the rebels in both Jewish Revolts and was a monastery in Byzantine times. Built by Herod, this magnificent structure was intended to serve as a fortified palace and after his death was to be his mausoleum. However, no evidence of Herod's tomb has been discovered.

The distinctive conical shape was achieved by mounding up rubble on top of a hill. This unique building rises 60 m (195 ft) above the summit of the natural hill and consists of two parallel circular walls, 62 m (202 ft) in diameter. The walls are dominated by a circular tower, estimated originally to have been 16 m (52 ft) high. Three semicircular towers are built on to the outer walls.

Access to the palace was only by an underground stairway, rising up from the base of the hill to a vaulted entrance into the garden courtyard. The interior of the palace was divided into two sections. In addition to the garden courtyard, there were luxurious living quarters, at least two storeys high, with a bathhouse on the lower level. The floors were decorated with mosaics in geometric patterns, while the walls were plastered – the lower half painted in coloured panels and the upper sections ornamented with white, moulded stucco.

Lower Herodium was equally magnificent, dominated by a large pool at its centre. This also served as a reservoir and was large enough not only for swimming but also for small boats. Surrounding the pool was an ornamental garden, several palace buildings and a bathhouse.

Within the mound around the upper palace was a warren of hidden passages, in part using underground cisterns of the time of Herod. These were constructed by the followers of Bar Kokhba during the Second Jewish Revolt. In the palace, remains were found of a synagogue and a *mikveh* as well as several small ovens built to serve the needs of the rebels. Many artifacts – especially weapons – were found, as well as coins issued by both groups of rebels. Later, in Byzantine times, a monastic settlement was built on top of the ruins. Today, the isolation of the site makes it all the more spectacular – a monument of Herod's imagination.

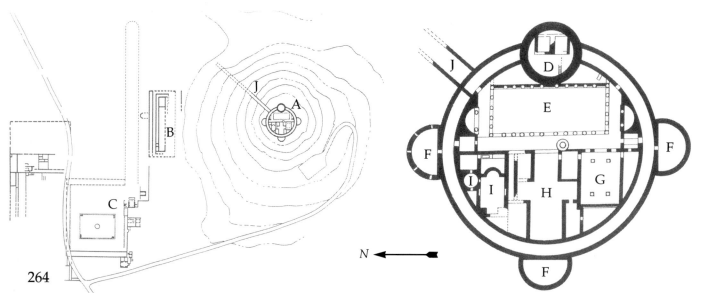

A Herodium
B Lower palace
C Pavilion of the pool
D Main tower
E Courtyard
F Semicircular towers
G Synagogue
H Cross-shaped hall
I Bathhouse
J Entrance passage

264–265 *The unique conical shape of the desert fortress of Herodium in the hills of Judaea is visible from a long distance. At the top of the artificial mound was the palace-fortress, while at its foot were other buildings and a large pool which* served both for bathing and as a reservoir. Herod built this palace not only as a place of refuge close to Jerusalem, but also as his mausoleum. Josephus describes Herod's funeral procession, but no evidence of his tomb has been found.

HERODIUM: THE STRONGHOLD OF KING HEROD

King Herod built Herodium for two reasons: first, he wanted a memorial to the place where he had won an impressive victory over the Hasmonaeans and their supporters; and second, he intended the fortress to be his mausoleum after his death. However, archaeologists excavating the site have not found Herod's tomb. In the last weeks of the Second Jewish Revolt, the fortress also provided a refuge for the Jewish rebels led by Bar Kokhba. The stronghold is built in the shape of a cone on top of what was already an isolated hill top. During its construction, earth was taken from the inside and poured over the walls to form a steep-sided rampart. Access was by a stairway through a long tunnel that ended in a large vaulted entrance in the outer wall, next to the palace garden.

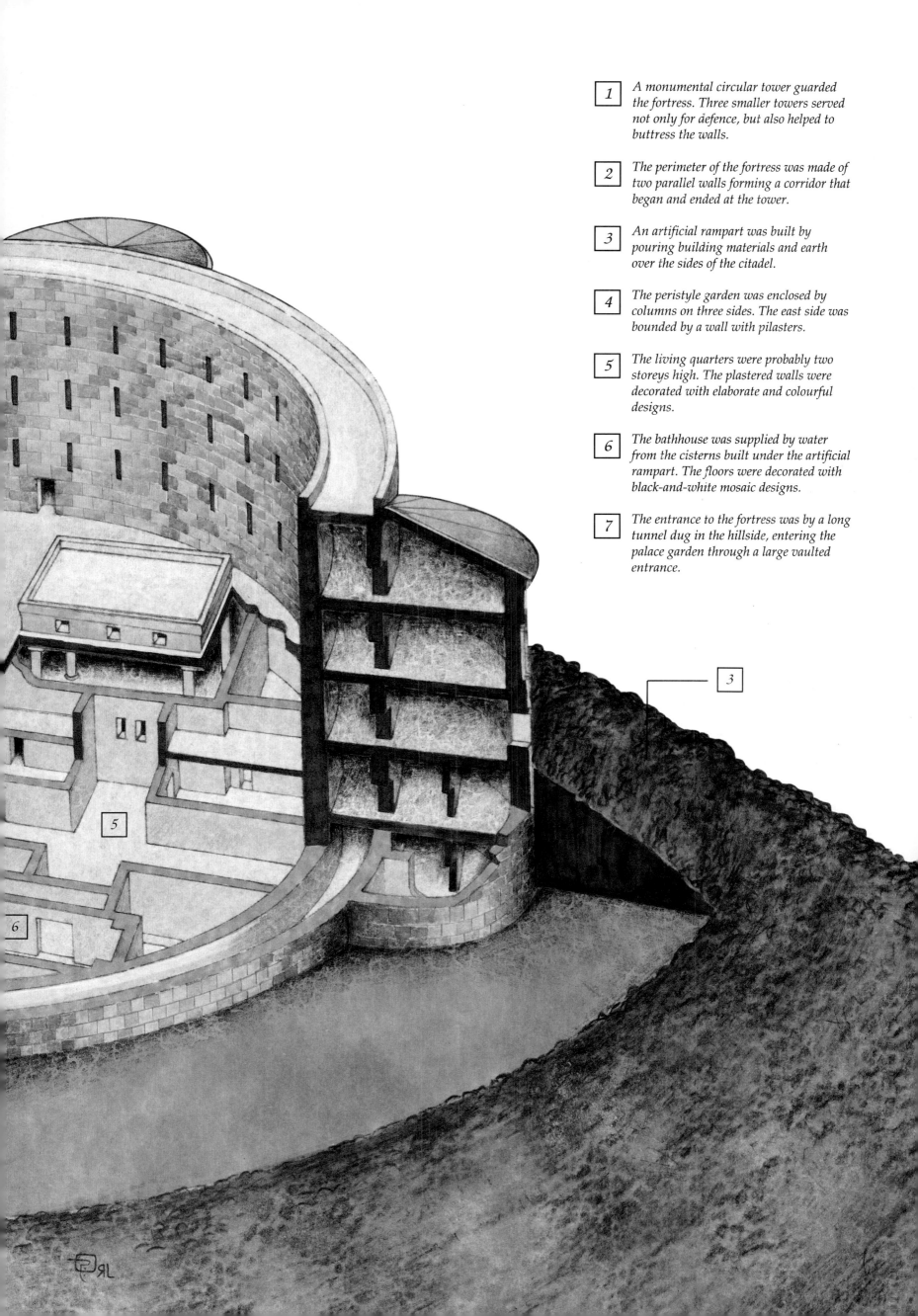

1   A monumental circular tower guarded the fortress. Three smaller towers served not only for defence, but also helped to buttress the walls.

2   The perimeter of the fortress was made of two parallel walls forming a corridor that began and ended at the tower.

3   An artificial rampart was built by pouring building materials and earth over the sides of the citadel.

4   The peristyle garden was enclosed by columns on three sides. The east side was bounded by a wall with pilasters.

5   The living quarters were probably two storeys high. The plastered walls were decorated with elaborate and colourful designs.

6   The bathhouse was supplied by water from the cisterns built under the artificial rampart. The floors were decorated with black-and-white mosaic designs.

7   The entrance to the fortress was by a long tunnel dug in the hillside, entering the palace garden through a large vaulted entrance.

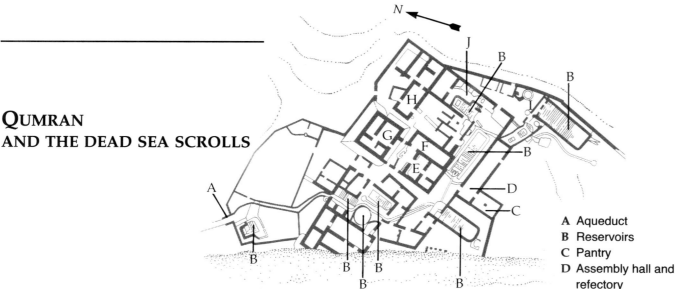

QUMRAN
AND THE DEAD SEA SCROLLS

A Aqueduct
B Reservoirs
C Pantry
D Assembly hall and refectory
E Room with benches
F Scriptorium
G Tower
H Kitchen
I Potter's kiln
J Laundry

The ancient community at Qumran has been linked with the documents known as the Dead Sea Scrolls which were found in nearby caves, and many scholars also see a connection with the ancient Jewish communal sect, the Essenes. However, it should be noted that no other site in Israel has caused so much controversy. One suggested interpretation is that Qumran was a caravan stop for the large numbers of travellers on the 'Salt Road' between Jerusalem and Arabia and the Horn of Africa. Others have proposed that the site was a winter villa for some of the wealthy of Jerusalem and yet others consider it a military fortress.

Located on a plateau on a spur of land extending east on the coast of the Dead Sea, Qumran is probably the City of Salt, one of the six cities in the wilderness of Judaea referred to in Joshua (15, 61–62). The area was first inhabited in the Israelite period, probably as a desert fortress, and was abandoned on the fall of the kingdom of Judah. From the second century BC until the suppression of

the First Jewish Revolt, the site was continuously occupied except for an unknown period after an earthquake in 31 BC. While archaeological evidence supports the conclusion that Qumran was a communal site, no direct connection has been found between it and the Essenes, or between the Essenes and the group described in the Dead Sea Scrolls.

The main entrance to the complex was through a gate, next to which was a two-storey tower; there were two other entrances. The unfortified wall of the compound was formed by the backs of houses and the walls enclosing courtyards. Communal buildings included a very large kitchen with five fireplaces. Nearby is a long hall, which has been called the refectory, and adjacent was a smaller room which contained the remains of more than 1000 clay vessels: jars, dishes, jugs, plates, bowls and cups, which could have been used in communal meals. There was also a potter's workshop at the site. A long assembly room was excavated which may have been a scriptorium since a writing table and three inkwells were discovered.

The system of water supply for the community was quite sophisticated. An aqueduct brought the water in, first into a decantation basin where it was purified; from there it was fed into seven cisterns by a series of channels. A cemetery immediately adjacent to the settlement contained over a thousand graves. Arranged in orderly rows, each grave is marked by a small mound of stones. The burials are almost all on their backs with their heads pointing to the south. The excavated graves mostly

268 (left) One of the caves where Dead Sea Scrolls were discovered in 1947. The arid desert conditions preserved the delicate parchments of biblical texts and documents of the community at Qumran.

268–269 (right) The scrolls were discovered in caves at Qumran, in the Judaean Desert overlooking the Dead Sea. Because of its remote location, the Judaean Desert provided a place of refuge – and safekeeping.

contained the remains of men, though there were a few women and children at the edges of the cemetery.

The Essenes are mentioned by the ancient Jewish historians Philo of Alexandria and Flavius Josephus, as well as briefly by Pliny the Elder. According to these sources, the Essene sect exceeded 4000 members, with membership restricted to men. They lived in communal houses scattered throughout Palestine. A period as a novice preceded admittance as a full member of the sect. New members gave the sect all their property and pledged their subsequent earnings to the group.

It is generally agreed that the Dead Sea Scrolls were hidden in the caves in about AD 68 to 70 by the inhabitants of Qumran. Some of the scrolls, as well as other ancient documents discovered earlier, like the Damascus Scroll, describe a set of rules for communal living and a system of beliefs different from mainstream Judaism of the time. The 'Manual of Discipline' outlines the rules of communal life, while another scroll, 'The War Between the Children of Light and Darkness', gives an apocalyptic interpretation of events that will precede the end of the world.

The last word has not been said with regard to Qumran. The recent release of the Dead Sea Scrolls to the wider world of scholarship should afford many new interpretations. Some scrolls may still be in the hands of the Bedouin or be privately owned. More likely, there may still be scrolls awaiting discovery in the caves in the cliffs of Qumran.

270 (top) This inkpot found in excavations at Qumran supports the hypothesis that many of the Dead Sea Scrolls were written by scribes of the Qumran community.

270 (centre) A phylactery, or tefillin, dating from the first century AD and found in one of the Qumran caves. It still contains four small, folded parchments of religious texts.

270 (right) These tall jars contained the scrolls found in the caves at Qumran. They helped to preserve the documents, some of which survive as complete texts.

271 (right) A parchment document discovered in one of the caves in the Judaean Desert. The study of these texts has provided a wealth of information concerning life in first-century Judaea.

271 (left) Bronze vessels, a mirror and a house key left in the 'Cave of Letters' in the Judaean Desert by the followers of Bar Kokhba during the Second Jewish Revolt. As the name suggests, documents were also preserved in this cave.

MASADA,
THE CITADEL
ON THE DEAD SEA

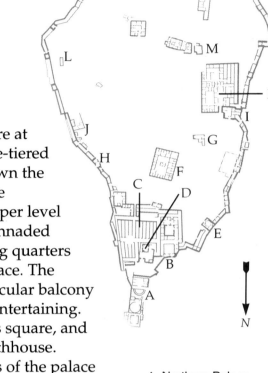

Masada, the desert fortress built by Herod, has become one of the most poignant symbols for the Jewish people. In AD 73, 960 men, women and children committed suicide rather than surrender to the soldiers of the Roman Tenth Legion. This was the last chapter in a rebellion that had resulted in the destruction of Jerusalem three years earlier.

Masada was first used as a fortress by the Hasmonaean kings. In 40 BC, Herod left his family there for safety when he fled to Rome to escape the forces of the Parthian-supported pretender, Antigonus. Under siege, Herod's followers were saved when a sudden rain refilled the cisterns. They were rescued shortly after and Herod managed to reclaim his kingdom. Herod obviously saw the advantages of Masada and built an elaborate fortress and palace there to protect himself from the threat of the rebellious Jewish people who were never reconciled to his rule.

Still the most impressive structure at Masada is the three-tiered palace terraced down the northern side of the summit. On the upper level was a circular colonnaded building with living quarters built into the cliff face. The next level had a circular balcony and was used for entertaining. The third level was square, and boasted a small bathhouse.

The interior walls of the palace were decorated with brightly coloured frescoes, some of which can still be seen today. They are painted with floral and geometric motifs, and designs intended to resemble marble. Mosaic floors were laid in black-and-white geometric patterns.

While the Northern 'hanging' Palace was clearly for entertainment, and also for the exhibition of Herod's wealth and power, the Western Palace was more functional.

A Northern Palace
B Water Gate
C Storerooms
D Bathhouse
E Synagogue
F Large building
G Byzantine church
H Snake Path Gate
I Western Gate
J Zealots' living quarters
K Western Palace
L Open cistern
M Pool
N Columbarium
O Mikveh
P Southern Gate
Q Cistern
R Large pool
S Southern bastion

272 (left) The view of the fortress of Masada from the north, with the Dead Sea in the background. The flat top is surrounded on all sides by steep cliffs, separating it completely from the surrounding plateaus of the Judaean Desert.

272–273 (above) The view of Masada from the south, with the large rectangular pool in the foreground. Remnants of the casemate walls that surrounded the fortress can also be seen.

273 (right) A collection of ostraca written in Hebrew with personal names or nicknames. The one in the lower left corner is inscribed with the name Ben Yair, the leader of the rebels besieged in Masada by the Romans in AD 73.

It consisted not only of the royal apartments and service rooms, workshops and storerooms, but also rooms used for administrative functions, such as state receptions. The floors were richly decorated with mosaics and there is evidence that some parts of the palace were several storeys high. There were also three smaller palaces nearby. Even today, the large, four-roomed bathhouse is especially impressive and is one of the best preserved in Israel. The entrance room, or *apodyterium*, was adorned with frescoes and a black-and-white tiled floor. The warm room, or *tepidarium*, led into the stepped pool of the cold room, or *frigidarium*. In the hot room, the *caldarium*, the small pillars holding up the floor over the heating chamber, the hypocaust, are still well preserved.

Close to the bathhouse was a large complex of storage rooms used for keeping food and wine. One storeroom was specially fortified for guarding valuable objects, such as weapons or treasure. This area of Masada, including the palaces, bathhouse and storerooms, was separated from the remainder of the summit by a wall and gate.

Water supply was the greatest problem for a site that might need to house a thousand people at any one time. Masada is not only in a desert with very scarce seasonal rainfall, but it is also on the high plateau of a mountain, surrounded on all sides by steep ravines. A system was devised which brought rain water from dams in nearby valleys to 12 cisterns on the lower slopes. From there, water could be carried by men or donkeys up a winding path, and through the Water Gate to reservoirs on the top.

Despite being an almost inaccessible, remote and steep-sided site, Masada was also fortified with high walls. The walls enclosed all but the northern tip of the mountain and were casemate – with an inner and outer wall separated by rooms. In total, these walls are 1386 m (4550 ft) long, with 70 casemate rooms, 30 towers and four gates.

When the Jewish rebels took over Masada during the First Jewish Revolt against Rome, they made extensive changes to the Herodian complex. To accommodate a large number of families, all the rooms in the exterior casemate walls were put to domestic use and many rooms in the palace were subdivided. The rebels also built two *mikvehs* and there is evidence that one room may have been used as a *beth midrash*, or room for religious study. The site of the synagogue has been partially reconstructed, it was orientated towards Jerusalem and may have been built by the Zealots over a previous synagogue of the time of Herod. Fragments of clothing, including prayer shawls and leather sandals, pottery and parts of baskets have survived in the very dry climate. The rebels minted their own coins and these were discovered in abundance at the site. The remains of 14 scrolls with texts of the Bible were found in various places in the ruins. Over 700 ostraca (pottery sherds with writing) were also discovered. They were mostly written in Hebrew or Aramaic but also, rarely, in Greek or Latin.

274 (opposite) The Hanging Palace on the northern point of Masada was constructed for the personal use of King Herod. The circular colonnaded hall on the top tier was used for lavish entertainments, as was the second tier. The third tier, rectangular in shape, had a small bathhouse.

275 (above) A corner column with a Corinthian capital from the lowest level of the Hanging Palace. The plaster that covered the surfaces of the columns and walls is still visible in places. It was painted in bright colours to imitate marble panelling.

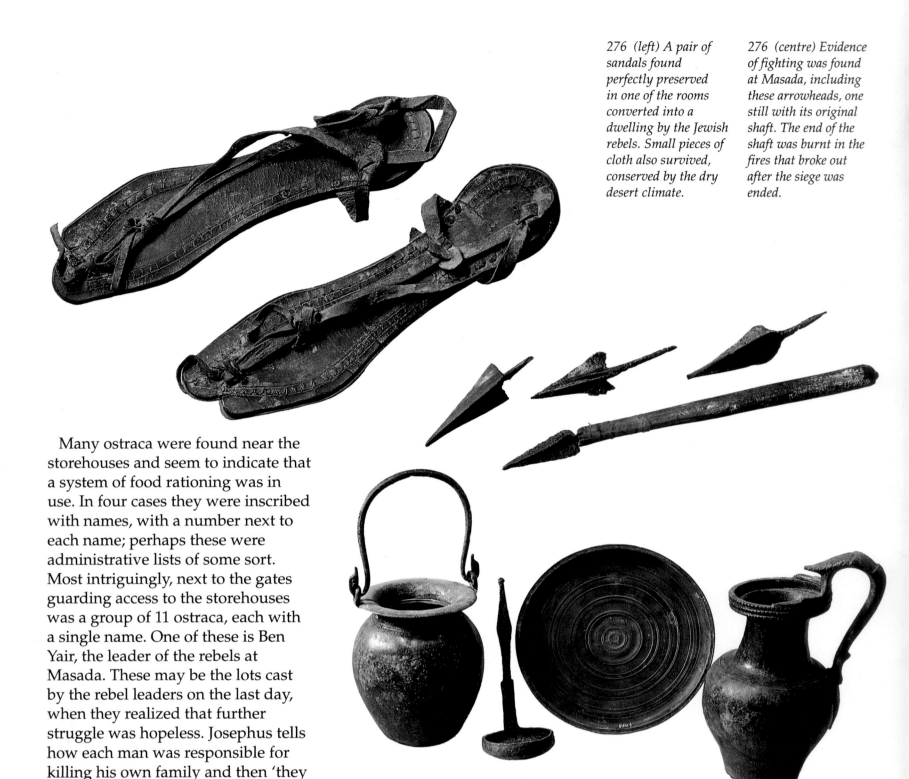

Many ostraca were found near the storehouses and seem to indicate that a system of food rationing was in use. In four cases they were inscribed with names, with a number next to each name; perhaps these were administrative lists of some sort. Most intriguingly, next to the gates guarding access to the storehouses was a group of 11 ostraca, each with a single name. One of these is Ben Yair, the leader of the rebels at Masada. These may be the lots cast by the rebel leaders on the last day, when they realized that further struggle was hopeless. Josephus tells how each man was responsible for killing his own family and then 'they made the same rule for casting lots for themselves, that he whose lot it was should first kill the other nine, and after all, should kill himself'.

Evidence has been found that confirms Josephus' account of the siege of Masada by the Roman general Flavius Silva and the Tenth Legion. The Romans built eight fortified camps around the base of the mountain and a circumference wall with 12 observation towers. The Jewish rebels could neither enter nor escape. The steep, winding Snake Path was not practical for a large number of soldiers and the siege machines needed to break through the fortress walls. Flavius Silva therefore built a huge ramp on the western side of the mountain. Stone-throwers were positioned on a nearby promontory to provide cover fire and protect the soldiers building the ramp. Once the ramp was completed, the huge siege-breaking machines could be dragged into place and a battering ram succeeded in breaking through the wall. The rebels made one last attempt at defence and hastily put up an ineffective wall of wooden planks and dirt, but once this was breached by the Roman soldiers, Masada fell.

THE HANGING PALACE AT MASADA

The Hanging Palace at Masada was another architectural feat of Herod's engineers and was used purely for entertainment. On the top level was a round hall with columns topped by Corinthian capitals. It was connected by a covered staircase to the next level, another round building with a distinctive roof similar to that of Absalom's Tomb in Jerusalem. The lowest level was rectangular in plan and included a small bathhouse. The interior walls and columns were covered with brightly coloured plaster, much of it designed to imitate marble.

1 *The upper level was adjacent to the palace buildings, a large bathhouse and storerooms.*

2 *The three levels were connected by a covered stairway.*

3 *The second level had a distinctive conical roof.*

4 *The lower level was graced by an interior courtyard decorated in brightly coloured plaster.*

5 *The small bathhouse.*

THE FORTRESS OF MASADA

The fortress of Masada had a special meaning for Herod. In 40 BC, when he was fleeing from Antigonus and the Parthian forces, he left his family at Masada and continued on to Rome. The refugee family, along with a protective force of 800 men, nearly died of thirst before a sudden rainstorm refilled the cisterns. Masada's position, on a flat-topped mountain, made it an ideal fortress. A casemate wall surrounded the perimeter, and towers were placed at strategic intervals. Later, after Herod secured his throne, he built elaborate palaces for his guests. The northern palace complex was separated by a wall from the rest of the summit. It enclosed an administration building a palace, an elaborate bathhouse, storerooms and the Hanging Palace.

1. A large pool used for the storage of water.

2. One of the towers spaced around the walls at strategic locations.

3. The gatehouse and main entrance to the fortress.

4. Casemate walls were built around the summit.

5. The Western Palace, used for the accommodation of Herod's guests.

6. The synagogue, one of the oldest in Israel.

7. A large administrative building or palace.

8. The large bathhouse.

9. The Hanging Palace.

10. The storerooms were within the wall guarding the Northern Palace complex.

11. Part of the casemate walls converted by the Jewish rebels for their living quarters.

12. Various buildings, including one holding a pool.

13. The Southern Gate, and a mikveh.

280 (left) The interior of the large water cistern discovered at Masada. Water was brought via an aqueduct to cisterns on the lower slopes of Masada, and then carried to the summit.

280 (below) The small columns of the hypocaust (heating system) supporting the floor of the caldarium, or hot room, of the large bathhouse.

280–281 (right) The northern palace complex was separated by a wall from the rest of the fortress. It enclosed the hanging palace, the large bathhouse, the storerooms, as well as other palace buildings.

*281 (left) The
columbarium,
perhaps used to hold
urns containing the
ashes of non-Jewish
soldiers who died at
Masada.*

*282–283 (overleaf)
The Hanging Palace
at the northern point
of Masada provided
Herod's guest with
spectacular views
of the Dead Sea.*

284–285 (above)
Shivta became a large
sprawling town in the
Byzantine period,
when the Nabataeans
were forced to adopt
a more settled form
of life.

284 (right) Mamshit
is located in the
central Negev. It
appears on the
Madaba Mosaic map
and was an important
trading town in
Byzantine times.

AVDAT, MAMSHIT AND SHIVTA: NABATAEAN CITIES OF THE DESERT

The Nabataeans were a unique people: largely nomadic, they made their living from trading and serving as guides for the caravans that crossed the desert. Described by the Greek historian Hieronymus as more wealthy than other Arabian nomadic tribes, they numbered no more than 10,000 people. They developed highly sophisticated systems for the collection and conservation of water in the hostile desert environment. The most spectacular Nabataean site is Petra, now in Jordan.

The spice trade lay at the centre of Nabataean wealth and they held a monopoly on it for many centuries. Spices came from as far away as India and the Far East, as well as from Arabia, and were brought by Nabataean traders overland to ports on the southeastern shores of the Mediterranean. By the first century BC, Nabataean trade encompassed a system of caravan stops which had bathhouses, temples and even banking services so that silver would not have to be carried long distances. Highway robbery was still a major danger and the Nabataeans also developed a military system.

Several towns in the Negev lay at the centre of the trade routes that extended as far south as Arabia and as far north as Damascus and Tyre. The most completely excavated of these caravan stops is the ancient town of Oboda, named after a Nabataean king, King Obodas II (30–9 BC). Its Hebrew name Avdat is derived from the Arabic, 'Abdah'. The acropolis at Avdat has been excavated and some of the remains of the white limestone temple built in the reign of Obodas II are still

visible, although much of the stone was reused in the construction of two Byzantine churches. North of the acropolis was a military camp, square in shape. Also still evident are breeding enclosures for the camels ridden by the Nabataean soldiers. In the Byzantine period the houses included rooms cut into the soft rock of the site, which were used as storerooms and workshops.

Nabataean culture changed dramatically after the Romans encroached on the routes previously monopolized by the Nabataeans. By the middle of the first century AD, the Nabataeans were forced to abandon their nomadic way of life and to settle in towns, relying on agriculture for their livelihood. They early became adept at the raising of horses. Along with the reliance on agriculture came the development of sophisticated systems of irrigation.

Mamshit was a Nabataean town built at the site of a caravan stop after the transition to a settled way of life during the late first and second centuries AD. The houses were built in densely packed blocks separated by wide streets and open spaces and thus in many ways resemble in form a tent city. The system of water collection is well preserved and can be seen today in a wadi near the town, where a series of three dams trapped water from the few torrential rainfalls each year.

Shivta, located on the road between Oboda and Nessana, doubled in size after the Nabataeans turned to agriculture. At Avdat and Shivta Israeli scientists built experimental farms to study ancient methods of desert agriculture.

285 The Byzantine North Church at Shivta was a large building with a monastery attached. Evidence shows it became a place of pilgrimage.

286–287 (overleaf) Avdat (or Oboda), was important as a civic and religious centre at the junction of several important trade routes. The Byzantine North Church, with its columns still standing, lies above the podium of a Nabataean temple.

SELECT BIBLIOGRAPHY

HISTORY AND ARCHAEOLOGY OF THE HOLY LAND

Aharoni, Y. and Avi Yonah, M., *The Macmillan Bible Atlas*, New York and London 1977.

Alexander, D. and P. (eds), *The Lion Handbook to the Bible*, Oxford and Sutherland, NSW 1993.

Barnavi, E. (ed.), *Historical Atlas of the Jewish People*, London 1992.

Ben-Arieh, Y., *The Rediscovery of the Holy Land in the Nineteenth Century*, Jerusalem 1979.

Ben-Tor, A. (ed.), *The Archaeology of Ancient Israel*, New Haven and London 1992.

Benvenisti, M., *The Crusaders in the Holy Land*, Jerusalem 1970.

Connolly, P., *Living in the Time of Jesus of Nazareth*, Oxford 1983.

Court, J. and K., *The New Testament World*, London and Melbourne 1990.

Dothan, T., *The Philistines and their Material Culture*, Jerusalem 1983.

Dothan, T. and M., *People of the Sea. The Search for the Philistines*, New York, 1992.

Finegan, J., *The Archaeology of the New Testament*, Princeton 1992.

Glueck, N., *Rivers in the Desert*, New York 1959.

Harris, R.L., *Exploring the World of the Bible Lands*, London and New York 1995.

Josephus, Flavius, *Jewish Antiquities; The Jewish War*, H. St J. Thackeray (trans.), Loeb edition.

Kenyon, K., *Archaeology in the Holy Land*, London 1979.

Levine, L.I. (ed.), *Ancient Synagogues Revealed*, Jerusalem 1981.

May, H.G. (ed.), *Oxford Bible Atlas*, Oxford 1985.

Mazar, A., *Archaeology of the Land of the Bible 10,000–586 B.C.E.*, New York 1990.

Millard, A., *Treasures from Bible Times*, Tring and Belleville 1985.

Millard, A., *Discoveries from the Time of Jesus*, Oxford and Batavia Illinois 1990.

Murphy-O'Connor, J., *The Holy Land. An Archaeological Guide from Earliest Times to 1700*, Oxford 1992.

Ovadiah, R. and A., *Mosaic Pavements in Israel*, Rome 1987.

Penslar, D.J., *Zionism and Technocracy. The Engineering of the Jewish Settlement in Palestine, 1870–1918*, Bloomington 1991.

Prawer, J., *The Latin Kingdom of Jerusalem European Colonialism in the Middle Ages*, London 1972.

Pringle, D., *The Churches of the Crusader Kingdom of Jerusalem*, I, Cambridge 1993.

Pritchard, J.B. (ed.), *Times Atlas of the Bible*, London 1987.

Rasmussen, C.G., *NIV Atlas of the Bible*, Grand Rapids, Michigan and London, 1989.

Riley-Smith, J. (ed.), *The Atlas of the Crusades*, London 1991.

Rogerson, J., *The New Atlas of the Bible*, London and New York 1985.

Rogerson, J. and Davies, P., *The Old Testament World*, Cambridge and Melbourne 1989.

Shanks, H., *Judaism in Stone. The Archaeology of Ancient Synagogues*, Jerusalem 1979.

Shanks, H. (ed.), *Ancient Israel. A Short History from Abraham to the Roman Destruction of the Temple*, Washington DC and London 1989.

Shepherd, N., *The Zealous Intruders. The Western Rediscovery of Palestine*, London 1987.

Stern, E. (ed.), *New Encyclopedia of Archaeological Excavations in the Holy Land*, I–IV, Jerusalem 1993.

Sukenik, E.L., *Ancient Synagogues in Palestine and Greece*, London 1934.

Tsafrir, Y. (ed.), *Ancient Churches Revealed*, Jerusalem 1993.

Tubb, J.N. and Chapman, R., *Archaeology and the Bible*, London 1990.

Yadin, Y., *Bar-Kokhba*, London 1971.

CARTOGRAPHY AND OLD PRINTS

Avi-Yonah, M., *The Madaba Mosaic Map*, Jerusalem 1954.

Bourbon, F., *Yesterday and Today. The Holy Land, Lithographs and Diaries by David Roberts R.A.*, Bnei-Brak, Israel 1994.

Donner, H., *The Mosaic Map of Madaba*, Kampen, Netherlands 1992.

Laor, E. (ed.), *Maps of the Holy Land, Cartobibliography of Printed Maps, 1475–1900*, New York and Amsterdam 1986.

Nebenzahl, K., *Maps of the Bible Lands. Images of Terra Sancta through Two Millenia*, New York 1986.

GEOGRAPHY AND NATURAL HISTORY

Aharoni, Y., *The Land of the Bible. A Historical Geography*, Philadelphia 1979.

Borowski, O., *Agriculture in Ancient Israel. The Evidence from Archaeology and the Bible*, Winona Lake, IN 1987.

Hepper, N., *Illustrated Encyclopaedia of Bible Plants*, Leicester 1992.

Walker, W., *All the Plants of the Bible*, New York 1979.

JERUSALEM

Avigad, N., *Discovering Jerusalem*, Oxford 1984.

Bahat, D., *The Illustrated Atlas of Jerusalem*, New York and Jerusalem 1990.

Ben-Arieh, Y., *Jerusalem in the 19th Century. The Old City*, Jerusalem and New York 1984.

Burgoyne, M.H., *Mamluk Jerusalem*, London 1987.

Corbo, V., *Il Santo Sepolcro di Gerusalemme*, I–III, Jerusalem 1981–82.

Couasnon, C., *The Church of the Holy Sepulchre in Jerusalem*, London 1972.

Creswell, K.A.C., *Early Muslim Architecture*, I–II, Oxford 1932–1969.

Gibson, S. and Taylor, J.E., *Beneath the Church of the Holy Sepulchre, Jerusalem*, London 1994.

Hamilton, R.W., *The Structural History of the Aqsa Mosque*, Oxford 1949.

Harvey, W., *Church of the Holy Sepulchre*, Jerusalem, London 1935.

Jerusalem Revealed, Archaeology in the Holy Land, 1968–1974, Jerusalem and New Haven 1976.

Kenyon, K., *Digging Up Jerusalem*, London 1974.

Mazar, B., *The Mountain of the Lord*, Garden City, NY 1975.

Peters, F.E., *Jerusalem the Holy City in the Eyes of Chroniclers, Visitors, Pilgrims and Prophets*, Princeton 1985.

Prag, K., *Jerusalem (Blue Guide)*, London and New York 1989.

Richmond, E.T., *The Dome of the Rock in Jerusalem*, Oxford 1924.

Shiloh, Y., *Excavations at the City of David (Dedem 19)*, Jerusalem 1984.

Vogüé, M. de, *Le Temple de Jerusalem*, Paris 1864.

Wilkinson, J., *Jerusalem as Jesus Knew It. Archaeology as Evidence*, London 1978.

Yadin, Y., *Jerusalem Revealed, Archaeology in the Holy City 1968–1974*, Jerusalem and New Haven 1976.

ARCHAEOLOGICAL SITES
ACRE

Dichter, B., *The Orders and Churches of Crusader Acre*, Acre 1979.

BAR'AM

Jacoby, R., *The Synagogues of Bar'Am*, Jerusalem 1987.

BELVOIR

Benvenisti, M., *The Crusaders in the Holy Land*, Jerusalem 1970.

BETH ALPHA

Sukenik, E.L., *The Ancient Synagogue at Beth Alpha*, Jerusalem 1932.

BETH SHEAN

Fitzgerald, G.M., *Beth Shan Excavations 1921–23. The Arab and Byzantine Levels III*, Philadelphia 1931.

Rowe, A., *The History and Topography of Beth Shean I*, Philadelphia 1930.

Yadin, Y. and Geva, S., *Investigations at Beth Shean. The Early Iron Age Strata (Qedem 23)*, Jerusalem 1986.

BETH SHE'ARIM

Avigad, N., *Beth She'arim III. Catacombs 12–23*, Jerusalem 1973.

Mazar, B., *Beth She'arim I*, Jerusalem 1973.

Schwabe, M. and Lipshitz, B., *Beth She'arim II. Greek Inscriptions*, New Brunswick 1973.

BETHLEHEM

Hamilton, R.W., *A Guide to Bethlehem*, Jerusalem 1939.

Harvey, W., *Structural Survey of the Church of the Nativity Bethlehem*, Oxford and London 1935.

CAESAREA

Frova, A., et al., *Scavi di Caesarea Maritima*, Milan 1965.

Holum, K.G., et al., *King Herod's Dream. Caesarea on the Sea*, New York and London 1988.

Raban, A., *The Harbours of Caesarea Maritima*, Oxford 1989.

CAPERNAUM

Corbo, V., *The House of St Peter at Capernaum*, Jerusalem 1970.

Orfali, G., *Caphernaum*, Paris 1922.

Tzaferis, V., et al., *Excavations at Capernaum I, 1978–1982*, Winona Lake, IN 1989.

HERODIUM

Corbo, V., *Herodium I. Gli edifici della reggia fortezza*, Jerusalem 1989.

Netzer, E., *Herodium. An Archaeological Guide*, Jerusalem 1987.

MASADA

Cotton, H. and Geiger, J., *The Latin and Greek Documents (Masada II)*, Jerusalem 1989.

Netzer, Y., *The Buildings, Stratigraphy and Architecture (Masada III)*, Jerusalem 1991.

Yadin, Y., *Masada*, London 1966.

Yadin, Y. and Naveh, J., *The Aramaic and Hebrew Ostraca and Jar Inscriptions; Y. Meshorer, The Coins of Masada (Masada I)*, Jerusalem 1989.

MEGIDDO

Davies, G.I., *Megiddo*, Cambridge 1986.

Fisher, C.S., *The Excavation of Armageddon*, Chicago 1929.

Guy, P.L.O., *New Light from Armageddon*, Chicago 1931.

Kempinsky, A., *Megiddo. A City-State and Royal Centre in North Israel*, Munich 1989.

MONTFORT

Benvenisti, M., *The Crusaders in the Holy Land*, Jerusalem 1970.

NABATAEAN CITIES

Negev, A., *Personal Names in the Nabatean Realm*, Jerusalem 1991.

NAZARETH

Bagatti, B., *Gli Scavi di Nazareth I*, Jerusalem 1967.

Folda, J., *The Nazareth Capitals and Crusader Shrine of the Annunciation*, University Park, PA 1986.

QUMRAN

Callaway, P.R., *The History of the Qumran Community Investigation*, Sheffield 1988.

Cook, E.M., *Solving the Mysteries of the Dead Sea Scrolls. New Light on the Bible*, Grand Rapids, MI 1994.

Laperrousaz, E.-M., *Discoveries in the Judean Desert 6–7*, Oxford 1977–1982.

Milik, J.T., *Ten Years of Discovery in the Wilderness of Judea*, London 1959.

Vaux, R. de, *Archaeology and the Dead Sea Scrolls*, London 1973.

Vermes, G., *The Dead Sea Scrolls. Qumran in Perspective*, London 1977.

SAFED AND MERON

Meyers, E.M., et al., *Excavations at Ancient Meiron, Upper Galilee, Israel*, Cambridge, MA 1981.

SEPPHORIS

Miller, S.S., *Studies in the History and Traditions of Sepphoris*, Leiden 1984.

Waterman, L., et al., *Preliminary Report of the University of Michigan Excavations at Sepphoris, Palestine, 1931*, Ann Arbor, MI 1937.

TIBERIAS

Dothan, M., *Hammath-Tiberias. Early Synagogues and the Hellenistic and Roman Remains*, Jerusalem 1983.

PERIODICALS

Biblical Archaeologist, 4500 Massachusetts Avenue NW, Washington DC 20016–5690, USA.

Biblical Archaeology Review, Biblical Archaeology Society, 4710 41st Street NW, Washington DC 20016, USA.

Eretz, The Geographic Magazine from Israel, P.O. Box 565, 53104 Givatayim, Israel.

Israel Exploration Journal, Israel Exploration Society, P.O. Box 7041 Jerusalem, Israel.

Palestine Exploration Quarterly, Palestine Exploration Fund, 2 Hinde Mews, Marylebone Land, London W1M 5RR, England.

ILLUSTRATION CREDITS

INDEX